CREATING STRATEGIC LEVERAGE

CREATING STRATEGIC LEVERAGE

Matching Company Strengths with Market Opportunities

Milind M. Lele

John Wiley & Sons, Inc.

NEW YORK • CHICHESTER • BRISBANE • TORONTO • SINGAPORE

Copyright © 1992 by Milind M. Lele

Published by John Wiley & Sons, Inc.

All rights reserved. Published simultaneously in Canada.

Reproduction or translation of any part of this work
beyond that permitted by Section 107 or 108 of the
1976 United States Copyright Act without the permission
of the copyright owner is unlawful. Requests for
permission or further information should be addressed to
the Permissions Department, John Wiley & Sons, Inc.

This publication is designed to provide accurate and
authoritative information in regard to the subject
matter covered. It is sold with the understanding that
the publisher is not engaged in rendering legal, accounting,
or other professional services. If legal advice or other
expert assistance is required, the services of a competent
professional person should be sought. *From a Declaration
of Principles jointly adopted by a Committee of the
American Bar Association and a Committee of Publishers.*

Library of Congress Cataloging-in-Publication Data

Lele, Milind M.
    Creating strategic leverage: matching company strengths
with market opportunities / Milind M. Lele

ISBN 0-471-63142-6

Printed in the United States of America

10 9 8 7 6 5 4

For
Evangeline, Anand, and Saurabh

Acknowledgments

An author incurs many debts, few of which he can repay and none in full measure. During the journey this book represents, many persons gave unstintingly of their time, their ideas, and their support. Particular thanks to

- John Deighton, Abbie Griffin, Paul Schoemaker, and Mark Shanley, colleagues at The University of Chicago's Graduate School of Business, for many discussions and in-depth comments
- Deans Robert Hamada and Al Madansky at The University of Chicago for giving me the opportunity to teach at the GSB over an extended period, thereby enabling me to test the various ideas in this book
- Philip Kotler of Northwestern University and Tom Nagle of Boston University for their comments
- Jim Allison, Wiley Caldwell, Dan Cwynar, Mike Dunn, Sushim Dutta, Sam Felton, Ashok Ganguly, Sam Hill, Nagesh Mhatre, Peter Moe, Allen Rehert, Alan Schultheiss, and Mike Smithson for taking the time to critique the manuscript at various stages, share the benefits of their corporate experiences and, in some cases, even allowing me to use their organizations as "guinea pigs" for testing and refining these concepts and techniques
- Ron Code and Jonathan Brookner of SLC Consultants, Inc., for supporting my research and writing, even though it meant additional work for them
- Several sets of researchers, in particular, Elaine Olshefsky, Ramesh Subramaniam, Julie Goldberg, Virgina Cram, Jim Gordon, Nick

Mitchell, Sarah Connor, and Ed Snajdr for their invaluable help in finding the right citations, statistics, and other supporting evidence

- My students at the GSB, with particular thanks to the Business 450 classes of 1984, 1985, and 1986 for their enthusiastic support (despite rather strict grading!) and the spirited dialogues and discussions which were invaluable in hammering these ideas into shape

- Sara Drummond for her editorial support and cheerful willingness to meet the deadlines of an erratic author, and Beth Bartoszek for her help in supervising the production of the final manuscript; and

- John Mahaney, my editor at John Wiley & Sons, Inc., for his continuing support and faith in a manuscript that was supposed to have been finished in 1988!

My apologies to anyone who was inadvertently omitted. All these individuals contributed immeasurably to improving this book; any remaining mistakes are mine alone.

Contents

TWO
ANALYZING STRATEGIC LEVERAGE

THREE
EXPLOITING STRATEGIC LEVERAGE

Introduction

With this book, I want to change the way managers think about their company's long-term direction, using a new concept called "strategic leverage." In the last three decades, academics and practitioners have conducted extensive research into the field of strategy. As a result, a number of techniques and frameworks for formulating strategy have emerged. However, none of these techniques enable a manager to *systematically* answer the question, "Over the long term, where should I concentrate my company's scarce resources?" My book is focused on this fundamental issue.

I first became aware of this need nearly 10 years ago, when I started teaching strategy to executives and MBA students at The University of Chicago's Graduate School of Business. I wanted to convey the idea that successful strategists concentrate on only a few—one, two, or at most three—areas over the long term and that a strategist's skill lies in selecting the "right" areas.

To illustrate my point, I asked this question: "Where should a marketing executive of a travel agency selling to large corporate clients focus his attention?" Much to my surprise, few participants—including many seasoned veterans—realized that, in fact, the marketing executive's choices were limited and offered little return as compared with investments in sales or operations. Furthermore, their responses varied and appeared to be based primarily on experience, bias, or other factors—*not* on any systematic analysis of the industry, the company's competitive situation, or its resources. (ALL)

I repeated this exercise with many different groups but invariably got the same results. Gradually I realized that managers —at all levels—

usually assumed that they could change anything, and they seldom considered what the payoffs would be.

Upon researching this phenomenon further, I found that the necessary tools and techniques to answer this central question were lacking. Not *one* of the widely used planning techniques—the various portfolio matrices, the industrial economics (Porter) model, the work of the Profit Impact of Market Share (PIMS) researchers, and others—addressed this fundamental question of strategy, namely, "Given a particular industry and a company within that industry, in which (few) areas should a firm's managers concentrate their long-term attention and resources?"

This realization started six years of research with the aim of developing a systematic process for answering the above question over the widest possible range of industry and company situations. I drew upon cases and studies of more than 20 diverse industries and the strategies of almost 50 companies in these industries; statistically based academic research; theoretical papers especially in industrial economics, game theory and marketing; and last but not least, on my own consulting work during the last 20 years with U.S. and international companies.

Gradually, a framework began to emerge: Industry structure and company competitive position determine industry payoffs; payoffs, in turn, determine the constraints on a company and, through these constraints, influence a company's strategic choices; and finally, these relationships are interactive and change over time. The finishing touch came when I defined the concept of "strategic leverage," synthesizing the various subframeworks into a coherent whole.

This book makes a number of important contributions to the field of strategy. First and foremost, it addresses the fundamental question overlooked by other techniques, namely, "Where should a company concentrate its scarce resources in a given industry and competitive situation?" As a consequence, it creates a coherent synthesis of several widely used techniques. It introduces the concept of a company's "freedom of maneuver," which vividly illustrates how industry structure affects real-life decisions. It also incorporates industry dynamics into strategy, thus helping managers anticipate and plan for changing conditions.

The concept of strategic leverage helps managers get to the heart of strategy questions quickly and consistently. As a result

- discussions of strategy are more productive, as extraneous or irrelevant issues can be identified and quickly set aside;

- little tactical or strategic confusion exists, because the process of precisely identifying a <u>company's area of leverage</u> also makes its choices abundantly clear; and most important;
- managers are less likely to squander the company's resources on the wrong areas or to chase after unattainable goals.

A step-by-step approach to determining where a company has the greatest leverage also stimulates strategic creativity. As participants realize how their choices are limited by various industry or competitive forces, they begin to ask, "How can we change this situation more in our favor?" Hitherto unconsidered, even "taboo" strategies often emerge from these discussions, widening the company's choices.

Especially in large, multidivisional companies, discussing and formulating strategy can get quite chaotic due to the seemingly endless variety of frameworks. Managers throw out phrases such as "the BCG matrix clearly indicates," or "we'll use a differentiation strategy," or "the Porter model makes it clear" like so many incantations. More often than not, such discussions create heat but shed precious little light on what the division's or business unit's strategy *is*. I show how these techniques relate to one another and incorporate them into an overall framework. This eliminates fruitless discussions about the validity of various approaches and provides a common "language" for discussing strategic issues throughout a large, diversified company.

Mangers frequently appear oblivious to how industry structure and their company's competitive position restrict their strategic and tactical flexibility. The concept of a company's freedom of maneuver makes the operational implications of structure and position crystal clear. Moreover, by analyzing freedom of maneuver, managers can learn, for example, how much latitude they have in changing relative prices. If the answer is "Very little," they can concentrate their attention elsewhere. Or they can probe further and learn what factors restrict their freedom in pricing and whether (and to what extent) they can influence these forces. Understanding maneuver also helps managers identify areas competitors have overlooked and which they can use to radically change their company's position and profits.

By and large, existing frameworks for developing strategy are relatively static. They provide little explicit guidance on how to anticipate and adapt to the dynamics of an industry. But in this book, industry dynamics form an explicit part of the various frameworks. I analyze how a company's strategic leverage changes as an industry evolves and examine, in detail, the implications for a firm's long-term objectives, its strategies, and its tactics. I show how a company's leverage changes over time and examine the underlying forces responsible. This analysis highlights how the focus of managerial attention needs to change as the industry evolves. Managers can use the results to better anticipate shifts in their own industries that will require major changes in their company's strategic direction.

In addition, this book makes several specific contributions. It introduces the notion of a firm's "motives" for entering a new segment, market, or industry. It asks managers, "Are you entering merely because 'it's there' and the opportunity appears too lucrative to pass up? Or are you entering because your company's key strategic interests—existing markets or control of core competencies—are threatened?" This prevents discussions of entry from becoming dominated by financial considerations and re-emphasizes the importance of strategic concentration.

I also show the limitations and pitfalls of "generic" strategies, namely, differentiation, cost leadership, and focus. Often used as convenient labels to describe a company's or business unit's proposed approach, these terms sometimes obscure the lack of a real direction. I show who can and cannot successfully execute a differentiation strategy, what are the dangers of pure cost focus, and what it takes to capture and maintain a successful niche. Then I examine the implications for a company's long-term objectives and highlight the importance of selecting feasible or attainable objectives while the market is still evolving.

Finally, I introduce a powerful tool called the Structure-Position map. This forces managers to address several key issues: "What do we want to *be* in this market? Why? What makes us believe we can achieve this goal? How realistic is this goal? What changes to industry structure, our position, or both would we have to make in order to achieve this objective? What are our realistic choices?" The Structure-Position map categorizes a company's long-term choices and shows how these change as the industry evolves and the company's position changes. While it is not intended to be applied mechanistically, the Structure-Position map provides a simple way to plot a company's current and future direction and stimulate discussions about strategic issues.

Organization

The book falls naturally into three parts. Chapters 1 through 3 introduce the concept of strategic leverage and describe the basic paradigm relating leverage to industry structure and company competitive position and to a firm's objectives, strategies, and tactics. Two sub-themes that will be repeated throughout the rest of the book are also introduced, namely, the concept of freedom of maneuver, and the likely returns of such maneuvers.

Part Two is the heart of the book. Here I explain how industry structure and competitive position affect the nature and terms of competition and how these, in turn, determine maneuver, returns, and leverage. First, I show how the five forces of competition affect a company's freedom of maneuver. Next, I discuss the returns of three generic strategies. I then analyze how a company's strategic leverage changes as the industry evolves. Finally, I discuss the implications of these changes for different players' objectives, strategies, and tactics.

The final section of the book shows how companies can exploit their strategic leverage. Using the Structure-Position map, I summarize the earlier analyses of leverage. I then show how product, channel, and pricing tactics can be used to exploit a firm's strategic leverage by increasing its freedom of maneuver, maintaining its control over a market, or even changing the terms of competition in its favor.

Approach

This book is intended for practitioners—divisional general managers seeking to improve their unit's performance; corporate executives concerned with evaluating the long-term direction of their various businesses; security analysts studying the prospects of industry participants; advisers to management on questions regarding the overall direction of a business or industry; and teachers and students of business and marketing strategy.

A key feature of my approach is the use of in-depth industry examples. Over several years of teaching these techniques, I have found that such examples are essential for the participant or the reader to fully appreciate the power and utility of these concepts. I have deliberately avoided specialized or contrived situations. Instead, I use industries such as travel agencies, airlines, overnight package delivery services, consumer durables, industrial fasteners, industrial equipment, and others that

- are familiar to readers either from personal experience or through the business or financial press;
- require little or no specialized knowledge of industry structure; and
- represent a wide range of industry structures and company competitive positions.

I believe readers will find these discussions interesting, both in themselves and for the insights they provide into the various analytical tools and frameworks.

Depending on the reader's background and knowledge of strategy, certain parts of the book will prove more interesting than others. The first part (Chapters 1 through 3) is fundamental and should be read by all. Managers who are thoroughly familiar with Michael Porter's work can skim through Chapter 4, while others will find it instructive. Corporate executives and planners should definitely read Chapters 7, 8, and 10, which contain the main strategic frameworks. Divisional managers and marketing executives will find something to interest them in all the chapters; a suggested plan is to read Parts One, Two, and Chapter 10 from Part Three, dipping into the chapters on tactics as time and their interests permit.

CREATING STRATEGIC LEVERAGE

PART ONE

UNDERSTANDING STRATEGIC LEVERAGE

1

Strategic Leverage: A New Paradigm

In this book, we introduce and develop the idea of a company's *strategic leverage*. The concept of strategic leverage provides managers with a new and powerful tool for making the most of their company's opportunities in any market. It also shows managers how to create new opportunities by changing the terms of competition or even the structure of the industry itself. Furthermore, the concept of strategic leverage synthesizes several hitherto unrelated but widely used planning tools and techniques. Thus it offers managers, for the first time, a coherent framework for thinking about their company's long-term direction.

We define a company's strategic leverage as "maneuver" multiplied by "return." By maneuver we mean the company's freedom to change its position in the market relative to its competitors. Return refers to the changes in revenue, market share, or both that result from such maneuvers. If a company can change its position *and* the market provides a significant return for such changes then, by our definition, the company's strategic leverage is high; otherwise it is low.

A company can change its relative position in a market along any one of five principal dimensions, namely, target market(s), product, place (or channels), promotion, or price. In practice, however, a company's freedom to change its position, its *freedom of maneuver,* varies considerably along these five dimensions. How much freedom a company has depends on the structure of the particular market and on the company's position within the market. For example, in the overnight package delivery market, all participants' flexibility in changing prices or services is limited by competition. As the leader, Federal Express need not always lower

3

prices or promise faster delivery to meet Airborne, but Airborne must match Federal Express' every move or risk losing share.

The *returns* for any changes in relative position (maneuvers) also vary considerably, depending on the market and the company's competitive position within the market. By investing heavily in advertising relative to other brewers, in the late 1960s, Philip Morris took Miller from an also-ran to second place in the U.S. beer industry. But similar investments in advertising for an industrial product like a lubricant would have no effect; there are no returns to advertising in such markets. Returns also change over time, as demonstrated more recently by Miller's inability to slow Anheuser-Busch's relentless growth in share despite heavy advertising expenditures.

Understanding Strategic Leverage Is Essential

A thorough understanding of strategic leverage is absolutely essential if a firm is to survive—let alone prosper—in a competitive environment. In the short run, ignorance about leverage may create only minor problems. However, over the long term, such ignorance is dangerous if not downright ruinous:

- Amana went from market leader to distant follower in the microwave oven industry because it did not recognize how strategic leverage had shifted from product and promotion to channels and pricing.

- Midway Airlines lost over $30 million in a fruitless attempt to provide "first-class service at coach prices," overlooking the fact that it had very little room for maneuver (and therefore very little leverage) in pricing, given the major airlines' commanding market positions.

- Deere in farm equipment and Miller in beer systematically exploited their leverage with the result that Deere went from a solid but unexciting second to undisputed leader, and Miller moved from fifth to second in share.

- Canon used technology to increase its freedom of maneuver (and therefore its leverage) in the dimensions of target market, product, and place, with the result that it succeeded in office copiers where previously IBM and Kodak had failed to make any headway against Xerox.

We can summarize the importance of strategic leverage in two ways: First and foremost, leverage is central to strategy decisions. Secondly, leverage adds value to the strategy process.

Leverage Is Central to Strategy Decisions

A comprehensive knowledge of leverage is essential for determining which tactics and strategies are feasible, which objectives are attainable, what resources and skills ("competencies") are necessary, and how to "creatively disrupt" an industry for the company's benefit.

Identify Feasible Tactics and Strategies. Understanding strategic leverage requires managers to systematically analyze their company's maneuver—its freedom to change its position relative to competitors—in all five dimensions. This identifies specific changes or tactical moves that are not feasible due to

- Constraints imposed by industry structure, such as strong buyers who dictate product specifications and restrain prices, the presence of substitutes, and so forth
- Likely competitive reactions, for example, determined industry leaders who control the terms of competition closely, or the absence of mobility barriers to a niche making it difficult to raise prices without inviting entry by the major players.

These restrictions on tactics, combined with a knowledge of the likely returns, provide detailed insights into which long-term shifts in position, which *strategies,* are feasible.

Midway Airlines is a vivid example of how studying leverage can identify feasible strategies and tactics. Chapter 5 contains a detailed analysis; here we will briefly summarize the key features.

Midway is a small, regional airline with its main hub at Chicago's Midway airport. It competes with the major national airlines, especially United and American, on various routes. Upon analyzing strategic leverage, we find that Midway has very little latitude in changing prices or the quality/price ratio, especially in the lucrative business flier segment. As a regional airline in a secondary airport location, Midway cannot set its prices equal to or above the majors. Nor can Midway set its prices significantly below those charged by American or United without risking retaliation, particularly if it offers equal or higher quality services. Thus, its freedom both to set prices and to change service features is restricted, and any attempts along these lines, such as Midway's Metrolink™ service, are very likely to fail.

Midway has more freedom in target market, channels of distribution, and (nonprice) promotion; of these, promotion offers little return due to the nature of demand and Midway's small size. Midway's real opportunities lie in selecting target markets (e.g., large, Chicago-based corporations) and changing channels (e.g., selling direct to corporate accounts) to create a long-term advantage.

Define Attainable Objectives.   In the process of analyzing strategic leverage, managers gain considerable insight into the nature of industry payoffs—likely gains and losses of individual players in response to various moves—and into the dynamics of the industry. These insights, in turn, allow managers to evaluate how leverage will change as the industry evolves and, by extension, which objectives are attainable and which are probably beyond their reach.[1]

Amana's situation in the U.S. microwave oven industry during 1976 to 77 illustrates how leverage helps define attainable objectives. Although Amana was the early innovator and industry leader in the early 1970s, by 1976 it was in second position behind Litton. Had Amana's managers possessed the tools to analyze their company's leverage, they would have found that it was changing rapidly. Specifically:

- Returns for any investments from product (features) or promotion (advertising, cooking schools, etc.) were declining due to increasing standardization of offerings and greater consumer awareness.
- Increased reliability meant less need for after-sales service and permitted a wider range of channels of distribution.

Thus, leverage was shifting from product and promotion—areas where Amana was particularly strong—to channels and price, where Amana was weak. These shifts in strategic leverage, taken in conjunction with the rate of industry growth and the changes in industry competition, would have indicated to Amana's managers that regaining industry leadership was probably not feasible, given their high costs and absence from the mass merchandiser channel. Further, they would have found that even retaining their present position as the second/third player would require substantial investments and drastic changes to their system of exclusive distributors; and that finding an attractive and lucrative niche such as high-end, feature-rich appliances sold through high service outlets might be their best alternative. (Chapter 13 contains a detailed discussion of Amana's constraints and choices.)

Determine Required Competencies.   Analyzing strategic leverage shows a manager along which dimensions he or she can profitably change a company's position. Once these areas have been pinpointed, the manager can ask, "What resources or capabilities—what competencies—do we need in order to exploit this opportunity?" By comparing these required competencies with the firm's existing capabilities, managers can determine if and to what extent they can exploit market opportunities.

For example, in the case of Amana the competencies required to exploit the opportunities in the microwave oven market were (1) a strong retail brand identity, (2) the ability to lower product costs, and (3) experience and expertise distributing through mass merchandisers like Sears, Penney's and K-Mart. While Amana's brand identity was very strong, its product and selling costs were high, and it had historically disdained mass merchandisers. Consequently Amana was poorly positioned to exploit this opportunity.

Enable "Creative Disruption."   A careful analysis of strategic leverage provides an indepth look at the prevailing terms of competition, the current "rules of the game." In turn, this shows managers where major groups of competitors or even the entire industry may be vulnerable, that is, where the industry's "fault lines" are located. Such knowledge, when combined with superior technology, marketing, or other competencies, enables a clever competitor or entrant to engage in "creative disruption" by drastically changing the terms of competition to its advantage.[2]

Canon's penetration of the copier industry and the manner in which Philip Morris took Miller from fifth to second are classic examples. IBM and Kodak had previously tried (and failed) to compete with Xerox head-on, using similar tactics—direct sales and service, leasing, focusing on large accounts. Canon avoided direct attacks. Instead, it "changed the rules of the game" and ultimately the game itself. Canon first used its technological capabilities to create a reliable cheap copier requiring no service. It then used dealers, avoiding the expense of direct sales. Finally, it sold rather than leased.[3]

Philip Morris similarly changed the rules of the game in the beer industry. Prior to its entry, competition was gentlemanly and low in intensity. Philip Morris acquired Miller Beer and proceeded to demolish the old "clubby" atmosphere. Ignoring the traditional stress on beer quality and the focus on bars/pubs, Miller/Philip Morris repositioned the brand and dramatically increased advertising spending. Before the others could respond, Miller had captured 20 percent of the beer market.

Leverage Adds Value to the Strategy Process

The concept of strategic leverage also makes it easier to design, compare, and communicate strategies inside an organization. Analyzing leverage enables managers to systematically identify key issues and concentrate upon them. It also helps classify situations in other, often unrelated, industries, thereby increasing managers' knowledge and strengthening their insights. Finally, leverage creates a common vocabulary and "language" within the organization, enabling very disparate groups to discuss strategic issues productively.

Concentrate Attention on Key Issues.   Strategic leverage enables managers to systematically and completely identify how they can and cannot change their market positioning and what are the likely returns for such changes. Once this is complete, managers can determine what objectives and strategies are even feasible, and under what conditions the leverage might change to their advantage or disadvantage. This places strategic issues in perspective. For example, if there is little return from changes in price (as in the case of industrial supplies like heat transfer fluids), expanding capacity (to lower costs and, therefore, prices) should take lower priority to segmenting the market or changing the terms of competition by using totally different channels of distribution.

Classify Diverse Industry Situations.   The concept of leverage forces managers to look below the surface of an industry and examine the underlying economic drivers in a systematic fashion. This provides a "filter" when searching for analogs. Instead of restricting ourselves to related industries, technologies, or customer characteristics, we ask, "Where can we find situations where the pattern of leverage is or was similar to our current situation? What can we learn from these cases?"

Consider the case of AT&T versus MCI in the long-distance telephone service industry (described in Chapter 3) and United Air Lines versus Midway (Chapter 6). On the face of it, these two situations have very little in common. However, on analyzing them, we find that Midway's and MCI's freedom of maneuver and therefore their strategic leverage are restricted in exactly the same way and for many of the same reasons. Consequently, we can compare their actions and analyze common patterns for future reference.

Create a Common Language.   The concepts and analytical techniques of strategic leverage are not industry specific. As a result, they create a common vocabulary and a "language" for discussing strategic choices and issues. Such a language is extremely valuable in communicating laterally as well as up-and-down the organization.

The concept of strategic leverage helps lateral communication both within a division or strategic business unit (SBU), as well as between diverse units of a large corporation. For example, it allows different functional areas such as manufacturing, product engineering, logistics, and marketing to appreciate how their actions affect leverage and, therefore, have strategic impact. Rather than argue about their functional strategies, they can jointly explore how the organization as a whole could exploit or change its strategic leverage and therefore its competitive position. Similarly, diverse business units can compare their separate industry situations along the lines of AT&T versus MCI and United versus Midway with one difference: One business unit may have capabilities or resources that could assist the other in significantly changing its strategic leverage.

Similarly, the language of strategic leverage makes discussions between corporate and business units more fruitful. In a large, diversified company it is not feasible for corporate managers to have a detailed knowledge of all the industries in which their company participates. Without an analysis of strategic leverage, corporate reviews are, of necessity, confined mostly to financial issues. The tools and techniques of leverage provide a common language for both sides to have a meaningful discussion of the strategic problems faced by the individual business unit. Corporate managers can now ask, "What forces are constraining your leverage? What do you intend to do about it? What are the risks involved in changing your leverage? How can we use our overall technological, marketing, and operations resources to achieve 'creative disruption'?"

The Strategic Leverage Paradigm

Our starting point is the definition of leverage as the product of the firm's freedom of maneuver and the returns for any maneuvers. Freedom of maneuver in turn depends upon the structure of the industry and the company's competitive position. The returns for any changes in position depend on the size and manner in which total industry payoffs are divided. These payoffs are defined by the industry's terms of competition, that is, by the structure of the industry and the competitive positions of the various players (see Figure 1.1).

Simplifying these interrelationships leads to our central paradigm relating structure, position, and the terms of competition with leverage and the firm's strategic choices (Figure 1.2). Structure and position define the nature of the game and the terms of competition. The terms of

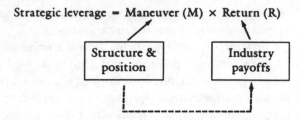

Figure 1.1 The concept of strategic leverage.

competition determine the company's strategic leverage. In turn, lever-age influences the selection of objectives, strategies, and tactics. These relationships also work in reverse: A company's actions can change indus-try structure or competitive position, thereby changing the nature or the terms of competition and, ultimately, the company's leverage and, by implication, its strategic choices.

Our paradigm provides a systematic, logical framework for analyzing leverage and determining the implications for a company's objectives, strategies, and tactics. We start by evaluating structure, using the tools of industrial economics. Once we understand structure, we can identify

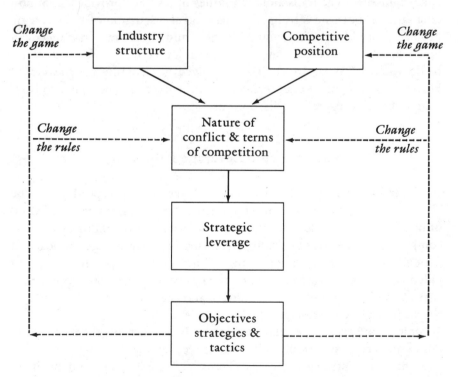

Figure 1.2 The strategic leverage paradigm.

likely constraints on the firm's maneuver, such as powerful buyers, high degree of industry rivalry, mobility barriers, and so forth. The next step is to study the competitive positions and past behavior of the various players. This enables us to determine the nature and terms of competition and, by extension, the likely returns for changing the company's position along any of the five principal dimensions.

We can now define the company's leverage in considerable detail. This enables us to determine which tactics can affect our overall positioning, and which strategies are even feasible or attainable. At this point, we have essentially two choices: *exploit* or *change*. We can elect to choose from the various strategy choices available. Alternatively, if the feasible choices are not appealing, we can try to change either the rules of the game, or the game itself. The second approach often involves considerable risks, including the possibility that, if this *approach* fails, the company may be forced out of the industry. At the very least, it runs the risk of substantial losses.

While we can use this approach on a case-by-case basis to design strategy, marrying it with industry evolution transforms the strategic leverage paradigm into a prescriptive framework of great power. This framework helps managers determine what they *should* concentrate on in developing their strategies. Once managers have located their company on this framework, it enables them to define feasible objectives, strategies, and tactics. It assists managers in anticipating changes in industry dynamics. Last but not least, it facilitates creative thinking regarding changing the terms of competition or even the structure of the industry in order to change strategic leverage to the company's benefit.

The Importance of Industry Evolution

Changes to industry structure cause corresponding changes in the nature and the rules of the game. These in turn affect the company's leverage and, ultimately, its objectives, strategies, and tactics. What is more, changes to industry structure follow a fairly regular pattern, one which has been researched extensively.[4] We can use the results to analyze the interactions between structure, position, and leverage in detail. The main highlights are the following (chapters indicated in parentheses discuss these issues in more detail):

- Industry evolution changes the nature of the game—the payoffs—in a predictable fashion.
- Specifically, the sequence is "win/win" to "limited warfare" to "win/lose" and finally, "lose/lose," corresponding to the

emerging/growth, early maturity, mid-to late-maturity, and decline stages of industry evolution (Chapter 2).

- Competitive position becomes increasingly important as the industry moves into maturity (Chapters 3 and 7).

- Strategic choices such as differentiation or focus become progressively more limited as the industry evolves from growth into maturity and, finally, decline (Chapters 6 and 7).

- A firm's maneuver—its ability to change the five key variables of target market, product, place, promotion, and price—also becomes progressively restricted as the industry evolves (Chapters 5 and 7).

- The returns for any changes decrease and tend to be concentrated along just one or two of the five principal dimensions (Chapters 6 and 7).

- The company's strategic leverage tends to concentrate along one or two main dimensions.

- Tactical issues—how to exploit available leverage—gradually overshadow strategic ones, unless a firm is successful in changing the leverage (Chapters 10 through 14).

With the aid of these and related findings, we can determine *in advance* how a company's leverage changes over time and how this affects its strategy.

Relationship to Prior Work

Our concept of leverage synthesizes three separate and very different approaches to strategy, namely, Porter's scheme of the five forces of competition, the Profit Impact of Market Share (PIMS) approach, and game theory.[5] Further, it builds on these concepts to create a complete, self-contained framework for designing company strategies and tactics.

In 1980, Porter introduced his scheme of the five forces of competition that shape strategy. In the process, Porter converted the tools and techniques of industrial economics into a framework for competitive analysis. We make extensive use of these concepts for analyzing the structure of an industry, for evaluating a company's competitive position, and for determining its freedom of maneuver. Thus our notions of maneuver and, to some extent return, are based solidly upon the extensive literature of industrial economics (the Porter model).

We use the research carried out by the Profit Impact of Market Share (PIMS) project (initiated by the Harvard Business School) for

- Evaluating the relative competitive position of a company
- Analyzing how returns change as the industry goes from growth to maturity and then to decline
- Assessing the attractiveness, feasibility of a company's strategic choices at different stages of industry evolution.

Finally, our notion of industry "payoffs" is rooted in game theory, particularly the idea of an industry as a many-player, nonzero sum game, although our use of terms such as "win/win," "win/lose" may make purists shudder! We relate industry payoffs to industry structure and examine how they influence return, maneuver and therefore leverage.

What's Different

We believe that the concept of leverage (1) makes the interrelationships among these three schools of thought explicit, and (2) synthesizes them into a coherent tool for analyzing and designing business unit strategies.

Makes Relationships Explicit. Industrial organization (the Porter model) and game theory are interlinked through the concept of maneuver; we cannot really understand a company's freedom of maneuver in an industry until we know the underlying forces of competition, the industry payoffs, and how the two affect each other. Knowing only one or the other is not enough to determine maneuver. For example, structurally the beer and the residential long-distance telephone service industries are very similar. Both have strong leaders with major shares of the market (Anheuser-Busch and AT&T, respectively), in both industries buyers and suppliers are weak, large advertising expenditures make entry difficult, substitutes have limited effect, and rivalry is controlled. However, the beer industry's payoffs are essentially "win/lose," in part because overall consumption is declining, but more importantly because Anheuser-Busch is pushing relentlessly for increased share. The long-distance industry, on the other other hand, is in "limited war"; AT&T, the leader, is relatively content to maintain the status quo. Thus the freedom of maneuver of the aspiring players, Miller Brewing and MCI respectively, is substantially different.

Game theory and the market share concepts researched by PIMS are linked through the concept of the "return" for a particular maneuver. Assuming that a company *can* change its relative position in one of the five main dimensions—target market, product, place, promotion, or price—the PIMS data tell us the *historical* returns for such a change, given the state of industry maturity and the market position of the company. We must still modify this information by assessing the pay-offs of our particular game; whether it is being played as "limited war," "win/lose," or "lose/lose"; the intentions of the various participants; how desperate a particular company may be; and so forth. The Japanese attempt to make a major change in the price/performance ratio had less impact in the heavy equipment industry (as compared with consumer electronics or automobiles) because (1) the industry was more mature (PIMS) and (2) the competition—Caterpillar—was much more deter-mined to maintain its share and leadership of the market (game theory).

Creates a Coherent Tool.   We believe that, taken individually, these three approaches to strategy design are not complete; they provide little detailed guidance to managers and practitioners about how to develop a market-based strategy. The Porter model, for example, contains a wealth of analytical techniques for studying the structure of an indus-try. But how a manager translates his or her understanding of industry structure into specific objectives, strategies, and tactics is far less clear. The PIMS approach shows the likely benefits of increasing share, yet provides little explicit guidance on how one achieves this happy state of affairs. Finally, while game theory concepts provide insight, applying any of its tools in practice is beyond the knowledge and capabilities of most managers.

The strategic leverage paradigm provides a systematic progression from industry structural analysis to an evaluation of the firm's competi-tive position and its implications, then to a detailed examination of the industry "game," the firm's leverage and finally to specific objectives, strategies, and tactics. Further, because it is interactive, it gives managers insight into the likely effects of proposed strategies on industry structure and competitive position. Combined with knowledge of their company's strategic leverage, this enables managers to determine whether and how they could change the industry to their advantage.

Strategic Leverage and Core Competence

Prahalad and Hamel have introduced the notion of the core competen-cies of a corporation.[6] They define a core competence as one that (1) provides potential access to a wide variety of markets, (2) makes a significant contribution to the perceived customer benefits of the end product, and (3) is difficult for competitors to imitate. They go on to say that ". . . in the long run, [a company's] competitiveness de-rives from an ability to build, at lower cost and more speedily than competitors, the core competencies that spawn unanticipated products." Strategy design, from this perspective, becomes the process of identifying, investing in, and exploiting the core competencies of the corporation to generate superior profits.

The Two Approaches Are Mutually Supportive.   Strategic leverage defines requirements, while core competencies identify possibilities. Thus, they complement each another. Managers should not design strategy solely around a firm's core competencies while ignoring strategic leverage, nor should they focus exclusively on leverage and ignore the firm's core competencies.

Lacking a proper appreciation of leverage, the firm is likely to misapply its core competencies. At the very least, resources are likely to be wasted while managers determine by trial and error where their firm's competencies are best applied. For example, we could argue that IBM had many of the core competencies necessary to compete in the laptop market: IBM is a leading manufacturer of large memory chips, it has high brand recognition, and it has expertise in sophisticated manufacturing techniques such as surface-mounting of components. Yet IBM has apparently never understood where the market offers strategic leverage, as confirmed by its repeated introductions of products that were underpowered and overpriced, its reluctance to use "discount" channels, and its anemic response to price competition.

Nor is knowledge of leverage alone sufficient. Unless managers understand their core competencies, they cannot know whether and to what extent they can exploit the available leverage. Consequently, they are likely to either miss opportunities or become complacent, thereby failing to respond as leverage changes. In the late 1970s, Amana could have retained its position in the microwave oven market, had it chosen to shift to mass merchandisers and changed its sales and pricing tactics. However, neither Amana nor its parent Raytheon had low-cost manufacturing expertise or the ability to work with mass market channels, core competencies essential for exploiting these opportunities. As a result, they were poorly positioned to capitalize on the leverage available.

Leverage Aids in Identifying Core Competencies.   By analyzing a company's strategic leverage in a given segment or market, we can identify what capabilities—*enabling* competencies—are required in order to exploit the leverage. Examining these enabling competencies across diverse groups of industries begins to identify common themes. These themes point to the core competencies the firm should be investing in, acquiring, or nurturing.

To pursue the Amana/Raytheon example further, in the microwave oven industry, the enabling competencies (in the late 1970s) were brand identity, high-quality/low-cost manufacturing, and skill at mass merchandising. A similar analysis of the large kitchen appliance market—refrigerators, cooking ranges, washing machines—might have shown Raytheon that the enabling competencies were a strong dealer network and high-quality/low-cost manufacturing. If a third industry in which Raytheon participated (or wished to enter) had high-quality/low-cost manufacturing among its enabling competencies, it would suggest to Raytheon that, perhaps, high-quality/low-cost manufacturing is a core competence that the company should cultivate further.

Summary

In this chapter, we outlined the main features of the strategic leverage paradigm. We will now examine the individual elements of this framework in detail, examine their interrelationships, and develop various tools and techniques for designing strategies and tactics using strategic leverage.

Our focus throughout the book is on market or industry strategies, as contrasted with internal, company (or resource-based) strategies. We believe that managers must first understand how industry structure and competitive position define their company's leverage. Next, they must carefully analyze how segmentation, product changes, channel selection, and pricing tactics can be used to exploit leverage. Only then will they fully appreciate what their firm's resources and capabilities—technology, capacity, cost position, organizational flexibility—can *and cannot* achieve.

2

Industry Structure and Strategic Leverage

The structure of an industry has a profound effect on a company's strategic leverage. Structure determines how industry payoffs will be divided. Structure influences the terms of competition. Finally, structure, in combination with the nature of industry payoffs and the terms of competition, defines a company's freedom of maneuver.

Consider a local travel agency with a mixture of vacation and business customers, one of many that may be found in any city. For such a firm, the structure of the travel agency industry matters far less than the state of the local economy. There is none of the urgency of a few competitors hotly pursuing the same accounts. The firm has almost unlimited freedom in its strategic leverage; within its own financial limits, it can target whatever segment of the market it desires, advertise anywhere, set prices as it pleases, and offer all or only a few services. Such competition as exists is friendly, almost cozy.

By contrast, the marketing vice-president of a large corporate travel agency with offices across the country serving Fortune 500 clients ignores industry structure at his peril. The very size of the individual accounts ensures that other, equally well-financed firms will be competing fiercely for the business. Further, serving these accounts requires substantial investment in branch offices, reservation and accounting systems, and skilled personnel—fixed costs that become severe liabilities in a downturn. At the same time, the firm's customers expect, or may even demand, significant "rebates," or refunds, on the commissions the agency receives from *its* suppliers—airlines, hotels, and car rental companies.

Consequently, the firm's margins and profitability are squeezed relentlessly by its need to maintain a large overhead structure (to serve its customers and to remain competitive) and by its clients' insatiable appetite for reducing their travel costs through low-cost flights (meaning smaller commissions) and larger rebates (still smaller commissions).

Nor does our vice-president have much freedom in his choice of business strategies. He cannot concentrate on individual segments of this market because, as he soon finds out, none are large or distinct enough. Nor can he change the marketing mix—the combination of product, price, promotion, and place—that his firm offers. To remain competitive, his company must offer the same products and services provided by its rivals. If he invests in additional services, such as more individualized billing or easier access for making reservations, he soon finds out that customers will not pay a premium for such services. Nor can he look to these investments to provide a long-term competitive advantage—his competitors will quickly match any new offerings that catch on with clients. Spending money on advertising is not advisable, except as a minimum, maintenance expense; large firms do not make their decisions on the basis of advertisements. Using intermediaries such as other agents and brokers to market the firm's services merely dilutes margins without increasing revenues or profits. Finally, he has very little freedom in pricing; raising prices is not feasible because they are set by his suppliers, and reducing rebates will cause his firm to lose accounts.

In fact, as our marketing vice-president soon finds out, he can do very little to increase his firm's profitability through his marketing plans. In corporate travel, the real strategic focus is on *operations*—buying blocks of airline seats and hotel rooms in advance at deep discounts, using information systems to minimize transaction-processing costs, controlling personnel costs through careful scheduling, and so forth. Despite his title and perquisites, he has far less freedom of maneuver than the owner of the local travel agency.

The two firms also face different payoffs and, as a result, have very different strategic objectives. For the local travel agency, business is not a "I win, you lose" game; if it loses an account to a crosstown rival, the repercussions are minor. Consequently, its owner worries very little about market share and industry growth; his objectives are primarily *internally* focused—profitability, cash flow, and revenue growth. On the other hand, with a fixed number of accounts and the same firms chasing after them, the corporate travel agency's gains and losses come at the expense of its rivals. Therefore, losing a major account has a significant impact, while the loss of two or more accounts could conceivably be disastrous. Thus, the corporate travel agency's management focuses on *external* measures such as market share, account control, and growth relative to the industry as a whole.

Industry Structure: The Key

The reasons for these wide differences become apparent when we analyze the structure of the two industries. The local travel agency operates in an industry that is relatively formless: it is easy to enter (and exit) the market, neither customers nor suppliers have much clout, there are few substitutes for the services offered by the agency, and rivalry is low (see Figure 2.1). The actions of one firm have little or no effect on any of these economic forces; therefore, managers in such a fragmented industry have considerable freedom in choosing their business strategies. The limits on their behavior are primarily *internal,* that is, how well the firm is capitalized, the abilities of its key salespeople, and management's willingness to take risks.

By contrast, the corporate travel industry is highly structured. Entry into the market is difficult, requiring substantial investments in facilities and people before any corporate client will even consider placing its business with a firm. Customers have considerable muscle; they spend large amounts of money, are sophisticated in purchasing, and could bring these activities in-house (integrate backwards) if they so choose. Finally, competition is intense partly because the buyers—the Fortune 500

	Local Agency	National Firm
Nature of marketing "war"	"Win/win" or live and let live	"Win/lose"
Constraints	Practically none	Very little freedom to choose segments, change services, spend on promotion, use agents or vary prices
Terms of competition	Gentlemanly	Could become cut-throat
Industry structure	• Many small buyers • Many competitors of varying sizes • Few substitutes • Entry is easy *A fragmented industry*	• A few large accounts • Rivals few, similar in size • More substitutes • Entry is difficult *A concentrated industry*

Figure 2.1 How industry structure affects marketing strategy.

firms—want it that way and also because the large resource requirements ensure that only a few firms will be capable of operating in this market. Here the limits on the objectives and strategies of an individual firm are imposed by these *external* economic forces.

These two examples represent two extremes in the interaction of industry structure and company strategy—from very little impact in the case of the local travel agency to almost total domination in corporate travel. Most industries are not as highly organized as the corporate travel market; consequently, industry structure doesn't have the same stifling effect. But in every situation, we can understand the relationship between structure and strategy when we recognize the following:

- Structure defines the nature of the industry "war."
- Structure decides the industry's terms of competition.
- Structure determines a firm's "freedom of maneuver."

Structure Defines the Industry "War"

Conflicts—both commercial and military—can be of many types, from extended truces marred only by occasional skirmishes, to limited wars, to all-out or "total" warfare. In commercial conflicts, the structure of the industry largely determines the nature of the industry "war" that will be fought by the various participants.[1] Sometimes, as in the case of the local travel agency, the conflict will be minimal and limited to a few participants in one or two segments of the market. In other cases, industry warfare will be widespread, especially when participants find out that their gains or losses come at the expense of the other players. Such appears to be the situation in the corporate travel industry.

To appreciate the nature of the conflict—the type of industry war that will occur—we must analyze how the gains and losses of the various players add up. In some industries, *total* gains and losses add up to a constant sum; one company's increase in share, revenues, or profits occurs at the expense of the others. When this is the case, firms are likely to wage "total war," resulting in intense competition.[2] More often, the total gains and losses are not constant; everyone gains (or expects to gain) by participating in the market. Under these circumstances, we can have a variety of conflicts—cooperative actions (to the extent allowed by the antitrust laws), total warfare, or even situations where *all* players lose revenues and profits.

The nature of the conflict has a direct bearing on the objectives that an individual firm should set for itself when determining its business strategy. A firm that insists on playing "winner take all" in an industry where conflict is minimal risks precipitating an all-out war, one that may not be desired by the other parties and that the initiator may have no hope of winning (as Texas Instruments found out in the home computer market). Thus, understanding the nature of the industry war is a crucial first step in choosing a firm's overall business strategy.

The Four Generic Types of Industry Payoffs

We can classify industry conflicts into one of the following categories, depending upon industry payoffs: win/lose, lose/lose, win/win, and standoff, that is, truce, stalemate, or limited warfare (see Figure 2.2). Win/lose or stalemate occurs in industries where the payoffs are constant or zero; in other markets any one of these four outcomes is possible.

Win/Lose.   This is the classic "winner takes all" conflict. In such industries, share, revenue, and profit gains come at the expense of other competitors. The structural characteristics of industries where such total "war" occurs are the following:

- Total industry revenues and/or profits are constant or are growing very slowly.
- There are significant economies of scale in production, distribution, and/or promotion.
- The number of firms participating in the industry is (relatively) limited and stable.
- Individual participants have, or can obtain, information regarding the relative positions of the major players.

Player 1

		Win	Lose
Player 2	**Win**	Win/Win	Win/Lose or Cooperative equilibrium
	Lose	Win/Lose or Cooperative equilibrium	Lose/Lose

Figure 2.2   The four generic types of industry wars.

The intensity of the conflict will depend on two interrelated factors: the degree of agreement on the "rules" and external economic forces. Under some circumstances, the players will agree—explicitly or tacitly—to compete only along certain dimensions, such as product and promotion, and avoid other tactics, such as price-cutting. At other times, such agreements may never happen or, if they exist, may be disregarded by one or more players. When this occurs, we have indiscriminate or total "war" in which nothing is sacred and no tactics are out-of-bounds.

The intensity of the competition is also affected by several external forces such as the ease with which new players can enter the market, whether existing players can leave easily, the relative proportions of fixed and variable costs in the production process(es), and the degree of homogeneity in the corporate values and cultures of the individual companies.

The U.S. steel industry is a classic example of a market where the payoff is win/lose. Overall industry sales and profits have been stagnant for the past 15 years, while domestic producers have been losing market share to imports. The beer industry is another example of a win/lose market; the majors have been gaining share at the expense of the smaller regionals and of each other.[3]

Lose/Lose.   As the term indicates, here industry payoffs are declining. In these situations, all parties lose revenues and profits; it is very difficult for an *individual* company to gain at the expense of the others. In such industries, competitive activities such as price changes, increases/decreases in advertising expenditures, and channel consolidations are immediately matched, and often exceeded, by the other players. The net result is to further reduce industry profitability. Industries where the nature of the payoff is lose/lose have some or all of the following characteristics:

- Total industry profits are very low, zero, or negative.
- Industry revenues are declining or, at best, steady.
- Product technology is at or past its peak.

Competition in such situations varies from sporadic to intense. Industry characteristics make it difficult for participants to agree to some (tacit) rules of conduct; while such agreements are often desirable, legal and economic forces tend to make them short-lived. Often, all it takes for the agreements to be broken is a temporary dip in revenues.

The North American farm equipment market is a good example of a lose/lose payoff. From 1980 to 1986, total industry revenues dropped more than 30 percent and profits were nonexistent. Yet consolidation came very slowly because of high exit costs, and price competition was intense due to the high fixed costs of idle manufacturing capacity.

Win/Win.   When everyone gets something for participating in the industry, conflict is at a minimum. Most of the players are too busy making money and do not perceive their gains and losses as a direct result of the actions of their competitors. Consequently, existing conflict is local—small skirmishes between one or two players competing in a particular segment of the market. Industry characteristics are some or all of those listed:

- Total industry revenues and profits are growing rapidly.
- There are numerous players of varying sizes.
- Products and services are not standardized.

Note that win/win does not mean that all participants win equally; it is only important that all parties perceive that they gain to some extent.

In the early 1980s, personal computers and long-distance telecommunications were prime examples of win/win markets. Total industry revenues were growing (very rapidly in the PC market), and most of the firms shared in the growth, to some extent.

Limited Warfare.   This occurs when all players recognize that (1) they can't do better individually than they can by belonging to a group, tacitly or explicitly, and (2) all the various groups recognize that one particular arrangement is the best they can achieve. *Stalemate* occurs when all parties are too exhausted to fight and realize that additional expenditures in advertising, price-cutting, and so on are not likely to change the status quo. *Truce* is a recognition that stalemate is likely and that, therefore, some restraints are necessary if the various firms participating in the industry are to avoid catastrophe. Finally, in some cases, all the players recognize that, *both individually and collectively,* they have more to gain by restraining or restricting the scope of competition; this leads to *limited warfare.* As we will discuss later, these three conditions can occur under various circumstances. Further, they may or may not be stable or long-lasting, depending on such factors as the capabilities and resources of the participants, technological evolution, the emergence of substitute products or services, and the entry of new participants, either directly or through acquisitions.

Detroit in the 1950s and 1960s practiced limited warfare: General Motors was the undisputed leader with approximately 60 percent of the market, Ford was number two, and Chrysler was number three, with American Motors a very small fourth. The Big Three generally avoided head-to-head competition, especially on price. All three firms followed similar policies in key areas such as labor negotiations and settlements, dealership terms, and margins and product design.

Structure Defines the Terms of Competition

Every industry has certain rules, a set of tacit agreements among the participants that define the *terms of competition* in the industry.[4] These rules determine the *dimensions* along which industry participants will compete, the *intensity* with which they will compete, and the *stability* of the terms of competition. Managers who fail to understand the rules in their industry risk

- Wasting resources (e.g., by spending money on advertising when the key area of competition is channels)
- Precipitating unwanted warfare (e.g., by causing a full-scale price war when all they wanted to do was reposition a brand)
- Failing to anticipate and adapt to changes (e.g., by following historical patterns and underspending on advertising).

The rules are not created haphazardly or by accident. Rather, they arise from (1) the economic realities underlying the industry, (2) the industry's evolution over time, and (3) the motivations and objectives of the various participants.

Industry structure defines the terms of competition to a considerable extent. To fully understand this relationship, we must first analyze the nature the industry payoffs. These, in turn, determine the areas in which firms will compete, how hard they will fight, and how likely they are to change the rules without warning.[5]

How Industry Conflict Affects the Terms of Competition.   Table 2.1 summarizes the implications for the terms of competition in each of the four types of industry conflicts, specifically:

- *Win/win.* In this case, all we can say with confidence is that the intensity of competition will be low. To understand which dimensions of market position will be key or how stable the terms of competition are, we must analyze the role of each of the five forces of competition in that industry.

Table 2.1 How the nature of the marketing "war" affects the terms of competition.

Terms of Competition	Nature of Conflict			
	Win/Win	Win/Lose	Lose/Lose	Limited Warfare
Key dimensions	—	—	Price	Product, promotion
Intensity	Low	Medium to high	High	Medium to low
Stability	—	—	Low	—

- *Win/lose.* All we can say is that the intensity of competition will be moderate to high, depending on the size of any storage costs or exit barriers.

- *Limited warfare.* Typically, the principal dimensions of competition will be product/brand extensions and promotional expenditures. Price *is not* a key area of competition; the whole objective of limited warfare is to control price competition.[6] The intensity of competition is moderate, because the leading players work to maintain the status quo and control any fighting. The long-term stability of such arrangements is the one unknown; it depends upon such factors as the long-term objectives of the various participants and the cost structure of the industry.

- *Lose/lose.* By contrast, in this case, we can be quite specific about the terms of competition. The key dimension is almost always price, the intensity is on the high side, and the overall stability of the terms of competition is low. The causes are the same ones that created the lose/lose situation in the first place, such as high fixed or storage costs, capacity added in large increments, substantial exit costs, and so forth.[7] In all such cases, firms need more sales volume, so they cut prices to stimulate demand. But demand is typically limited; consequently, reducing prices merely increases industry losses, making all the participants more desperate and less predictable.[8]

Table 2.1 provides only the broad outlines of how industry structure affects the terms of competition. To learn the finer details, we must analyze the relationship of the other forces of competition—buyer power, supplier power, substitutes, and market barriers—to three elements—intensity, stability, and key dimension—defining the rules of the game. The results are summarized in Table 2.2.

Table 2.2 How industry forces affect the terms of competition.

Terms of Competition	Industry Forces				
	Buyer Power	Supplier Power	Substitutes	Barriers to Entry	
				Exit Easy	Exit Hard
Key dimensions	Product, promotion	—	Price	Product, promotion	Price
Intensity	Medium	Medium	Medium to high	Medium	Medium to high
Stability	—Medium to high—		Low to medium	High	Low

- *Buyer power.* When buyers are powerful, the principal focus of competition is price. Strong buyers dictate product design, are not particularly affected by promotion, and minimize the use of channels. Powerful buyers find it in their self-interest to keep the intensity of competition under control and the terms of competition stable. Occasionally, product design may become a key area of competition as industry participants seek to neutralize buyer power or buyers' needs change. (See Chapter 4.)

- *Supplier power.* In this case, the intensity of competition is moderate, and stability is usually moderate to high. Strong suppliers generally find it in their self-interest to keep their customers divided but viable enough to remain a profitable market.

- *Substitutes.* Other things being equal, strong substitutes tend to increase the intensity of competition. The principal dimension of competition is price, the intensity is moderate to high, and overall, competition is less stable. Substitutes usually place a ceiling on the prices that can be charged. When this is coupled with slow or declining demand, as is often the case, pricing becomes a key area of conflict as firms cut prices to maintain market share. Competition also tends to be less stable because (1) the rate of substitution is unpredictable, (2) some firms adapt to the new technology faster than others, and (3) firms often have differing objectives, with some companies willing to exit quickly, while others wait till the bitter end.[9]

- *Barriers to market entry.* The impact of these must be examined in conjunction with exit barriers in the industry. If entry is difficult and exit is easy, the industry will, in all probability, stabilize over time into a small group of firms that compete on product and promotion but not on price.[10] Competition will be moderately intense and stable. On the other hand, if both entry and exit are difficult, industry participants will tend to focus on price; competition will be intense and most likely unstable, as weaker players resort to desperate measures to maintain share. If entry is easy and exit difficult, the situation is even worse.

Structure Determines Maneuver

Industry structure affects freedom of maneuver through the restrictions that the five forces of competition place on a firm's freedom to change the market position relative to competitors. These restrictions can be direct or indirect. *Direct restrictions* occur primarily in two areas— product design and channel selection:

- *Product design.* Once a standard or "dominant" design emerges, a firm has much less flexibility in changing product-related variables. (See Chapter 11.)
- *Channel selection.* When channels have power, they can (and usually do) restrict a firm's ability to decide which channels it will use. They may also limit its latitude in pricing decisions. (See Chapter 4.)

Indirect restrictions can affect virtually every aspect of market position; however, the areas most commonly affected are target market, and promotion and pricing:

- *Target market.* Industry structure affects a firm's ability to defend specific niches through the presence or absence of viable mobility barriers.
- *Promotion and pricing.* One or both of these variables may be restricted by the presence of substitutes, which limit price increases, or by industry rivalry, which demands that a firm match its competitors' advertising and promotional spending.

How industry payoffs affect maneuver is heavily influenced by the nature of the industry conflict. Specifically, if the conflict is

- Win/win, then there are few or no external constraints, and any limits are due to internal, resource-related restrictions
- Win/lose, then freedom of maneuver is restricted, but it may be difficult to determine the particular constraints as they often change over time

- Standoff/limited warfare, then the constraints on the maneuver are usually quite explicit and understood by all parties
- Lose/lose, then there is very little flexibility at all.

The U.S. Breakfast Cereal Industry

This industry provides a vivid example of the way in which structure defines the nature of the industry conflict, decides the terms of competition, and limits a firm's freedom of maneuver.

The U.S. ready-to-eat (RTE) cereal industry[11] got its start around the turn of the century when C.W. Post introduced Post's Grape Nuts cereal, followed rapidly by Post's Toasties and Kellogg's Toasted Corn Flakes. By 1905, four out of the five major techniques for producing RTE cereals (which we will call just "cereals" for convenience) were in use. These cereals rapidly displaced hot cereals in popularity, with the result that, by 1939, they accounted for nearly 65 percent of total category sales by dollar volume. By 1977, this proportion had risen to more than 85 percent. Demand has been stable for the last 15 years, with poundage output (net of sugar additions for presweetened cereals) growing at the rate of the consuming population.

Industry Structure

Since the mid-1930s, four firms have accounted for more than 85 percent of industry sales, making it one of the most concentrated industries in the United States.[12] Kellogg is the share leader, General Mills is in second place (with roughly half of Kellogg's share), General Foods (Post) is third, and Quaker is fourth. In terms of the five forces of competition, the situation is summarized:

CRITICAL MASS BARRIERS

- Barriers to market entry are high and consist primarily of advertising costs. Estimates vary, but in the late 1980s, the fixed advertising costs of launching a new, national brand of cereal were around $30 to $35 million for the first year. Economies of scale, per se, are not a major barrier to market entry.
- Buyer power is low. Consumers have little or no power, while the power of channels, namely the supermarket and grocery chains, is limited by the high levels of advertising and strong brand identities.
- Supplier power is nonexistent. The suppliers are fragmented and cannot effectively exercise any power on the four major players.

- Substitutes such as pancakes, toast, and so on, have little effect on pricing.
- Rivalry is moderate. The industry does not have high fixed or storage costs, exit barriers are low, and capacity is not augmented in large increments.[13]

Further, contribution margins are high, averaging 48 percent of revenues net of freight costs. When we apply the framework developed in the previous sections, we come to the following conclusions:

- *The nature of the conflict is limited warfare.* Given stable demand and the fact that cereals account for a small fraction of a family's food bill, each of the participants will conclude that price competition is likely to be counterproductive. The odds are that it will not stimulate demand to any significant extent, while the other players will be forced to retaliate to maintain share. Therefore, lowering prices will merely reduce revenues and profits without any gains in share.
- *Competition is moderate, stable, and focused on product and promotion.* This follows from Table 2.2. The desire to limit price competition and the importance of grocery chains leaves only target markets (i.e., niches), product, and promotion as the key dimensions of competition. The leading producer's (Kellogg) strong market position—its share is equal to that of the other three participants put together—ensures that competition will be both moderate and stable.
- *Freedom of maneuver is also limited.* There are explicit restrictions on channel choice due to the pre-eminent position of the large grocery chains and the importance of getting and holding shelf space in the stores. There are implicit limits on pricing due to the desire to prevent all-out price wars, which are counterproductive.

Industry Conduct

When we examine the industry's historical behavior, we find that it follows closely the pattern described above. Specifically, the industry has behaved as an oligopoly, with one firm (Kellogg) acting as the price leader and with competition restricted to product innovation or proliferation, and non- or limited-price promotional campaigns.

Pricing. From the mid-1960s, the industry has de-emphasized price competition, with the result that cereal prices have remained stable and have even outpaced overall consumer price increases. Kellogg has been the clear price leader: "Out of [the] 15 unambiguous price increase rounds between 1965 and 1970 . . . Kellogg led 12."[14] Further, other aspects of price competition—rebating, discounts, private labels—were severely limited:

- Competition using "in-pack" premiums, such as baseball cards, toys, and so forth, was vigorous in the late 1940s and early to mid-1950s, but has been controlled and limited since. It escalated briefly in 1968 but was controlled immediately.
- Trade allowances to the supermarkets and to the end purchaser have been limited since the 1950s. As a General Mills advertising agency observed, ". . . . historically, the cereal industry has resisted pressures to enter into the allowance battles which most other package goods categories wage continuously."
- "Couponing" has been used extensively since it offers several advantages over straight price cuts: It is less expensive, as most purchasers do not bother to redeem coupons. It allows precise targeting to repeat customers and helps build loyalty. Finally, the high costs of couponing keep the use of this tactic under control.
- Private-label competition is nonexistent. A 1966 study found that, for a sample of 212 food products, cereals had exceptionally few private labels. This is not an accident; the leading producers, Kellogg and General Mills, have consistently refused to supply private-label brands, and the other producers have generally followed suit. In 1968 and 1969, Ralston did try to build its private-label corn flakes business, forcing Kellogg to retaliate with substantial price cuts, ultimately limiting such competition.

Advertising and New Products.   These two areas are the focal points of competition in this industry. Advertising expenditures average 7.3 percent of sales in the industry, second only to toiletries (10.2 percent). The average for all consumer goods industries is 5.7 percent. There is extensive use of segmentation, with products and advertising campaigns designed expressly to meet the perceived and actual needs of different buyer groups.

These promotional expenditures go hand-in-hand with extensive brand proliferation. In 1950, the six leading firms offered a total of 26 brands. Over the next 20 years, 84 brands were introduced, with the result that in 1973 there were 80 brands in distribution (see Table 2.3).

Table 2.3 Brand introductions in RTE cereals.

Year	New Brands Introduced	Total Brands Six Firms	Total Brands: Top Three Firms		
			Kellogg	General Mills	General Foods
1950		26	9	3	6
1955	7	33	12	4	8
1960	14	44	15	8	9
1965	13	55	18	11	12
1970	28	69	20	15	12
1973	22	80	20	19	15

Source: Adapted from F. M. Scherer, *Industrial Market Structure and Economic Performance* (Boston, MA: Houghton Mifflin, 1980).

Summary

We have presented the broad outlines of the interrelationships between the structure of an industry and the strategic leverage available to a company. We will defer a more detailed discussion to Part Two. In Chapter 3, we will discuss return, the other half of leverage, and describe how company competitive position influences the returns for various maneuvers.

3

How Competitive Position Restricts Leverage and Limits Choices

Competitive position influences strategic leverage through both maneuver and return. A company's competitive position in an industry restricts its flexibility in changing prices, raising or lowering advertising expenditures, redesigning products, or otherwise altering the terms of competition. Competitive position also affects the returns for such changes. How much additional revenue, market share, and, ultimately, profit, a company obtains as a result of these changes depends considerably upon whether it is a leader, a follower, or a niche player.

By restricting leverage, a company's competitive position also limits its strategic choices. These limitations become more apparent as an industry evolves over time. In a rapidly growing industry, competitive position has relatively little impact on strategic choices. Competitive position becomes progressively more important as the industry starts to mature and becomes a major factor as the industry enters into late maturity and decline.

AT&T versus MCI in Long-Distance Telecommunications

The U.S. long-distance telephone services market provides a graphic example of how a company's competitive position affects its leverage and choices. It also illustrates the fact that market share alone is not enough to evaluate a firm's position while highlighting other factors that should be considered.

In long-distance telecommunications, AT&T is the overall industry leader, while MCI ranks second. However, their relative competitive positions, leverage, and choices vary according to the market segment. In the residential and general business segment, MCI has much less leverage and very few choices; AT&T is clearly the dominant player. In the large business market, on the other hand, MCI is much better positioned, although still second to AT&T. As a result, MCI's leverage is greater, and it has more latitude in its strategic choices.

Background

The U.S. long-distance telecommunications market had been a regulated monopoly since 1913. This monopoly started to break down in the mid-1970s and formally ended on 1 January 1984 with the dissolution of the Bell System into seven regional companies and AT&T. The regionals (or "Baby Bells") were restricted to serving local communications needs, while long-distance services were the province of AT&T, the former parent. Further, competition in the long-distance market was encouraged in a variety of ways.

Long-distance revenues were composed of (1) access charges paid to local telephone companies for connecting two parties to a long-distance carrier's facilities, and (2) transmission and switching revenues (see Figure 3.1). Typically, the long-distance carrier charged the user for the access fees, then turned around and paid them to the local carrier. However, in some situations, the long-distance carrier connected directly to a customer's own telephone equipment (bypassing the local telephone company), thereby eliminating at least one set of access charges. Total revenues, net of access charges, were $28.1 billion in 1987 and were

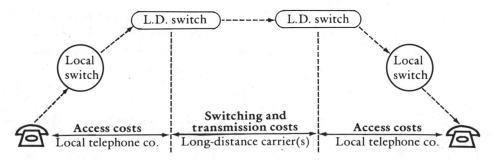

Figure 3.1   Access and switching and transmission charges.

growing at 6–8 percent annually. The industry grew rapidly in the years preceding and immediately following deregulation, but increasing price competition held revenues down, although usage still increased, albeit at a slower rate than before.[1]

Key factors determining the structure of the industry were (1) changes in technology that had dramatically reduced transmission costs, (2) the presence of third-party networks that enabled entrants to avoid high initial investments in establishing a nationwide transmission and switching network, (3) the structure of access costs. In the early days of long-distance telecommunications, the costs of constructing and maintaining a national network based on conventional copper cables was extremely high; in fact, this was one of the major reasons for the establishment of the Bell System as a regulated monopoly. Recent technological developments, in particular the advent of fiber optic cable, lowered these costs considerably and, at the same time, expanded the capacity of the network severalfold. This led several investor groups to construct partial or complete long-distance transmission networks across the United States, thereby creating a glut of transmission capacity.[2] Consequently, network costs were no longer the barrier to market entry they once were; would-be players could lease capacity almost as cheaply as the majors such as AT&T and MCI, who had created their own networks.

The other significant factor was the cost of access, that is, the cost of taking the signal to and from the long-distance carrier's equipment to the customer's premises (see Figure 3.1). This was particularly acute in the case of households and small businesses that were dispersed over large geographical areas; for such customers the local telephone company was virtually the only supplier of access. Access (and its associated costs) was much less of a problem in the case of large business customers because they were geographically concentrated and had high traffic volumes. This made it economical to bypass the local telephone company, for example, by installing microwave transmission equipment that sent traffic directly to the long-distance carrier's facilities.[3]

As a result of these changes, the structure of the long-distance market changed from a high fixed-cost industry to one in which, at least in some market segments, the fixed costs were low and entry was relatively easy.

Segments

The long-distance market was composed of three main segments—large national accounts, medium-sized regional firms (the "major markets"), and residential and small business customers (usually referred to as "residential"). The large national and residential segments each accounted for approximately 40 percent of total market revenues, with the balance being major market customers. (Figure 3.2 presents summary statistics regarding the overall market and individual segments.) The large national and residential markets provide the greatest contrast in terms of the effect of competitive position on leverage and choices; therefore, in the subsequent discussions, we will concentrate on these two markets.

The residential segment was truly a mass market, with more than 110 million subscribers nationwide and average revenues of $15/month. The typical customer had one or two phone lines and required primarily voice long-distance services, although data transmission needs were increasing, as more persons worked out of their homes. Access was provided almost exclusively through the existing local telephone company's network, and typically billing and collections were also subcontracted by the long-distance carrier to the local service supplier. A variety of channels—direct mail, telemarketing, resellers, affinity groups—were used to reach these customers. Advertising costs were significant. In 1988, total advertising expenditures within the industry were $250 million. With an advertising budget of $148 million, AT&T accounted for the major portion of this spending. MCI and Sprint were the other major contributors with advertising spending of $25.4 million and $27.5 million, respectively.[4]

The large national segment, on the other hand, was highly concentrated, with fewer than 400 customers. Revenues per customer averaged more than $4 million a month, with firms in information-intensive industries (banking, financial services, airlines) spending considerably more than that amount. National accounts usually had their own networks connecting different company manufacturing/operations sites, sales offices, and in some cases, major customers. While voice services such as long-distance telephone calls between two parties were important

Long-Distance Calls on AT&T Lines in 1989	Revenue (in $ billions)	Market Share (%)
Residential, small businesses, international, operator services	$25.0	73.9
800-Toll-free services	4.7	82.6
Services for large corporations and institutions (including WATS line and dedicated lines)	9.0	66.8
Other, unregulated services	0.5	21.6
Total AT&T long-distance market	$39.2	70.8

Figure 3.2   AT&T's position in long-distance
telecommunications—1989.

to national accounts, their needs for data transmission at ever-increasing speeds, real-time access to large central databases, image and in some cases video transmission, and such services as free inbound-calling for customers (800# calling), voice mail, and so on were growing rapidly. National accounts generally had a telecommunications department to design and manage their networks and negotiate with suppliers of equipment and services such as AT&T, MCI, and others. The largest telecommunications managers were virtually chief executives of sizable telephone companies; for example, the telecommunications manager for a major oil company managed a network with an annual budget of more than $1 billion, more than 1,000 employees, 80,000 subscribers scattered all over the world, and a host of the latest telecommunications technologies including a satellite-based network, optical fiber transmission, data security concerns rivaling that of the Department of Defense![5]

Competitive Situation

While a number of firms competed in these two markets, in 1983, AT&T and MCI were clearly the main players, with US Sprint (joint venture between GTE and United Telecommunications) a distant third. AT&T was the leader, with more than 70 percent of the market share in each of these segments. MCI had approximately 11 percent of the residential market and a slightly larger portion of corporate customers. As long as AT&T was regulated, there was a price umbrella under which other players, notably MCI, could flourish. The situation changed in 1984, although not completely, since AT&T still had to file its proposed price changes with the FCC, giving its opponents time to react. These restrictions were gradually eased, especially in the large national segment, where AT&T was allowed to offer contractual terms to match competitive moves without the necessity of regulatory approval.[6] The net result of these changes was to intensify price competition overall; however, there were significant differences between the two segments.

Residential Segment. There was an early flurry of price-based competition, especially in the "equal access balloting" phase, during which residential and small business customers were required to sign up with a long-distance carrier of their choice. Subsequently, there was intermittent price competition during which one or the other carrier would lower its prices to attract customers, and the other players would follow suit.

However, beginning in 1986, AT&T started to re-establish price and market leadership. First, AT&T lowered prices as much as 20 to 35 percent. In the process, it narrowed the price gap considerably, to between 5 to 10 percent in the case of most major players. AT&T also dramatically raised its advertising expenditures, from less than $30 million in 1983 to more than $140 million in 1988. This forced other competitors to follow suit or risk losing share; largely as a consequence of AT&T's actions, industry spending on advertising increased severalfold. Last but not least, AT&T sent clear signals to its competitors, particularly MCI, about its willingness to match any "undue" price competition.[7]

Large National Accounts.   By contrast, AT&T has found it difficult to establish or maintain its leadership in this segment. Price competition has been more severe, as the various players struggled to gain or (in AT&T's case) maintain share. Promotional activity has been relatively restrained; for the most part, entrants have been content to establish an image of quality, reliability, and a complete range of services, for example, toll-free calling and WATS (wide area telephone service). Entrants have even begun to set trends in service innovation, such as MCI's PRISM services for corporate accounts and US Sprint's all-fiber network, a feature of some interest to data-intensive users.

Strategic Implications

While MCI was the second-ranked player in both segments, its leverage and choices differed by segment. In the residential market, MCI's freedom of maneuver was considerably restricted, and it had to be alert to AT&T's various moves. On the other hand, in the large national account market, AT&T had less influence over MCI's actions, giving the latter more latitude. Here competitive position was less important than industry structure, especially buyer power, in restricting maneuver.

Maneuver.   Table 3.1 summarizes the restrictions on MCI's freedom of maneuver, in both the residential and national account segments.

- In the residential segment, product and price were both constrained by MCI's distinctly weaker position vis-à-vis AT&T. The latter had made it abundantly clear that it could, and would, retaliate if MCI's product/price ratio was substantially higher than AT&T's. The implications for pricing, in particular, were evident; AT&T had de facto established a "band" of between 5 and 10 percent below which MCI could not lower its prices without a counterattack. Implicitly this band also constrained service innovations; any service offerings that changed the price/performance ratio in MCI's favor threatened AT&T's position, causing it to retaliate.

Table 3.1   Constraints on MCI's marketing tactics.

	Residential	Large Business
Product	• Constrained by the need to stay within "acceptable" product/price ratios • Innovation is also constrained by competitive position	• More flexibility due to contractual nature of purchases • Somewhat more flexibility to create innovative offerings
Place	• Restricted by smaller volumes, and costs of reaching mass market	• More flexibility
Promotion	• Restricted by need to maintain promotion spending below AT&T's "reservation" level • Price promotions constrained by restrictions on pricing	• Constrained primarily by internal resources
Price	• Within 5–10% of AT&T's prices	• Few overt constraints due to complex nature of typical packages

- When it came to national accounts, competitive position did not particularly inhibit MCI's flexibility in changing service features or prices. This was due to (1) the contractual nature of the purchases and (2) the sophistication of the buyers. Corporate purchases of long-distance telephone services were made via contracts that were modified to suit individual customers' volumes and specific requirements. This inherently allowed greater latitude, both in pricing and in features/services covered under the contract. Companies could bundle, cross-subsidize, or otherwise change their offerings from one situation to the next, depending on the buyer's bargaining position, the desirability of the contract, and the supplier's immediate tactical objectives. The sophistication of the buyers made them less dependent on a leader such as AT&T to provide the "seal of approval" on specific features or services. (On the other hand, their very sophistication made it more difficult to differentiate services for any length of time.)[8]

- MCI's promotional spending in the residential segment was similarly limited from above by the need to maintain "limited war" with AT&T and, from below, by the need to maintain market awareness and share. If MCI's spending on nonprice promotional activities greatly exceeded AT&T's "reservation price," the latter would feel threatened and might be inclined to escalate its own efforts. However, given MCI's slender financial resources (as compared with AT&T), such competitive escalation of advertising was to be avoided if possible. By the same token, MCI could not afford to spend less than a certain amount, consistent with its market share, for fear of weakening consumer awareness with consequent damage to its market share.

- There were fewer competitive restrictions on (nonprice) promotions in the national account segment, in part because such promotional activities had little impact on buying decisions. Such limits as existed were due primarily to internal resources, for example, AT&T could afford to have extensive customer education and counseling services, while MCI had to be more restricted in its offerings.

- Competitive position had relatively little impact on the channels of distribution (including the direct sales forces); the major determinants were (1) the costs of reaching the mass market and (2) the need for extensive consultative selling to national accounts. Within these limits, MCI was somewhat more constrained in the mass market by its lower volumes, which raised its marketing costs relative to its larger rival.

There were constraints on AT&T, the industry leader, as well. In the residential segment, AT&T's pricing was constrained by the need to ensure that the price differential between itself and its closest competitors such as MCI and Sprint did not become too large, that is, that it did not become a price umbrella. At the same time, both self-interest and the (regulatory) difficulty of forcing major players such as MCI and Sprint out of the industry ensured that AT&T would not lower prices too far. With national accounts, AT&T's pricing was constrained by its prior record and by the need to maintain its quality image, which would be ruined by excessive or precipitate price discounting. Nor could the firm reduce its sales presence at these accounts without it affecting long-term relationships and, eventually, revenues. Other dimensions had few, if any, restrictions. Unlike MCI, AT&T could choose its own pace in service innovation, within reason, just as it could decide the competitive intensity of advertising and promotional expenditures.

Returns.   MCI's returns, in terms of additional revenues or market share, also vary by segment:

- Investments in service innovation offer greater potential returns in the national account market as compared with the residential segment. National accounts are likely to accept MCI's innovations more readily than residential customers. With the latter, MCI has to spend disproportionally more merely to gain parity with AT&T in terms of service features and perceived quality.

- The same investment in price changes offers greater returns in national accounts versus residential customers. Pricing tactics can be disguised more easily and large customers are more price sensitive. Conversely, in the residential market, price changes must be publicized if they are to have any impact. Once publicized, they can be matched resulting in little net gain.

- Promotional spending in the residential segment offers little return beyond creating awareness and perhaps generating trial by potential customers. Similar expenditures in the large national account market offer greater rewards if focused on sales presence, customer service, and account maintenance.

Choices.   Not surprisingly, MCI's strategic choices are also affected by the differences in its competitive position in the two segments. In the residential market, MCI has virtually no options but to faithfully follow where AT&T leads. While small-scale attacks are possible, MCI must avoid major confrontations; AT&T is simply too strong. In the large account segment, MCI can aim at bringing a strong across-the-board number two, "Pepsi to AT&T's Coke." Or it could choose to concentrate on a number of niches, or even pursue a cost-leadership strategy.

Competitive Position Restricts Strategic Leverage

As the examples suggests, our concept of competitive position is broader than just market share or relative share (the company's share divided by the leader's share). In our view, a company's competitive position is an index of its ability to influence or change the terms of competition. Thus, in the residential segment, MCI's competitive position is distinctly weaker than its share of that market would suggest. Conversely, MCI's position in the large account segment is stronger than what its share of the market would suggest. Our notion of competitive position includes not only market share and/or relative share but also such factors as

- Share of advertising/promotional expenditures
- Technological leadership
- Brand positioning
- Brand identity

- Relative cost positioning
- Control/share of channels.

How Position Affects Maneuver

The constraints placed on AT&T's and MCI's flexibility in changing price, promotion, and so on are typical examples of how position influences maneuver. Let us now discuss these relationships in greater detail for leaders, second/third players, and followers or niche players.

Leaders.   Companies that are industry or segment leaders have to ensure that their tactics do not inadvertently change the nature of industry conflict, thereby endangering their position within the industry. As a result, they find that tactical freedom of maneuver is restricted in several directions. They cannot afford *not* to make changes such as lowering prices or introducing new products for fear of eroding their competitive position and/or their ability to set the terms of industry rivalry. On the other hand, they cannot be overly aggressive if they wish to maintain "limited warfare." In summary, the restrictions on the five elements of market strategy are:

- *Target markets.* The leader's ability to change segments or concentrate on specific segments is restricted by the need to maintain its controlling position in major market areas. This hampers the leader in addressing new customer groups and may exclude it from some segments entirely.

- *Product.* If the leader is pursuing a differentiation strategy, its ability to change the product is restricted by the need to maintain its uniqueness in the customers' minds. At the same time, the leader has to be concerned about making its product line too broad, thereby spreading its sales and marketing efforts over too wide an area and leaving it vulnerable to being nibbled away by smaller competitors. If this were not enough, its prior efforts create "switching costs," for example, investments in spare parts, training facilities, sales and support personnel, which also make it more difficult to change product tactics. Xerox, for example, developed the cartridge copier but was reluctant to introduce it for fear of making obsolete its investment in a large in-field sales and service organization. Similarly, the leadership position constrained U.S. tire companies from making the switch in time from bias-belted tires to radials.

A cost leadership strategy similarly constrains product tactics. Extensions to the product line raise costs and divert resources from investments in cost reduction. Furthermore, the more a firm invests in production facilities and so on to lower costs, the more reluctant it is to switch to newer technologies or processes.

- *Pricing.* The leader's flexibility in changing prices is also affected by its market position. The larger the leader's share, the more reluctant it is to reduce prices as it has the most to lose (at least in the short run). An additional factor hampering the leader's ability to change prices is the fear of disruption and customer dissatisfaction. The longer a firm has been a leader, the more likely that significant price changes will cause disruption; therefore, the more reluctant it will be to make such changes. Pricing tactics are also restrained by the leader's desire to minimize industry conflict. If the firm lowers prices considerably, it may force lesser players to retaliate with matching price cuts, initiating a price war that may be difficult to keep under control.

- *Place.* Early on, the industry leader has the freedom to set the patterns of distribution. However, as the market matures, this flexibility is reduced by (1) a firm's investments in the status quo, and (2) the risk of substantial losses of revenue due to the inevitable delays in developing alternatives and the loss of revenue from the prior channels. However, other things being equal, the leader does have more flexibility than other participants in changing channel terms and conditions.

- *Promotion.* The leading firm's ability to change its advertising and nonprice promotional expenditures and activities is restricted by the need to maintain its market position. This is particularly important in industries where advertising is a key determinant of competitive intentions and intensity. In such cases, a leader's failure to devote promotional resources in proportion to its market position could be fatal. In industries where promotional activities play a lesser role, the leader has more flexibility; however, even in such cases it must be present at key events, for example, major trade shows, industry conferences.

Second/Third Players.   A leader's actions, in turn, restrict other participants' freedom of maneuver, especially if these changes threaten to disrupt firms' relative positioning. This is not as important in the case of niche players ("followers" in our terminology) but is definitely significant for firms that rank second or third. Consequently, these players find their maneuver restricted in both directions. If, for example, they increase their advertising or price promotions beyond a certain level, they risk retaliation by the leader. On the other hand, if they do not maintain their investments in these and other areas, they risk losing share to the leader or to niche players seeking to expand.

In addition, these players' freedom to change tactics is also restrained by internal limits on resources. These participants have to match the leader's activities in product development, promotion or channel margins, but on revenues and profits that are often substantially lower. The most extreme example of this dilemma is American Motors' attempt to match the Big Three automakers' model line-ups and distribution systems in the mid-1960s, with the predictable result that its share and profits both dropped. Even when the disparities between the firms are not so extreme, second/third players are often hard pressed to match the leader's moves.

Second/third players' freedom of maneuver is particularly restricted in the area of channels and pricing, especially when the industry situation requires that they "follow the leader." There is generally more freedom in product tactics and in nonprice promotional activities. However, here too, firms must balance their need to maintain their position relative to the leader against the potential revenues to be obtained by creating new products. MCI, for instance, must devote its resources to first matching the services AT&T is providing now as well those it is likely to introduce in the future. Only after these competitive requirements have been met can MCI consider developing new offerings (assuming it has any resources to spare). MCI must similarly match AT&T's moves in advertising and promotion, in proportion to its market position; this was demonstrated by the fact that the growth in MCI's advertising expenditures mirrored AT&T's increasing spending in this area (see Figure 3.3).

Followers. The effects of competitive position on marketing tactics vary depending on whether a firm is the fourth or fifth player in the industry or occupies a niche in which it is among the top two or three players. If it is an also-ran, for example, Chrysler in the global automotive industry, then it has even less freedom of maneuver than second/third players.

If, on the other hand, a firm occupies a strong position within a niche, it has more latitude. Within its niche, position and, thus, its room for maneuver are similar to that of the leader or second/third players in the

	AT&T[a] (millions)	MCI[b] (millions)
1990	592	141
1989	526	121
1988	548	110
1987	398	78
1986	481	88
1985	439	82
1984	456	73

[a] AT&T long-distance business communications advertising expenses only.

[b] Source: *Communications Trends, Inc.*

Figure 3.3 Comparative advertising expenditures.

industry as a whole. Further, if the niche is protected by strong mobility barriers preventing entry by the major players, then general industry forces have little effect on the follower's actions.

How Position Changes Returns

When we speak of the "returns" for a particular change in product, place, promotion, and so on, we are primarily interested in the impact on revenues, market share, or both. The question is, "If we change this variable by x amount, how much additional revenue and market share can we expect?" Such changes are ultimately linked to company profitability. However, likely returns in terms of profit also depend on internal factors, for example, efficiency, effectiveness, cost of capital, and so forth. For these reasons, we concentrate on external increases of revenue and market share.

A company's competitive position has a major effect on its returns for any changes to target market product, place, promotion, or price. Broadly speaking, the weaker a company's position, that is, the less it is able to influence or change the terms of competition, the lower the company's returns.

In the margarine and soft spreads industry, for example, Parkay was the leader while Chiffon was a distant fourth. Not surprisingly, Chiffon had to spend far more on "trade incentives"—advertising allowances to supermarkets for in-store coupons—as compared with Parkay, to achieve a given level of shelf space. In other words, Chiffon's returns in terms of shelf space (and therefore sales) were much lower than Parkay's for the same investment in channels.[9] MCI's returns, similarly, are generally lower than AT&T's. Furthermore, MCI's returns are lower in the residential segment, where its competitive position is weaker than in large accounts where MCI is better positioned.

Implications for Strategic Choices

By restricting leverage, a company's competitive position also places definite limits on its feasible strategic choices. These limits become stronger as the industry evolves over time. Our reasoning is as follows: As an industry evolves, the participants' overall freedom of maneuver, and the likely returns for such maneuvers, decline and become more focused along one or two dimensions. This reduction in the overall leverage, when combined with a weak competitive position (which further limits leverage), narrows the company's feasible choices considerably. Thus, in the ready-to-eat cereals market (a mature industry), Ralston-Purina as the fourth player can either co-exist with the leader or exit the market. Other choices such as trying to overtake General Mills or Kellogg, retreating to a niche, initiating a price war, and so forth, are either infeasible—very little leverage—or even suicidal, given Ralston-Purina's resources and competitive position relative to the major players. On the other hand, in a growing industry such as the personal computer market in the early-to-mid 1980s, a follower such Hewlett-Packard had more options. It could have tried to become second to IBM, displacing Apple, it could have focused on a niche, or it could even have tried to become a cost leader and carved out a distinct second/third position based on that strategy.

While the specific limits vary considerably depending on the structure and payoffs of the industry, we can make the following observations regarding how a company's position affects its choices, depending on the nature of industry conflict:

- *Win/win.* Here a company's competitive position has the least impact on its feasible choices. Market leaders and second/third players have considerable latitude in selecting their overall strategic direction. They can choose to pursue a differentiation strategy, try to become the low-cost producers, or concentrate their efforts on various niches. Followers typically have fewer options; essentially their choices are either to find a viable, lucrative niche or, in rare cases, try to capture the second/third positions.

- *Limited warfare.* At this point the major positions are usually becoming clear. Leaders and second/third players have already decided on their overall strategies, that is, differentiation or cost leadership, with the result that there is little latitude in terms of market positioning. Leaders can choose to either maintain the status quo, continue to expand more or less aggressively, or be content with defending their positions. In the U.S. beer industry, Anheuser-Busch has been relentlessly increasing its share, first at the expense of smaller regional brewers, and now by attacking Miller and Coors. In the 1960s and 1970s, Detroit, on the other hand, was trying to maintain the status quo—limited price competition, focus on larger cars, and a large variety of models and optional extras. The second/third players' choices are nominally similar, with one subtle but important difference: The industry leader typically has the initiative. These companies must respond to the leader's moves and must consider how the leader might retaliate to any aggressive moves. Other followers have basically only two choices, namely, find an appropriate niche or exit the industry. Niche players, similarly, have few choices other than to try to strengthen their position in the niche. If they are unable to do that, their best bet is usually to exit the industry, preferably at a profit.

- *Win/lose and lose/lose.* In either of these situations, the choices are very few indeed. The leader can try to reverse win/lose into limited price warfare by re-establishing price discipline within the industry. However, structural reasons such as strong buyers or high fixed costs may make restoring price discipline impossible. In such cases, they must choose between exiting the industry themselves or else forcing other players to exit. For all other participants, the question is, "Do we have a tenable position?" If the answer is "no," their only choice is to exit, trying to extract as high a price as possible. Trying to avert the inevitable merely prolongs the agony, as witness Massey-Fergusson's painfully slow (ruinously expensive) exit from the farm equipment market.

Summary

We have now outlined our major themes, namely, that understanding strategic leverage is essential in deciding a company's long-term goals and overall direction; that leverage has two components, maneuver and return; that if either maneuver or return are low, the company has very little leverage; that industry structure defines maneuver and, through industry payoffs, the returns; and that competitive position further constrains leverage and a company's feasible choices.

We will explore these major themes and related sub-themes in the next section of the book. We will also introduce tools and techniques for analyzing maneuver, returns, and leverage, as well as identifying feasible strategy choices.

4

How Competitive Forces Affect Leverage

We will begin our study of leverage by examining how the various forces driving industry competition affect a company's leverage. Our approach will be to look at each of the competitive forces and the conditions under which each one is likely to be significant. Then we will analyze how that force influences the structure of the industry. Finally, we will examine how the competitive force affects a firm's leverage by considering how it influences the various dimensions of target market, product, place, promotion, and price.

Our starting point is the standard industrial economics or Porter model for analyzing the structure of an industry (see Figure 4.1). Industries that consistently earn above-average profits do so because of one or more of the following:

- Their customers (buyers) are weak.
- Their suppliers are weak and cannot raise their prices.
- Customers have few effective substitutes for the products and services provided.
- Competition in the industry is not intense.
- It is difficult to enter the industry.

Similarly, in industries where profitability is below average, the converse is true.

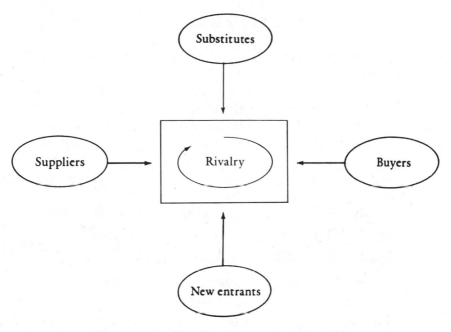

Figure 4.1   The five forces of competition.

Besides influencing industry structure, each of the five competitive forces also affects one or more elements of the target market, known as the 4Ps—product, place, promotion, and pricing. Strong buyers are likely to prevent industry consolidation, as in automotive ancillaries. Powerful buyers will also make product differentiation difficult or even irrelevant; typically, buyers will specify the product and base purchase decisions on price and delivery. They are not particularly influenced by promotion and usually keep the role of intermediaries to a minimum. By contrast, in the diamond trade, the key economic force is supplier power. De Beers runs the diamond cartel with an iron hand,[1] preventing any consolidation in diamond distribution and controlling wholesale (and to a lesser extent, retail) prices to ensure that diamonds retain their traditional investment value. Substitutes can limit or even end industry growth and place great constraints on industry pricing and promotion. If entry and exit are easy, the industry is likely to remain fragmented and in constant upheaval with new players entering and others leaving. In such an environment, product differentiation is very difficult as any promotional efforts are "muffled" by the constant turmoil and the fragmented nature of the industry. Finally, when rivalry is intense, price and promotion are usually under great pressure.

Buyer Power

Powerful buyers can prevent industry consolidation by keeping the various participants fragmented. By integrating backwards, they can create "poor" competitors who are willing/able to accept lower returns. In turn, they affect leverage by shifting the emphasis away from product differentiation and toward price competition. Weak buyers, on the other hand, have little effect on industry structure and on the 4Ps. The relationship between buyer power and the 4Ps also works in the other direction: Potentially powerful buyers may be successfully neutralized by using appropriate strategies and tactics.

When analyzing the relationship between buyer power and the 4Ps, focus on the following questions:

- What are the factors determining buyer power?
- Under which conditions will buyers exercise their power?
- How can buyer power be neutralized?
- What are the implications for industry structure and for leverage?

Determining Buyer Power

For a buyer or a group of buyers to have power over an industry, they must have alternatives for the industry's products or services, these alternatives must be economically feasible, and there must be an inequity in the relationship between the buyers and the industry participants, that is, the industry participant must need the buyers more than the buyers need the industry participant.

Buyers are powerful under some or all of the following circumstances:[2]

- There is a large relative volume of purchases.
- Products are standard or undifferentiated.
- There are few switching costs.
- Buyers can integrate backwards.
- Inputs are not key to quality.
- The buyer has access to full information regarding industry cost, technologies, and demand levels.
- The buyer controls access to the ultimate end customer.

The Power of Intermediaries.   In a number of situations, the buyer is an intermediary who controls access to the end user. For example, in U.S. long-distance telephone service, the local exchange provider such as

Ameritech or NYNEX is a powerful intermediary, especially in the case of residence subscribers. In this industry, long-distance service is provided by a long-distance carrier such as AT&T, MCI, or Sprint. Each of these companies has to establish a point-of-presence, a distribution point, in a given service area. In turn, this point-of-presence connects to the local exchange switch, to which all the subscribers in the area are also connected (see Figure 4.2).

In this case, the local exchange company (for example, Ameritech or NYNEX) has considerable power vis-à-vis the long-distance carriers because it controls access to the ultimate end user. But this power varies considerably by segment. Bypassing this intermediary to access the vast majority of residence and small business users would be prohibitively expensive—the long-distance carriers would have to set up an alternative local telephone company. On the other hand, in the case of large concentrated users, such as a major corporate headquarters or a large university campus, it becomes economically and technologically feasible to "bypass" the local telephone company; thus, its power is considerably less.

Exerting Buyer Power

Even though a group of buyers is powerful, they may not choose to use their strength, for example, if they want to maintain viable sources of supply. Buyers will be predisposed to use their power when

- The item is a large portion of their purchases.
- They are not overly concerned about maintaining viable sources.
- Their profits are low relative to their suppliers.
- Their profits are being squeezed.

The last two factors are particularly strong incentives.

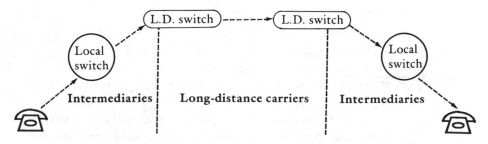

Figure 4.2 Intermediary power—the case of long-distance telephone service.

Neutralizing Buyer Power

In some situations, the bargaining power of buyers can be reduced or neutralized through a number of different strategies. The specific approach varies, depending on whether the buyer is an intermediary or an end-user customer.

When Intermediaries Have Power.   In this case, the choices are to "leap frog" over them, co-opt them, or eliminate them entirely.

- *"Leap frog" over them.* Federal Express is an example of this approach. Before Federal Express, the actual end user had no say in choosing the carrier for his package. Users typically called their shipping departments, which then took care of it. In essence, the intermediary, the shipping clerk, really made the decision. Federal Express appealed to the end user by saying, "When it absolutely, positively has to be there overnight, call us," bypassing the shipping clerk altogether. This is classic "pull" marketing.

- *Co-opt them.* Buyers who are co-opted do not exercise their power. For example, there is an almost symbiotic relationship between the chief financial officers of large corporations and the leading "Big Eight" public accounting firms. In many cases, the CFO started his professional career with the CPA firm that audits his corporation's books. Therefore, he is familiar with the firm's concerns and sympathetic to its problems and needs. As a result, the firm is not predisposed to exert its bargaining power in what is increasingly seen as a standardized service.[3] Dow Chemical has similarly co-opted chemical engineers into specifying Dow products for use in heat-transfer applications by supplying products to engineering schools at no charge. As a result, the engineer-to-be takes it for granted that "Dowtherm™ is the product you specify." Using this strategy, Dow has captured over half of the market in what is essentially a commodity chemicals business.

- *Eliminate them.* Finally, intermediaries can be neutralized by eliminating the need for their services. This can be done by integrating forwards or by changing the manner in which products are distributed so as to eliminate the need for the functions traditionally performed by the distributor. In the 1970s, Cessna Aircraft Company bought out its independent regional distributors, thereby gaining total control over its distribution system. Several large appliance manufacturers have looked into consolidating their distribution system, making the dealer merely an ordering point. In this scheme, customers would walk into a dealership and decide which models they would like and how they would pay for them. The units would be shipped from the factory directly to the buyer, with installation (if necessary) by the dealer.

When the End Customer Has the Power.   Here the choices are to try to differentiate the product, create switching costs, choose the "right" buyers, or become the low-cost producer.

- *Differentiate the product.* This can be done by changing the intangible services surrounding a tangible product (or by changing the tangible products surrounding an intangible service).[4] Generally, this approach is successful only in combination with another strategy, such as co-opting the intermediary (influencer, specifier); against truly powerful buyers, differentiation, per se, is not likely to be very successful over the long term.
- *Create switching costs.* Many contractors and builders are reluctant to switch from Caterpillar equipment because of their large investment in Cat parts and spares, which would become obsolete if they changed to Komatsu. Large corporations are similarly loath to switch from IBM computers due to the costs of converting their huge installed base of software and data.
- *Choose the "right" buyers.* Not all buyer groups are equally powerful; this fact can be used to neutralize buyer power by isolating and concentrating on segments of the market that are less powerful.
- *Become the low-cost producer.* Finally, buyer power can be neutralized in the long run by concentrating on costs and gradually driving out other, less efficient, suppliers. This changes the balance of power—buyers now have only a few suppliers and cannot play them off against each other as previously.

Using Buyer Power to Affect Leverage

If buyers are inherently weak or can be neutralized, they will not have much influence on industry structure. On the other hand, strong buyers will do their utmost to keep the industry fragmented and profits only moderate. It is in their self-interest to siphon off any above-market profits by forcing prices down or integrating backwards.

We can determine the implications for leverage by considering two cases—one where buyers *can* be neutralized, the other where buyers *cannot* be neutralized—and examining their effect on the 4Ps. The results are summarized in Table 4.1.

When buyers can be neutralized, product and promotion become key variables, with price and place playing only secondary roles. Product design and promotion will be the basic tools for neutralizing buyers. Place (channels/intermediaries) is likely to become a bottleneck, particularly if shelf space is limited. This merely heightens the importance of product and promotion; they become essential for gaining and maintaining the firm's share of shelf space.

When buyers cannot be neutralized, the focus shifts to price and product cost. The goal is to produce a standard product—the one specified by the purchaser—at minimum cost. There is little point in trying to differentiate the product because buyers will not pay any premium, that is, there is no return along this dimension. Any investments in product development should be aimed at eliminating needless costs (from the buyers' perspective) from the design and in manufacturing. Promotion, too, has minimal leverage because the buyers:

- Are few in number (otherwise they would not be powerful)
- Specify the product's functions and often its design
- Have complete information regarding the various firms' products
- Will not let purchase decisions be influenced by advertising or promotional efforts aimed at differentiating the product.

Table 4.1 Implications of buyer power for leverage.

	Buyer Power	
	Can Be Neutralized	Cannot Be Neutralized
Product	*Primary variable* Produce a differentiated product	*Primary variable* Produce a standardized product at minimal cost
Place	*Secondary variable* Neutralize intermediary power by consolidating or "leap-frogging"	*Secondary variable* Reduce intermediary costs by minimizing distribution levels
Promotion	*Primary variable* Use "pull" strategy, co-opt buyers, create switching costs	*Secondary variable* Minimize expenditures, concentrate on maintenance advertising—institutional, print media
Price	*Secondary variable*	*Primary variable* Determines market share

For the same reasons, the use of intermediaries—place—offers minimal leverage because buyers will prefer to capture the margins typically given to the intermediaries for themselves. The primary use of intermediaries will be for the basic functions of physical distribution, *provided they are more efficient at it than either the buyers or the firms themselves.* Price, in this environment, is the key to market share, along with a strong salesforce that can minimize price erosion while capturing share.

The corporate travel agency example, discussed in Chapter 2, exhibits all of these characteristics. The product is standardized. Promotion is minimal—the number of potential customers is limited, the buyers are fully aware of the various agencies' capabilities, and contracts are awarded on a scheduled basis. There are no intermediaries; the firms use their own salesforces. Finally, the focus is on the amount of rebate a firm can offer its corporate clients—on the price. The strategic focus, therefore, is on internal operations, to minimize cost, and on account relations, to maintain market position via superior service.

Supplier Power

Supplier power is the mirror image of buyer power. Powerful suppliers can influence industry structure by preventing or slowing down industry consolidation, integrating forward and thereby creating "poor" competitors, and lowering industry profitability by raising the prices of inputs.

Determining Supplier Power

Suppliers are powerful in situations where purchasers have few alternatives, the alternatives are not economically feasible, and/or there is a basic inequity in the relationship in favor of the supplier, that is, purchasers need the suppliers more than suppliers need the purchasers.

We can summarize the specific conditions under which suppliers have power over an industry as follows:[5]

- Suppliers provide a unique input.
- The supplier group is dominated by a few firms or is more concentrated than the buying industry.
- The industry is not an important customer.
- There are few or no substitutes.
- There are significant switching costs in substituting alternative materials/services.
- Suppliers can integrate forward.

The U.S. Federal Reserve System's (the Fed) relationship with the government bond dealers is a good example of supplier power at work. The Fed "recognizes" only a handful of such dealers, who are then obliged to report their transactions in detail and maintain an adequate capital position. The Fed itself is the sole arbiter of who is (and is not) allowed to do business directly with the central bank and restricts the number carefully. Overall, ". . . the Fed wants them to make money"[6] to ensure an orderly market for federal securities.[7]

Using Supplier Power to Influence Leverage

Weak suppliers will have no impact on industry structure. Strong suppliers, on the other hand, could hamper industry consolidation. Should the industry appear to be very profitable, they may try to integrate forward and capture some of the profits for themselves, potentially creating "poor" competitors. Alternatively, they may try to capitalize on industry profitability by raising prices.

Strong suppliers affect leverage indirectly, by increasing product costs and restricting pricing flexibility. The strategy then should be to neutralize supplier power by testing to see if the industry's customers will accept substitutes and by working closely with product design to reduce dependence on supplier inputs.

- *Test for substitutes.* When sugar producers raised prices too high, Coca-Cola and Pepsi both changed their formulas to use fructose, which was cheaper. They test marketed these formulas and found consumers willing to accept them.
- *Change the design.* Coke and Pepsi, in effect, changed their designs—their formulations—to make use of the lower-cost substitute.

Substitutes

Substitutes are products that are competition for the industry as a whole, not merely for individual firms. Substitutes affect industry profits by restricting the industry's ability to raise prices. They can also provide opportunities for future growth by enabling the firm to broaden its products or markets.

Substitutes are of two types: those that already exist and those that come into existence due to external factors.

- *Substitutes that already exist.* Examples of such substitutes abound: fructose (corn syrup) for sugar, soya-based cheese for "natural" cheese, aluminum for steel in beverage cans, and fossil fuels for coal in electrical power generation. They place a ceiling on the prices that can be charged, thereby limiting industry profitability.

- *Substitutes that come into existence.* Industry pricing, buyers' cost pressures, or technological evolution often create substitutes where none existed before. AT&T lost its market for long-distance TV transmission due to its exorbitant pricing policies, which were based on (1) an assumption of a continuing monopoly and (2) regulatory policies that favored certain segments at the expense of the heavy users. As a result, it was cheaper for the major networks to launch their own satellites than pay AT&T's rates. Newspapers, under severe cost pressure, have substituted computerized typesetting equipment for Linotypes™; they were willing to accept higher capital costs to eliminate the labor costs and operational problems of the unionized printing shops. Finally, technological evolution creates substitutes where none existed previously; for example integrated circuits replaced transistors, which replaced vacuum tubes; word processors are replacing typewriters, and so forth.

Substitutes Affect Leverage

By limiting pricing flexibility and profitability, existing substitutes intensify competition within the industry, and indirectly, increase the bargaining power of buyers. They may even destroy the industry, particularly if the marginal cost of producing the substitute is very low. If this is the case, the industry is forced to set its prices well below its costs to maintain market share, or it can keep prices up and lose share. Either way, the industry loses. An example of such substitution is the jute industry, which lost its major customers, the carpet companies, when they started using polypropylene in place of jute as backing for carpets. Polypropylene was a by-product created of petroleum refining. When it was applied to carpet backing, it became a competitor for jute whose marginal costs were extremely low—more than an order of magnitude lower than those of the jute producers. The result was inevitable; within a decade the share of jute in carpet backing had dwindled to negligible levels.

Substitutes that come into existence due to industry pricing or buyers' cost pressures may be competitive threats or opportunities, depending on whether they limit or eliminate existing markets, or they enable a firm to broaden its products or markets.

Table 4.2   How substitutes affect leverage.

	Substitutes	
	Currently Existing	Future Possibilities
Product	• Improve price/performance ratio • Look for new applications	• Track sources of potential substitutes • Incorporate/participate in developments
Place	• Reduce costs as much as possible	• Not too entrenched/ attached to a particular channel
Promotion	• Reduce costs as much as possible	—
Price	• Limit pricing flexibility	—

The implications for the 4Ps are summarized in Table 4.2. They differ according as the substitutes exist today or are future possibilities:

- *Currently existing.* Here product and price become key, while promotion and place are secondary. The focus in product design/ manufacturing must be on improving or maintaining the price/ performance ratio, where the price is set externally by the substitute products. In addition, alternative markets or applications where substitution does not occur or is less significant must be found. Other things being equal, expenditures on promotion and on intermediaries should be minimized, because these will merely reduce profits without creating any offsetting advantages.

- *Future possibility.* In this case, it is key to track the causes or sources of potential substitutes and, if possible, participate in promising developments. A corollary is not to become too attached to existing channels of distribution; these may be totally inappropriate for the substitutes, especially if they are based on new technologies. IBM's attachment to its direct salesforce may have hurt its ability to compete early on in the minicomputer market, where original equipment manufacturers, dealers, and remarketers were more cost-effective.

Barriers to Market Entry

Entry and mobility barriers create additional costs for potential entrants into new markets or market segments. Economies of scale raise the capital costs or alternatively, lower the available profit margins for later entrants. Switching costs lower the prices that newcomers can charge and still be competitive. Initial or absolute cost advantages may make it impossible to compete profitably in the industry.

By analyzing the nature of these costs, we can gain some insights into their implications for leverage. The relationship between entry barriers and leverage works in both directions. Just as the type of entry barrier affects leverage, so leverage can be used to create barriers to market entry. For this reason, incumbents should analyze these relationships to strengthen their defenses against potential entrants, whereas potential entrants need to study entry barriers to determine which dimension of the target market is key (see Table 4.3).

A number of factors can deter potential entrants to an industry. Sometimes these entry barriers may be negligible, as in the case of the local travel agency. On the other hand, they can be quite substantial as, for example, in the case of bulk chemicals. We can categorize the various barriers to entry as[8]

- Economies of scale in production or operations
- Product differentiation advantages of incumbents
- Switching costs faced by the buyers
- Access to customers being controlled by powerful intermediaries
- Initial or absolute cost advantages of incumbents
- Other cost disadvantages of potential entrants that are independent of scale.

How Entry Barriers Affect Leverage

Other things being equal, industries/segments that are difficult to enter tend to be more profitable. Such industries may also be more consolidated, and the overall intensity of competition is likely to be lower.[9]

Table 4.3 How entry barriers affect leverage.

	Product	Place	Promotion	Price	Target Market
Scale	—	—	—	—	Niche focus
Differentiation	—	—	—	—	Niche focus
Switching costs	Key	Minimal	Minimal	Key	
Access	Key	Bypass	Key	—	—
Initial or absolute cost advantage	—	—	—	—	Niche focus

The implications of these entry barriers vary depending on whether a firm is an incumbent or a potential entrant.

For incumbents, the message is clear: Increase leverage by creating new entry barriers or strengthening existing ones. For example, if economies of scale are not significant, change the product or operations design to create scale economies. Alternatively, strengthen differentiation through massive advertising, thereby making promotional spending a barrier to entry, much as the ready-to-eat cereal industry has done.[10] Economies of scale and differentiation are related to product and promotion, switching costs affect product and pricing, access determines channel choices/constraints, and initial or absolute cost advantages affect pricing. We can therefore easily determine what tactic to use in raising the height of a particular entry barrier.

For potential entrants, the barriers to entering a particular industry provide information not only about entering the industry, but also about which areas the firm should focus on and which ones it should avoid. The relationships between the entry barriers (with the exception of other cost disadvantages) and the five variables that determine relative position are:

- *Economies of scale and differentiation.* Potential entrants should focus on niches where entry will be easier.[11] We cannot say with any confidence what will be the effect on the other four variables.

- *Switching costs.* When these are high, buyers will be reluctant to change sources. This implies that the successful entrant will be one who can either minimize or eliminate the effect of these costs through pricing or product design. The product should be compatible with existing designs to the extent possible. Further, the price must be lower to offset the effects of any residual switching costs and to provide the buyer an inducement to change sources. A corollary to keeping the price low is that the firm should minimize promotion and place costs to the extent possible by choosing media and channels carefully. This was precisely how manufacturers of PC clones gained entry to the microcomputer market in 1985. Their designs were compatible with IBM's standards; this allowed purchasers to switch without worrying about losing their software investments. At the same time, the prices of the PC clones were significantly lower, providing a reason to switch. The clone makers used lower-cost channels (such as mail order) than IBM, and their promotional expenditures were also lower. So successful was this entry strategy that by 1986, clones accounted for 37 percent of the microcomputer market, displacing IBM.[12]

- *Access to customers.* To neutralize access as a barrier, that is, to increase leverage, the would-be entrant must focus on product design and promotion. The product design should allow the firm to bypass existing channels if need be, that is, increase the firm's freedom of maneuver. Similarly, the firm must use promotion to either induce existing channels to carry the product or, failing that, to induce customers to purchase the product from new, less familiar channels. Timex used this strategy to break into the U.S. wristwatch market in the late 1940s and 1950s. At that time, jewelers were the traditional channel for distributing watches; they refused to handle Timex products, which were cheaper and less profitable. For this reason, Timex decided to use corner drugstores and other retailers to market their watches. Their watches were rugged and reliable and did not require the channel to provide support services such as repair or cleaning. In fact, it was impossible to repair a Timex watch because the watches were riveted together to minimize production costs and keep prices low. Timex's advertising stressed their watches' quality and dependability and was aimed at removing any doubts customers might have about not buying their watches from a jeweler.[13]

- *Initial or absolute cost advantages.* These place limits on pricing; they also suggest that the new entrant not precipitate a pricing war by coming in lower than existing market prices. In addition, the entrant will probably have to concentrate on a niche in order to neutralize the cost (and hence, pricing) advantages of incumbents.

The impact of the other cost disadvantages varies considerably, depending on the specific industry situation; therefore, we cannot identify patterns that are valid across the board.

Rivalry

The intensity of competition in an industry is determined in part by industry-specific factors such as the presence of numerous or equally balanced competitors or technological characteristics that cause capacity to be added in large increments. Industry rivalry is also driven by the other four competitive forces, namely, buyer and supplier power, the importance of substitutes, and the height of entry barriers. By considering industry-specific factors in conjunction with the other four competitive forces, we can determine the intensity and the stability of competition within the industry. In turn, this defines the roles that price and promotion will play.

Rivalry within an industry is affected by such factors as how capacity comes on stream, whether industry growth has slowed, what the motivations of the various participants are, and so forth. Specifically,

competition in the industry is likely to be intense under any of the
following situations:[14]

- Numerous or equally balanced competitors
- Slow industry growth
- High fixed or storage costs
- Capacity that can be added only in large increments
- Diverse competitors with widely varying objectives
- High strategic stakes, whether perceived or actual.

Passenger airlines, long-distance fiber-optic transmission, and commercial airlines provide examples of these factors. The airline industry is a
classic example of both high fixed and high storage costs. Between 70
and 80 percent of an airline's costs are fixed, and unfilled seats are
revenue lost forever. In the fiber-optic cable industry, the major cost of
adding capacity is the cost of the right-of-way and of digging the necessary trench—not the cost of the cable. Once the trench is dug, the incremental costs of adding another fiber is very low. Consequently, capacity
is added in large jumps, leading to intense, even chaotic, competition.[15]
High perceived national and technological stakes have created cutthroat
competition in commercial airliners, to the point that John McDonnell,
the president of McDonnell Douglas, is reported to have said, "You are
driven by each deal to make the sacrificial price . . . [W]hichever manufacturer is the most desperate will get the next order."[16]

In addition, rivalry is also influenced by the other four forces of
competition, as these industry situations illustrate:

- Threaded fasteners, such as metal and wooden screws: This is a
  highly fragmented industry, with both entry and exit being very
  easy. Buyers and suppliers are weak, and there are numerous substitutes, depending on the application. As a result, rivalry is moderately high but chaotic.
- Automotive components like gears, door frames, stampings, wipers:
  Here, entry and exit are easy, but buyers are powerful. For this reason, rivalry is moderately high and stable; the buyers do not want a
  free-for-all.
- Ready-to-eat cereals, discussed earlier: Buyers and suppliers are
  both weak, entry is difficult, but exit is easy, as the bulk of the
  investment is in advertising and promotion, to create and maintain
  a brand image. Consequently, rivalry is moderate and stable.
- Cement used in construction: Entry and exit are both difficult,
  and buyers are strong. This creates intense but stable rivalry.

Rivalry Affects Leverage

Intense competition can cause the industry to consolidate, as the stronger players buy up or force out the weaker ones. Such consolidation is especially likely to occur in slow-growth or cyclical industries, as exemplified by the farm equipment industry in the 1980s and the recent wave of mergers in the U.S. domestic airline industry. In some cases, intense rivalry may even destabilize the industry, as participants become increasingly desperate in their efforts to improve their competitive position.

Figure 4.3 summarizes the impact of rivalry on industry structure. Intense rivalry and stable competition are typical of a mature, low-growth industry such as farm equipment. Intense rivalry, coupled with unstable competition, is the case in industries that are undergoing major structural changes, such as the home computer industry, which is still evolving. In some cases, such as the cereal industry, competitive intensity is low and the terms of competition are stable, reflecting a tacit agreement among the various participants to keep industry rivalry under control. Finally, as in the case of the local travel agency, rivalry is not very intense, but competition is unstable and doesn't follow any particular rules.

Industry rivalry affects leverage primarily through the limitations it places on promotion and price. Depending on the intensity and stability of competition, price points will either be set or else price will be a key variable. Promotion similarly will be limited or a major weapon. This creates the four possibilities shown in Figure 4.4.

- *All-out war.* Here price and promotion are both key variables and used extensively. Competition is intense and unstable; prices change constantly, advertising spending fluctuates, and promotions are rampant. A typical example is the periodic gasoline price

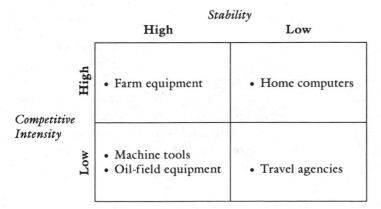

Figure 4.3 How rivalry affects industry structure.

		Price Key Variable	*Price* Points Set
Promotion	Key Variable	• All-out wars	• Branded packaged goods • Apparel
Promotion	Points Set	• Machine tools • Oil-field equipment	

Figure 4.4 How rivalry determines price and promotion.

wars in which the various oil companies tried to buy market share by repeatedly cutting prices, giving away gifts, and so forth.

- *Commodity or "bid" business.* Price is the key variable, but spending on promotion is minimal, either by tacit agreement or, more typically, because promotion has little impact. Here competition is intense but stable.
- *Gentlemen's agreement.* Price points are set and promotion is the key dimension of competition. Industry rivalry is moderate and stable. This is the case for branded packaged goods and, for the most part, in the apparel industry.
- *Friendly club.* Things are very cozy; price points are set and promotion is minimal. Such competition as exists is stable. The local travel agency fits into this category.

Summary

In this chapter, we focused on the basic interrelationships between specific competitive forces and individual components of strategic leverage. This provided us with insight regarding the strategic leverage offered by *individual* moves, that is, changes in channels or pricing, investments in product design to increase differentiation, and so forth. In the next chapter we will study the implications for maneuver in more detail. We will then analyze the returns and therefore the leverage of collections of moves that comprise various strategies.

PART
TWO

ANALYZING STRATEGIC LEVERAGE

5

Analyzing Freedom of Maneuver

In Chapter 4, we examined the relationships between the various competitive forces and leverage. We will now describe how to evaluate a given company's leverage in a particular market or industry.

Our starting point is freedom of maneuver. In this chapter, we present tools and techniques for analyzing a firm's ability to maneuver, that is, to change its position relative to its rivals along any of the five market dimensions. First, we examine the case of Midway Airlines in the air transportation industry. We show how Midway's ability to maneuver was restricted by industry structure and its own competitive position relative to the major airlines; we also discuss the implications for Midway's strategic choices. We then categorize the components of maneuver; in order to provide a detailed checklist for analyzing a company's freedom of maneuver. Next, we discuss how structure and position affect maneuver and how maneuver, in combination with company objectives, affects strategies and tactics. Finally, we present a quantitative technique for evaluating maneuver.

Why Midway Airlines' Metrolink™ Strategy Failed

Midway Airlines' experiences with its Metrolink™ service provide an excellent demonstration of the importance of understanding a firm's freedom of maneuver. After an early period of rapid growth, Midway Airlines invested more than $3.4 million to create Midway Airlines'

67

Metrolink[1] in an attempt to make inroads into the business travel market. The major airlines countered with lowered fares and other incentives, and Midway Airlines almost collapsed.[2] What Midway's management failed to realize was that its freedom of maneuver was sharply limited and that, therefore, the Metrolink strategy had very little probability of success. Specifically, it should have recognized the following:

- Midway's ability to choose its target markets was restricted by industry rivalry and the need for Midway to maintain a state of limited warfare if it was to remain profitable, let alone expand. In the business travel market, this meant Midway had to play cooperatively—similar fares, service offerings, promotions—on major high-density routes. It had more flexibility on lower density or "feeder" routes, which were less attractive to the majors; however, for the same reasons, they would not be very profitable for Midway. Industry rivalry was less of a constraint on the vacation/personal travel markets, except that the market was (1) highly seasonal and (2) extremely price-sensitive, thereby restricting Midway's (and the other players') margins and, in turn, its flexibility in changing prices or product offerings.

- Midway's latitude in changing service offerings or prices was limited by industry rivalry and the need to avoid direct competition with the majors, especially United Airlines. As discussed earlier, Midway had to keep its prices within a narrow band, far enough below the majors' prices to attract customers, but not so far as to invite counterattacks. (See Chapter 6.)

- The power exerted by intermediaries (travel agents), coupled with (1) the dominant reservation systems and (2) Midway's weak competitive position, made it virtually impossible to change channel margins, or roles.

Taken in conjunction with the overall structure of the domestic airline industry and Midway's relatively weak competitive position, these restrictions on Midway's freedom of maneuver narrowed its strategic choices considerably:

- Given industry structure and the ongoing consolidation, Midway's long-term choices were either sell out or create/find a defensible niche.

- In choosing a niche, Midway had to contend with the fact that (1) there were virtually no mobility barriers, and (2) entry barriers into individual segments were asymmetrical, that is, the majors could enter a regional route at lower cost than Midway or other regionals could enter a national route. Combined with Midway's relatively weak competitive position, this meant that Midway had to avoid direct competition with the major airlines and participate in limited warfare.

- These two requirements, along with the restrictions on Midway's ability to change the marketing mix, meant that Midway had to find a combination of target markets, routes, service levels, and prices that wasn't perceived as a threat by the larger carriers. Alternatively, Midway could select niches/strategies where the major airlines' cost of retaliation would exceed their expected revenue losses.[3]

The main strategy of Metrolink included:

- Targeting *business*—not vacation—travelers
- Concentrating on the major destinations such as New York, Boston, Philadelphia, Washington, DC
- Offering "first-class" service—four-across seating, more leg room, better food
- Pricing at the same level as regular coach fares.

In other words, the Metrolink strategy that Midway adopted from 1983 to 1984 violated the requirements in almost every way. It put Midway in direct competition with the majors in a vital segment, it deviated from limited warfare by offering service/price combinations that were aggressive, and, furthermore, it was aimed at key routes where the majors' expected revenue losses would be high, making retaliation inevitable.

The Dimensions of Maneuver

We measure a firm's freedom of maneuver in terms of the five components of market position—target market, product, place, promotion, and price. The more latitude a firm has in choosing or changing each of these components, the greater its freedom of maneuver. By this definition, the small local travel agency, discussed in Chapter 2, has considerable free-dom of maneuver; it can change any or all of these five elements in its marketing strategy. Conversely, the large corporate travel agency dealing with Fortune 500 firms has very little leeway; its target markets, service offerings, levels of performance, and pricing are all governed by the intense rivalry in its segment of the travel industry.

To fully understand a firm's "maneuverability" in a given market, we must analyze the degree of latitude it has in each of these five areas. For example, to measure flexibility in pricing, we need to know if a firm can set or change its prices or if it must follow established "price points," whether or not competitive forces constrain its prices relative to the industry leader's price levels, how much freedom it has in setting discount schedules and trade (channel) margins, and so forth. (See Figure 5.1.)

Target Market.   The main component is a firm's freedom to choose its target markets and/or its market segments. Industry leaders usually

Principal Dimension	Components
• Target market	• Target markets • Market segments
• Product	• Product designs, quality levels • Design standards and/or levels of service • Product line width/complements • R&D expenditures, focus • New product introductions & timing • Delivery schedules
• Place	• Types, numbers of channels • Terms and conditions • "Shelf space" • Degree of exclusivity • Territorial coverage • Sales expenditures • Sales focus
• Promotion	• Expenditure levels • Types of promotions • Media choices, frequency
• Price	• Price structure, levels • Discounts and trade terms • Frequency, duration of price promotions • Pricing of complements, support

Figure 5.1   The dimensions of maneuver.

have the most freedom, while smaller players, typically restricted to specific segments, are much more constrained, for example, United versus Midway Airlines.

Product.   A number of factors affect maneuver along the product dimension. Dominant designs or industry standards can restrict freedom of maneuver in product design, as is occurring in the CAD workstation market, where UNIX is emerging as the standard embraced by all major users (an example of buyer power).[4] Similarly, a firm's ability to control product line width may be restricted by buyer power, forcing it to offer optional features, service support packages, and so on; industry rivalry can also have the same effect. Relative competitive position can limit the degree of flexibility in the timing of new product introductions and/or in delivery schedules. For example, in personal computers, IBM can set its own pace to a considerable extent while compatible or clone manufacturers must wait for IBM's introductions and then deliver within a short time window dictated by industry rivalry.[5]

Place.   The number and type of channels and the terms and conditions are often constrained by a combination of intermediary power and/or rivalry, as in the ready-to-eat cereals or the soft drink industry. The ability to control the "shelf space" in the channels is usually limited by a firm's competitive position. Other things being equal, industry leaders have more freedom than niche players or other participants; for example, Kellogg's has more flexibility than Ralston Purina. Another factor is whether a firm can control the markets served by the channels. This is a function of intermediary power and product design. A particularly important component of maneuver is the degree of flexibility enjoyed by a firm in allocating sales resources, both company employees and dealer/distributor personnel. Industry rivalry and competitive position can limit a firm's discretion in allocating its own sales personnel by requiring it to match industry leaders in terms of frequency of coverage, compensation, support services, and so forth. The ability to control dealership sales resources is limited by the relative power of intermediaries and the position of a firm; industry leaders generally have more flexibility in this area than other players.

Promotion.   The level of promotional expenditures and types and frequency of promotional activities are often restrained by industry rivalry or the nature of the conflict. Particularly when there is a state of limited warfare, the industry leader is likely to police promotional activities to ensure that price discipline is maintained as Kellogg did when it retaliated against Ralston Purina's use of trade discounts and "excessive" couponing.

Pricing.   Understanding a firm's flexibility in pricing is essential both to avoid unintended price wars and to successfully defend market positions or niches. Two factors are particularly important: *relative price levels* and *price thresholds.* Relative price levels, the differential between a firm's prices and those of leaders/other players, are governed by

- Competitive forces, especially buyer power and rivalry
- Stage of industry evolution, with the overall price differential decreasing as the industry moves into maturity and, later, decline
- A firm's competitive position, with leaders having more flexibility than other players
- A firm's overall strategy, with differentiated competitors (across-the-board or niche) having more flexibility than cost-focused firms, and price competitors having the least freedom of all.

These considerations apply to both intermediary (wholesale) prices and retail or end-user prices.

Price thresholds are points above (or below) which other players will retaliate with price changes/attacks. Typically, they are a function of the price differential or, more precisely, the product/price ratio differential, as in the case of Midway Airlines versus United. Such thresholds therefore limit a firm's freedom of maneuver, often severely. A firm's latitude in this area is determined by rivalry, buyer power, competitive position, and sometimes, by the presence or absence of mobility barriers.

Industry Structure and Competitive Position Affect Maneuver

It is critical to analyze the role of maneuver in determining a firm's strategies and tactics. To do this, we must recognize the following relationships (see Figure 5.2):

- Industry structure and evolution determine the overall constraints on maneuver within an industry.
- Company competitive position determines the firm-specific constraints on maneuver.

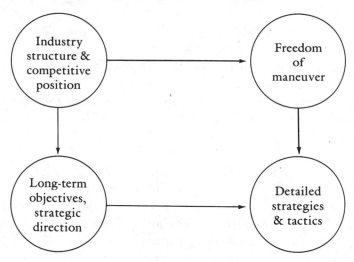

Figure 5.2 How freedom of maneuver affects marketing strategies and tactics.

- Industry structure/evolution and competitive position determine a firm's long-term objectives and strategic direction.
- Maneuver and long-term objectives/strategic direction determine the detailed strategies and tactics a firm should adopt at any given point in time.

Industry Structure

We have already analyzed how individual competitive forces affect a firm's ability to change target market, price, and so on. The concept of maneuver helps integrate these individual relationships and translate them into the following constraints on strategies and tactics:

- Buyer power has the most direct effect on maneuver by restricting industry participants' ability to differentiate the product and, consequently, their freedom in pricing. For example, the automotive companies restrict component makers' freedom in design and branding. Indirectly, buyer power can also place constraints on their use of intermediaries and the direction and focus of their promotional efforts.
- Industry rivalry similarly places tangible constraints on maneuver, especially on the various components of price, as well as on the levels and types of promotions, for example, the ready-to-eat cereal industry.

- Substitutes impose pricing constraints; they may also restrict the choice of target markets/segments.
- Supplier power and entry/mobility barriers, on the other hand, restrict maneuver in less direct, predictable ways; depending on the industry situation and the underlying technology, they may restrict product design, pricing flexibility, or the ability to bypass intermediaries (place).

Maneuver is further restricted by industry evolution and the nature of the conflict. Industry evolution places constraints on, progressively, the freedom to choose product designs, channels, promotional levels, and, ultimately, prices. Viewed in combination with the nature of the marketing conflict, we find the following patterns (see Figure 5.3).

Emerging and Growth Stages.   The nature of the conflict is win/win and there is considerable freedom of maneuver, usually well into the growth stage. The key strategic issue, as indicated earlier, is future positioning. Managers must analyze how their future flexibility might be limited as industry growth slows, and then determine how they can ensure adequate room for maneuver for their firms. They must bear in mind

	Stage of Evolution			
	Emerging	Growth	Maturity	Decline
Conflict				
Win/win	Relatively few external constraints on freedom of maneuver		-------Not applicable-------	
Limited warfare	--------------Not applicable--------------		• Strong limits on price, promotion • Constraints on channel terms • Product introductions, timing may be limited.	
Win/lose	--------------Not applicable--------------		• Few constraints on maneuver • Limits determined by five forces of competition	
Lose/lose	--------------Not applicable--------------		• Virtually no constraints	

Figure 5.3 How freedom of maneuver changes with industry evolution and the nature of the conflict.

that, in maturity, they will have few choices in terms of target market, product, or place; furthermore, place will become a crucial element in the late growth/early maturity phases. Some common mistakes that restrict a firm's subsequent flexibility in changing the elements of market position include:

- *Inadequate attention to target markets/segments.* The result is that a firm is poorly positioned to establish defensible niches. This is usually due to strategic myopia; a firm fails to recognize that differentiation and cost focus are not feasible strategies and, consequently, does not concentrate resources early on to identify or build defensible niches.

- *Lack of maneuvering room in product strategy.* Leaders as well as followers may find that they have not paid sufficient attention to product positioning in maturity, leading to limitations on their ability to create multiple brands flanking the main offering. Or they have not adequately controlled technologies or the positioning of flankers and/or complements, leading to potential share erosion or pricing problems. Or the packaging and pricing of support services restricts their ability to fight aggressively against "cream skimming." We will discuss these issues further in Chapter 12.

- *Failure to anticipate and curb the power of intermediaries.* A particularly common problem is excessive dependence on, or attachment to, a specific type of channel. Symptoms are exclusive distribution arrangements (especially when there is limited or no periodic review), prolonged efforts to counter "gray markets," reluctance to serve national accounts directly, or poor end-user pricing control. As we shall discuss in Chapter 13, companies must retain the freedom to change their channel strategies as the market matures and becomes more competitive. Therefore, such mistakes during the early growth stage will severely restrict a firm's ability to adapt to changing realities.

Maturity and Decline. In these two stages, freedom of maneuver varies depending on whether the nature of the conflict is limited warfare or win/lose. If industry conflict is limited, there are strong constraints on pricing tactics to ensure that competition is confined to nonprice elements such as product features and advertising expenditures. For the same reasons, price-oriented promotions are tacitly controlled, as are channel terms and conditions. Occasionally, there may be implicit restrictions on the timing of new model introductions and on the adoption of new technologies, as in the case of the U.S. automobile industry from

1950 to 1970.[6] When the situation is win/lose, however, there are relatively few restrictions on maneuver for the simple reason that participants have no incentives (other than their self-interest) to restrain price changes, expand/change channels, modify channel terms and conditions, invade segments served by other manufacturers, and so forth. Any limits on these activities are due almost entirely to the five forces of competition.

Finally, when the nature of the conflict is lose/lose, as in declining industries and during cyclical downturns, there are virtually no constraints on maneuver. Firms will make changes to nearly every feasible element of market position, raising advertising expenditures in frantic efforts to create "differentiation," cutting prices desperately, integrating forward, increasing sales expenditures, and especially in service industries, changing product designs/features.[7]

Competitive Position

A firm's freedom of maneuver is further limited by its relative competitive position. In Chapter 3, using PIMS data, we reviewed how a firm's position in the industry affected its profitability; we also analyzed how changes to market variables such as product quality, price, promotion, and marketing expenditures affected the market share of followers.

We can use this information to gain some insights into how market position affects a firm's freedom of maneuver. Specifically, we will concentrate on the late growth, maturity, and decline phases of industry evolution, in situations where the conflict is either limited or win/lose; only in these cases that we can draw some general conclusions. As discussed earlier, in the emerging or early growth stages, competitive position is not central to strategy formulation. Conversely, if the conflict is lose/lose, as in late decline or cyclical industries, firms have very little flexibility and any discussion of relative competitive position becomes moot.

Freedom of maneuver changes according to whether a firm is a leader or a follower. (See Chapter 3.) Overall, there are more constraints on maneuver when the conflict is limited. Leaders must maintain a "price umbrella"; this restricts their freedom in pricing, promotion, and setting terms and conditions for channels. They may also find their ability to select target markets restricted by the desire to avoid destabilizing industry prices. Followers' prices are constrained by the levels set by the leader(s) and by their own relative quality and market position. Their flexibility in changing other price-related components of maneuver is similarly restricted. When competition is unrestrained, there are considerably

Competitive Position

Maneuver	Leaders		Followers	
	Limited Warfare	"Win/Lose"	Limited Warfare	"Win/Lose"
Target market	Constraints due to need to maintain limited conflict		Constrained by need to create or defend niche(s)	
Product				
Width	Limited by (1) need to control rivalry & (2) avoid flanking	Internal limits due to concerns re cannibalization	Limits set by leader's positioning, available niches	
Introductions	Key variable in setting, enforcing pattern		Follow the leader	
Place				
Terms & conditions	Limited by price umbrella		Limited downward by need to avoid direct conflict	
Sales expenditures			More flexibility	Limited by internal resources
Promotion				
Levels & types	Limited downward by control requirements		Follow the leader	
Frequency			More flexibility	
Price				
Structure, discounts & frequency of changes	Limited downward by leadership role	Freedom to change prices may be limited by aggressor's actions	Stay within limits set by the leader	
Complements & support	More flexibility			

Figure 5.4 How competitive position affects freedom of maneuver.

fewer constraints on maneuver, and such limitations as exist are due to internal resources, or (in the case of leaders) the desire to avoid cannibalizing existing product lines. The overall patterns are summarized in Figure 5.4.

Company Objectives and Maneuvers Influence Strategy and Tactics

We can now analyze the relationship between freedom of maneuver and a firm's specific choices. A firm's long-term objectives and overall direction determine specific target markets, product positioning, and, in general, pricing policies. A thorough investigation of a firm's freedom of maneuver provides answers to detailed tactical issues such as, "How wide should our product line be? Which types of channels should (or shouldn't) we use? How far can we safely cut sales expenditures? What should be the focus and the level of our promotional efforts?" Of necessity, such analyses are industry- and situation-specific. However, we can make a number of detailed deductions in industries where the conflict is limited. In such situations, maneuver provides considerable insight into detailed marketing strategies and tactics. As would be expected, the conclusions depend on whether a firm is a leader or a follower and, in the case of leaders, whether it is pursuing a differentiation or a cost focus strategy.

Differentiated Leaders

When industry conflict is limited (and assuming the leader wants to keep it limited), the key tactical issues facing a leader using a differentiation strategy are

- Ensuring that the product/price ratio remains consistent with its long-term objectives
- Maintaining its price positioning relative to firms choosing a cost focus strategy, maintaining a suitable "price umbrella" in order to maintain limited warfare, and preventing any niche/focus players from mounting flanking attacks.

The issues are interrelated; any changes in product design, manufacturing quality, and so on, change a firm's relative positioning as do changes in prices by the firm, other competitors, or (most often) new entrants.

These two considerations, combined with the facts that (1) the firm is a leader, (2) its strategy is differentiation, and (3) it wants to keep price competition limited, enable us to make a number of deductions about the firm's marketing strategies and tactics (see Figure 5.5):

- *Target market.* While the differentiated leader must establish its presence in all major market segments, it must be careful to control

	Competitive Position		
	Leaders		Followers
	Differentiation	Cost Focus	
Target market	• Less freedom at either end of price range	• More flexibility re premium & specialty segments	• Restricted to defensible niches
Product			
Design & quality	• Restricted by dangers of flanking at either end	• Constrained by positioning of differentiated player	• Dictated by segment-specific needs
Width		• Limited by technology and positioning	• Restricted by need to concentrate resources & avoid conflict
Levels of service	• More freedom but time window is limited	• Follow differentiated player	• May be bounded from below by need to create service-related BME
Place			
Types of channels	• Constraints on using discount channels—"second brand" issue	• Constraints on using exclusive or "push" channels	• Confined to segment-specific channels
Terms & conditions	• Downward freedom limited by (i) limited warfare & (ii) need to create BMEs	• Bounded from above by cost focus	• Limited by leaders' actions
Sales expenditures	• Bounded from below to avoid creating flanking opportunities	• Limited by strategic direction	• Can be key to attacking "lazy" leader
Promotion			
Expenditures	• Minimum levels due to need to set, maintain pattern		• Limited by need to avoid conflict
Types	• Limits on price-oriented promotions	• Greater freedom for price-oriented promotions	

(continued)

Figure 5.5 How maneuver influences marketing strategies and tactics.

	Competitive Position		
	Leaders		Followers
	Differentiation	Cost Focus	
Price			
Structure discounts	• Restricted by positioning and need to maintain price umbrella	• Restricted by positioning vs. differentiated firm	• Constraints dictated by −segment needs −mobility barriers −leaders' capabilities, responses
Complements & product support	• Upper limits due to need to avoid flank attacks		

Figure 5.5   *(continued)*

the premium and low-end segments in order to (1) limit potential damage from flankers, and (2) ensure that its overall product/price positioning remains consistent under changing market requirements and competitive conditions. In the 1980s, General Motors consistently failed to watch its positioning in the luxury and mass market segments represented by Cadillac and Chevrolet, respectively, with the result that its share of the U.S. passenger car market slipped from 45 percent to under 36 percent. In the process, GM also lost its ability to control the terms of competition.[8]

• *Product.* The differentiated leader's choices in the area of *product design* and *quality* are restricted by the need to maintain its relative product/price position. This is especially important when technology or customer requirements change rapidly, or where changes in factor costs (especially labor rates) erode the leader's margins. Thus, in long-distance telephone services, AT&T must watch its offerings relative to MCI to ensure that it doesn't create a "gap" that MCI can exploit. Leaders have more freedom with respect to the timing of new product introductions and levels of service, but the time window is limited by the degree to which their customers are willing to wait for the leaders to adopt new innovations.

• *Place.* The differentiated leader faces definite restrictions on the *types* of channels it can use, the *terms and conditions* it should set, and the *level of sales expenditures* it should maintain. A differentiation strategy makes "discount channels" (such as off-price clothing stores, mail order catalogs) risky, because they lower a firm's perceived quality and hence its product/price positioning. The basic tradeoff is between brand extension and the creation of a second or "fighting brand."[9]

Differentiation and the need to keep price competition limited lowers the bounds on a leader's ability to set the pattern for channel terms and conditions. Excessive pressure on channel profits may destabilize the industry by minimizing or even eliminating smaller firms' pricing flexibility and initiating price warfare.[10] Such pricing pressures also reduce the channels' ability to help create and maintain a firm's differentiated positioning, thereby robbing the leader of an important barrier to market entry by new entrants.[11] Finally, the differentiated leader's flexibility in reducing sales expenditures is limited by the need to avoid creating flanking opportunities.

- *Promotion and pricing.* The differentiated leader's ability to reduce the *level* of promotional activities is limited by the need to set the pattern within the industry and also to maintain levels consistent with its market share position. Its flexibility with regard to the *types* of promotions is limited by its positioning, which restricts its use of price-oriented promotions.[12] These factors, together with the need to maintain a "price umbrella" for smaller players, also restrict freedom when setting price levels and terms.[13]

Cost-Focused Leaders

The cost-focused firm's freedom of maneuver is restricted by the need to ensure that its product/price ratio is consistent with the following relationship, namely,

$$\text{Price}_{\text{Differentiated}} > \text{Price}_{\text{Cost leader}} > \text{Price}_{\text{Reservation}}$$

At the high end, a firm's pricing and product design flexibility is restricted by its need to achieve overall cost leadership.[14] This precludes a firm from investments that would increase the differentiation of its products/services substantially, in turn limiting its price relative to differentiated leaders. If the cost leader's prices are significantly lower, it risks retaliation by differentiated players. In the airline industry, People Express isolated these constraints by setting its prices too low. Until recently, Northwest Airlines was a cost leader that had successfully avoided this trap. Today, however, Northwest is in trouble due to (1) intense competition, which has reduced this spread, and (2) its abandonment of pure cost leadership (high debt).

The objective of overall cost leadership also restricts a firm's flexibility in other areas, as summarized in Figure 5.5:

- *Target market.* While it must serve the major segments, the overall cost leader has more leeway with regard to premium and specialty segments, in contrast to differentiated firms.

- *Product.* In addition to the constraints described above, the cost leader's flexibility in product design is limited by its desire to continually reduce product costs. Typically, this necessitates a relatively standardized product and/or long production runs to achieve economies of scale, thereby limiting a firm's flexibility in meeting the needs of different segments. The emphasis on cost reduction (and, therefore, on economies of scale) may also limit the cost leader's ability to introduce new products rapidly.

- *Place.* A firm's goal of cost leadership limits its ability to use exclusive or "push" channels; they aren't consistent with a cost leader's overall positioning. For the same reason, there is a ceiling on channel terms and conditions and on sales expenditures in general.

- *Promotion.* Cost leaders have greater flexibility in price-oriented promotional efforts, although there is a lower limit on such promotions below which a firm risks initiating all-out price warfare.

Followers

As we might expect, there are many more limitations on followers' ability to choose and/or change their marketing strategies. They must concentrate on locating and occupying defensible niches. Their flexibility in product design and pricing is limited by the requirements of their chosen segments and the need to maintain limited warfare. The incentives they can offer their channels are constrained by the leader's activities (see Figure 5.5). Some of the key restrictions are:

- *Product.* The followers' freedom in selecting design features and quality levels is restricted by the needs of their segments. Further, the width of their product lines/service offerings is constrained by (1) the need to concentrate their resources in order to create/maintain mobility barriers and (2) the necessity of avoiding direct conflict with the leaders. Finally, the need to create mobility barriers also restricts their flexibility in reducing service levels.

- *Place.* Followers must choose "specialty" channels—narrow channels that are specific to their segments—as part of their efforts to create defensible niches. Channel terms and conditions tend to be limited by the pattern set by the leader; typically, niche players have to at least match the terms offered by the major firms and may have to offer improved terms to capture/retain "shelf space." Followers have *more* flexibility with regard to sales expenditures, which are limited primarily by a firm's internal resources and capabilities. Sales intensity becomes a key weapon for improving market share, especially if the leader is lazy or a large diversified firm is marketing a wide range of products through a single salesforce. In such situations, the focused niche player can gain significant share or even capture market leadership by increasing its sales expenditures and efforts.

- *Promotion.* Followers have to be careful when using price-oriented promotions due to their need to avoid direct challenges to the leaders. Further, the level of promotional expenditures is restricted by their relatively poor returns, as discussed in Chapter 3.

- *Pricing.* Perhaps in no other area are followers so constrained as they are in pricing. First and foremost, followers' flexibility in pricing is restricted by their overall positioning strategy. Firms focusing on premium segments must keep prices high enough to maintain their image of exclusivity or high quality, while those firms targeting low-end niches must keep their prices sufficiently accessible. At the same time, the heights of any mobility barriers affect their freedom very directly. Niche players protected by strong mobility barriers (such as the freight forwarders discussed in Chapter 6) have more license to set prices at whatever level they choose. In the absence of strong mobility barriers, followers must take care to ensure that their prices are not so high as to invite attack/entry by differentiated players or cost leaders. Last but not least, pricing flexibility is directly affected by the capabilities and responses of the leaders; followers in an industry where the leaders are weak or ineffectual have more latitude than their counterparts in industries where the leaders are determined to enforce pricing discipline more tightly.[15]

Maneuver and Differential Advantage

A firm's differential advantage is the difference between its strategic investments in the five market areas and its market share.[16] When we combine the concept of differential advantage with a firm's freedom of maneuver, we obtain additional insight into strategies and tactics. By evaluating differential advantage and maneuver, leaders can identify potential threats and anticipate changes in the nature of the conflict such as flank attacks by new entrants. Followers can similarly use the information to determine potential weak points of the major players and what changes are needed to their marketing tactics.

Defining Differential Advantage

Cook introduced the concept of differential advantage in marketing strategy to explain how market shares change in response to changes in a firm's relative expenditures on marketing. Specifically, the concept was that "[S]hare of units sold is a balancing mechanism, the center of gravity, of a free, competitive market. This center or balance point shifts in response to [the changes in] a firm's shares of strategic investments in product, promotion, place and price."[17]

He went on to add that "[W]hen a firm or group of competitors maintains a share of strategic marketing investments below its share of market quantity," this unit market share ". . . will be 'pulled down' in search of a new balance in consumer preferences." Conversely, when a firm spends more in marketing investments in relation to its unit share, over time the center or balance point will shift to reflect the difference, thereby increasing the firm's share.

We can appreciate the significance of differential advantage when we consider the case of the U.S. automobile manufacturers versus imports. In the year 1975, U.S. manufacturers had a unit market share of 84 percent as compared with 16 percent for all imports (European and Japanese). However, their share of strategic marketing investments in product, place, and promotion was significantly lower (see Figure 5.6). Only in the area of price did the domestic firms have an advantage, with a median weighted price of $3,838 to the imports' $4,208.[18] (This overstates their advantage, as it includes European imports that were typically priced higher than

	Market Share	Product	Place	Promotion	Price
Domestics	84.00%	74.70%	79.30%	68.70%	92.80%
Imports	16.00	25.30	20.70	31.3	6.40
Totals	100.00%	100.00%	100.00%	100.00%	—

From Cook, Victor J. Jr., "Marketing Strategy and Differential Advantage," *Journal of Marketing,* Vol. 47, Spring 1983, pp. 73 and 74. Reprinted by permission of the American Marketing Association.

Figure 5.6   Market share and share of investments.

	Market Share	Product	Place	Promotion	Price
Domestics	84.00%	−9.3	−4.7	−15.3	8.8
Imports	16.00	+9.3	+4.7	+15.3	−9.6

From Cook, Victor J. Jr., "Marketing Strategy and Differential Advantage," *Journal of Marketing,* Vol. 47, Spring 1983, pp. 73 and 74. Reprinted by permission of the American Marketing Association.

Figure 5.7   Differential advantage.

Japanese makes. In all probability, domestic manufacturers were at a disadvantage relative to the Japanese imports in this area as well.)

We can convert these differences in the strategic investments into the differential advantages of the imports over the domestics by using the following formula:

$$DA_i = x_i - m_1$$

Here DA_i represents the i-th component of differential advantage, x_i represents a firm's relative share of expenditures (in product, place, promotion, or price), and m_1 is a firm's market share in units. When we compare the domestic and imported car manufacturers (for the model year 1975), we find that U.S. manufacturers faced an average 9.8 percent disadvantage in product, place, and promotion (see Figure 5.7). With only a slight edge in pricing (which was deceptive, as discussed above), the domestics were poised on the brink of at least a 9 percent loss—from 84 percent to 75 percent—in market share if this pattern of strategic investments held. In fact, by 1981 imports had achieved a share of more than 26 percent, and in 1990, their share was nearly 30 percent of the U.S. market.[19]

Relationship to Maneuver

Measured in isolation, differential advantage provides very little information about the relative importance of the differences in product, place, promotion, and price. It also gives little insight into the feasibility of, or the potential strategic/tactical leverage in, making changes in any one of these variables. In terms of the automotive example discussed previously, differential advantage in and of itself does not indicate where domestic car manufacturers would get the greatest returns for incremental investments in marketing efforts.

However, when we examine the components of differential advantage as defined by Cook (see Table 5.1), we see that *differential advantage is*

Table 5.1   Measures of differential advantage.

Product-Related
- Research and development (money/employees)
- Patents (number issued and pending)
- Production capacity (value/ employees/units)
- Assortment (number offered)
- Plant inventories (value/units)
- Product performance (technical/ perceptual)
- Trademarks (value/number of brands)
- Warranties (value/terms)

Promotion-Related
- Media (money/number of messages)
- Salespersons (money/number/ calls)
- Promotion (money/number)
- Publicity (number of messages)
- Positioning (metric distance)
- Message (impact)
- Production (value)

Place-Related
- Retail outlets (number)
- Retail salespersons (number)
- Field inventories (value/units)
- Selling space (square feet)
- Shelf space (linear feet/spacings)
- Hours of business
- Special measures (e.g., flights per city pair)
- Trade support (dollar margins × volume)

Price-Related
- Relative price (1—(firm's price/ competitors' prices))
- Rebates/discounts (money)
- Trade margins (percent)
- Terms of sale (time/interest)
- Refund policies (recovery value)
- Transaction cost (money)

an operational measure of maneuver. In other words, by combining the information contained in differential advantage with an analysis of the freedom of maneuver in an industry, we can

- Define the relative importance of differences in strategic marketing investments in product, place, promotion, or price
- Interpret the significance of any shortfalls/excesses
- Determine the types and levels of marketing investments necessary to change market positions and shares
- Identify the long-term intentions of competitors, likely threats, and potential opportunities.

Viewed in this light, differences in relative investments in product and place are particularly important during the emerging and growth phases of an industry, while differential advantages in place and promotion and in promotion and price are key during the maturity and decline phases, respectively.

Differential Advantage and Competitors' Intentions

By using differential advantage in combination with maneuver, we can often obtain detailed insight into competing firms' long-term intentions and identify potential threats and likely opportunities.

Leaders.   If the market leader demonstrates a long-term pattern of maintaining a significant differential advantage, say, 15 percent higher than its market share in marketing investments, this signals (1) a firm commitment to the market and (2) possibly a desire to dominate the market. Especially in late maturity or decline, continuing investments in product development or promotion send an unmistakable signal that a firm intends to stay in the market well into the decline phase and to dominate the industry. (See Chapter 9.)

If the leader is consistently *underinvesting* in marketing, it is a sure sign of a lazy leader or one that is harvesting the market/product lines. Almost always, this indicates potential opportunities for followers or new entrants to gain share by maintaining their investments.

Followers.   If followers (or new entrants) are systematically investing substantially more in product, place, etc., than their market positions warrant, it is an unmistakable sign of a long-term intention to gain share at the leader's expense. By monitoring these investments, leaders can identify the market areas they are targeting and decide how to counterattack. If followers are investing less than their market position requires, it could be a signal that they want to exit the market.

Summary

Understanding maneuver is essential not merely to avoid wasting resources (inefficiency) but also to avert more drastic consequences (retaliation)!

Once a manager understands in which areas there is freedom to change a company's relative position, he can proceed to examine the likely returns from such changes. Alternatively, he can examine what industry forces restrict freedom of maneuver and attack those instead. In the next chapter, we will discuss how different "generic" strategies use a company's freedom of maneuver and the returns of each of these strategies. In Part Three, we describe some techniques for increasing a company's freedom of maneuver.

6

Likely Returns of the Three Generic Strategies

We have analyzed how industry structure influences maneuver and return, and examined freedom of maneuver at some length. We will now consider the returns of various maneuvers. For this purpose, we find it convenient to group possible maneuvers into three "generic" strategies. A company's returns for adopting one or the other of these three strategies vary considerably, depending on when the firm entered the particular industry; its current position and internal resources; the current structure of the industry; and the nature of the forces driving the industry.

Three Generic Strategies

Porter[1] identifies three generic strategies that firms can pursue in a competitive industry: (1) a firm can choose differentiation by creating products and services that are perceived as being unique in the industry; (2) a firm can opt for cost leadership, producing parity products more efficiently than all other firms in the industry, thereby obtaining above-average returns; (3) or else a firm can choose a focus approach, concentrating on selected areas of the market where it can provide superior products at lower cost (see Figure 6.1):

- *Differentiation.* A true differentiation strategy requires that a firm have a broad scope, that is, compete in all major segments; be perceived as offering unique, superior quality products and services

- *Differentiation*
  - Broad scope
  - Uniqueness across the board
  - Strong brand or name identity in the marketplace
  - Able to command a price premium
- *Cost leadership*
  - Broad scope
  - The low-cost producer in the industry
  - Standard, "no frills" offering
  - Parity or lower pricing
- *Focus*
  - Narrow scope of product line or limited market coverage
  - Tailored/specialized offering

Figure 6.1   Characteristics of generic strategies.

across-the-board; have a strong brand identity; and be able to command some premium in price. Among international airlines, Swissair is an example of a differentiation strategy,[2] while among the U.S. domestic airlines, American, Delta, and United appear to be following differentiation strategies.

- *Cost leadership.* Here, too, a firm competes in all major segments, but its prime focus is on lowering its operating costs by continuing investments in facilities and technology. The product strategy is "no frills"; a firm offers a parity product but makes no effort to position it as being unique. For this reason, the price of the product is at or sometimes slightly below the price of competing offerings. Continuing with the airline example, among the U.S. domestic trunk airlines, Northwest has followed a cost-leadership strategy consistently, while Continental is attempting to do so.[3]

- *Focus.* In contrast to the previous cases, a firm following a focus strategy concentrates on a narrow segment(s) of the market and produces a specialized offering. Within these two requirements, a firm can choose to differentiate itself in its segment or else concentrate on lowering its costs. Midway Airlines and Regent Airlines are two examples of firms' focus strategies among U.S. domestic carriers—one successful, the other not.

Implications for Maneuver and Leverage

Each of these approaches stresses different dimensions of market positioning. Consequently, they require varying degrees of freedom in maneuver and, as we shall see, their returns also vary considerably. A differentiation strategy emphasizes product and promotion. Channels play a supportive role; they must complement the product to ensure that it will be perceived as unique. Prices must be somewhat higher than the market average, for only then will a firm be able to afford the investments in creating and maintaining its unique positioning/brand identity.

Cost leadership, on the other hand, stresses price and, to a lesser extent, place. The product must be designed to meet minimum or "satisfactory" levels of performance; beyond that, the focus in design is on minimizing manufacturing costs. The keynotes are "utilitarian, functional" and not distinctiveness in design or styling. Promotion is also moderate in comparison with a differentiated firm. The really crucial choices relate to pricing. When setting prices, the cost leader must balance several considerations such as the following:

- *Price lower than the differentiated competitors.* The cost leader must maintain an appropriate distance between its prices and those of the differentiated competitors. Otherwise, customers have no incentive to choose their products over those that are (or appear to be) more distinctive or unique.

- *Price above "low-end" niche competitors.* Every market has its share of firms that concentrate on the highly price-sensitive segments. The cost leader must avoid being confused with such players; otherwise it risks tarnishing its image in the main areas of the market.

- *Avoid precipitating untimely price warfare.* Sudden price changes can trigger retaliation from low-end niche players who see their livelihoods threatened. Conversely, any reduction in the price differential vis-à-vis the differentiated firms could also create problems.

Radio Shack's difficulties in positioning its Tandy™ line of personal computers provides a good example of the difficulties faced by a would-be cost leader.[4] Radio Shack must (1) price the Tandy line well below IBM or Compaq, the differentiated firms, (2) price it above the low-priced "PC-clones," and (3) overcome its earlier reputation for poor, low-quality products.

Focus strategies typically cluster around either product and promotion in the case of high-end niche players or price and place in the case of the low-end competitors. The key here is consistency; the other components of the strategy must be consistent with the specific market focus. In other words, the channels and price must be consistent with a premium focus, and similarly, product design and promotion must fit in with the needs of price-sensitive customers. A common mistake is setting a low price for a premium niche product.[5] At the high end, pricing must reinforce the premium image and design.

Common Misconceptions

Managers suffer from several misconceptions when using this framework to analyze their own firm's or a competitor's strategy. They confuse a "price premium" with a "premium price." They assume a low-price position in the marketplace as evidence of a cost leadership strategy. Finally, they often find it difficult to distinguish between a differentiation strategy and one that emphasizes overall cost leadership.

Price Premium versus Premium Price.   A differentiation strategy requires that a firm charge some premium above the market in order to fund its investments in technology, product design, and promotion. However, this price should not be confused with the "premium price" charged by a niche supplier catering to upscale purchasers. A look at Figure 6.2 will help clarify the situation.[6] In a competitive market, customers can be segmented on the basis of perceived price and perceived quality as shown. The premium price segment is "high quality, high price," but it typically accounts for only 15 to 20 percent of the total market. The differentiated competitor (to meet the requirements of "broad scope"—see Figure 6.1) must position itself in the "high perceived quality, low perceived price" segment that accounts for 50 to 60 percent of the market. Here its pricing must be above that of nondifferentiated competitors yet below that of the premium-priced suppliers.

	Perceived Price	
	High	**Low**
High	Premium (15%–20%)	Best value (50%–60%)
Low	Opportunistic (5%–10%)	Cheap goods (10%–15%)

Perceived Quality (label at left, spanning High and Low rows)

Figure 6.2   Perceived price versus perceived quality matrix. (Percentages refer to segment shares in a mature industry.)

Low Price versus Cost Leadership.   Firms often confuse overall cost leadership with a low-price strategy. They are two very different approaches. Overall cost leadership concentrates on lowering operating or product *costs* (not prices) by systematic investments in facilities, capacity, and research and development. A low-price strategy seeks to enter a market or gain share by reducing prices. Under this approach, costs may or may not drop; if they do not come down, a firm will either have consistently lower profits or else be able to recoup its "investments" by gaining share. Among the U.S. domestic carriers, Northwest and Continental are examples of overall cost leadership and low-price strategy, respectively. Northwest has consistently invested in equipment, capacity, and efficiency. It has taken strikes rather than allow labor costs to go up. For this reason, its costs per passenger mile were among the lowest of the major unionized trunk carriers.[7] However, its fares are not noticeably lower than other "full-fare" majors such as United and Delta. Continental has consciously competed on the basis of *lower prices.* While its costs are low, in large part that is due to its ability to become a nonunionized carrier by declaring bankruptcy and not necessarily to any systematic investments in cost reduction.

Differentiation versus Cost Leadership.   Occasionally, these two strategies become confused. One cause of this confusion is management's understandable desire to stress efficiency.[8] But efficiency and cost leadership are not the same; cost leadership is a conscious attempt to focus the organization's efforts on systematically reducing or eliminating operating or product costs. Investments in improving product features, performance, or customer appeal, in this view, are secondary to investments in cost reduction. Thus, the two approaches stress fundamentally different aspects of strategy.[9] A more basic reason appears to be that cost leadership per se does not appear to be a viable strategy when differentiated competitors lower their costs close to the level of the overall cost leader. When this occurs, the cost leader can either (1) lower its prices to maintain the price differential, thereby lowering its profits, or (2) maintain its margins and risk blurring its identity in the marketplace. We discuss this conflict in more detail later in the chapter.

How Many Differentiated Competitors Can There Be in an Industry?

Differentiation is a particularly attractive strategy to marketing executives. It focuses attention on developing and maintaining the uniqueness or brand identity of a product, in the process employing tools marketing executives feel most comfortable with, namely, superior design, feature differentiation, and advertising. A differentiation strategy also allows a firm to charge above-average prices, something all managers believe in fervently.

How many truly differentiated competitors can you have in an industry? In other words, what are the returns for adapting differentiation? Or is there some upper limit to the number of differentiated competitors, suggesting that firms that cannot achieve that position in time should choose other strategies?

The answer depends on the degree of maturity of the underlying technology and the extent to which the industry is consolidated (which is closely related to technological maturity). Experience suggests that, as the technology and the industry mature, typically only two, but generally no more than four, companies can be considered to be truly differentiated competitors. The examples are numerous: Colgate and Crest in toothpaste, Moody's and Standard-Poors in bond-rating services, Deere and International Harvester/Case in farm equipment, and IBM and Apple in personal computers. It is difficult to find examples of *unregulated* industries in which there are three or more differentiated competitors. The airline industry—domestic as well as international—does have several differentiated players, but the international air passenger industry is still effectively regulated or cartelized, and the U.S. airline industry has already consolidated considerably, with the result that, at present, only American, Delta, and United can be considered differentiated competitors. Northwest and Continental are following cost leadership strategies, and USAir still isn't a trunk airline on the scale of the five majors. In some industries, there is only one truly differentiated company (in the sense of Figure 6.1): Caterpillar in industrial equipment (until Komatsu came along), Campbell's in canned soup, and IBM in mainframe computer equipment.

Rationale

The reasons for the limited number of successful differentiated competitors appear to lie in buyer behavior. Consumers typically purchase only those brands that are part of their "evoked set."[10] Brands or suppliers that are not in the evoked set get overlooked or purchased only infrequently, if at all. Typically, there are only four or at most five different brands in most consumers' evoked sets;[11] as a result, it is difficult for more than that number of firms to gain widespread acceptance as being distinctive and unique. In fact, given the diversity of perceptions, it would be difficult for more than two or three brands (or firms) to be part of the consciousness of a sizable fraction of the consuming population. This is the major reason packaged goods marketers fight so ferociously for "share of mind," for getting a part of the consumers' attention. If a firm cannot be part of the evoked set of the buyer group at large, then it cannot succeed in using differentiation as an overall strategy.

We find a similar situation in industrial buying behavior as well. In the past, most industrial purchases were traditionally split among two or three (rarely four) vendors, with the prime source receiving the major share, a second source receiving a smaller share, and a "swing" supplier (or occasionally two) receiving a small portion of the total business. This meant that there could only be a few—two to four—firms that would be prime or second sources for a significant portion of the market. Today, the trend in industrial purchasing is toward long-term relationships and far more single sourcing, further reducing the possible openings for differentiated suppliers.

These tendencies are reinforced as the technology matures. When the underlying technology is still evolving, there is considerable uncertainty and, therefore, more opportunity for establishing a differentiated strategy. However, once the technology matures, buyers settle on a few, selected choices, and it becomes much more difficult to establish a position that is unique (in the customers' eyes) from existing firms. Or, as we would put it, a company's freedom of maneuver along the dimensions of product and promotion shrinks considerably. Further, the technological differences between the various participants start narrowing;[12] thus, any innovations are likely to be quickly copied or even pre-empted by the major players, as they seek to defend their positions.

Implications

Given that the number of successful differentiated competitors in an industry is likely to be limited, this suggests that managers think long and hard about whether to use differentiation as a strategy at all, whether to shift from differentiation to either a focus or an overall cost leadership strategy, and how to position their firm as the industry evolves and the technology matures.

"Should We Use Differentiation as a Strategy at All?" This is the fundamental issue. Basically, the returns for a differentiation strategy are poor *unless* a firm is an early entrant and it already possesses some distinctive technology or market position. In most cases, it is the industry pioneers who have established successful differentiation strategies.[13] Later entrants generally have not been nearly as fortunate.

"Should We Change to a Focus or Cost Leadership Strategy?"   Unless a firm is well recognized as a technological leader or product innovator or has an extremely strong customer base, it may do better by abandoning attempts to differentiate itself. Instead, the firm should try to identify and build up its position in niches while these are still unoccupied or underserved. Alternatively, it could try to become the overall cost leader; however, this is riskier.

"What Should Be Our Long-Term Positioning?"   For a firm that has an early technological or performance advantage and a reasonably strong market position and, therefore, can successfully implement a differentiation strategy, the key issue is positioning. Sometimes this becomes self-evident as the industry evolves; Kellogg was one of the pioneers in ready-to-eat cereals, and its early growth made it a natural leader in the industry. In other cases, the outcome is not as clear-cut. One of the most important yet difficult decisions facing a firm that has been an early leader is whether to try to regain its leadership position or to use the same resources to establish a viable alternative while there is still time. Often the tendency is to rely on the firm's technological prowess. Unfortunately, this may not be enough, because the technology and the industry have matured to the point that further improvements do not significantly change market perceptions, or because the new leader has a stronger customer base. In such situations, discretion is the better part of valor. Many industry observers believe that John Sculley's greatest contribution at Apple Computer may have been to reposition it as an alternative or "second standard" to IBM and to abandon the attempt to regain its former position as the industry innovator and leader.[14] AT&T thus far has failed to establish itself as a distinctly unique competitor in microcomputers, for the simple reason that it entered the industry well after Apple and IBM were already entrenched as technological leaders and Compaq had carved out its position as the credible alternative source to IBM.

Despite the odds against it, differentiation remains a seductive strategy. Nothing else can explain the persistent attempts of industry latecomers trying to establish themselves as unique, notwithstanding the presence of several earlier entrants that have already carved out distinctive positions for themselves.

Is Pure Cost Leadership a Viable, Long-Term Strategy?

Differentiated players' costs are at or below the level of firms nominally pursuing cost leadership strategies. In other words, the differentiated firms are also the "low-cost producers."[15] This can occur due to systematic investments by the differentiated player, changes in product/process technology, or both. The net result is to reduce the potential return of a pure cost leadership strategy for the following reasons:

- A firm pursuing a pure cost leadership strategy of necessity must price its products below those of the differentiated producer to make up for its lack of uniqueness.
- If the differentiated firm reduces its costs to the level of cost leader, it can reduce prices to gain share *without compromising its profitability.*
- This places the cost leader in a very difficult position. If the cost leader firm cuts prices to maintain its position relative to the differentiated producer, its profitability suffers, reducing its ability to make continued investments in cost reduction.
- Conversely, if it maintains its prices (and margins), it loses its positioning relative to the differentiated producer and its market share suffers.

Economic Rationale

Differentiation—through superior technology, product design, advertising, or distribution—incurs costs over and above those of other, nondifferentiated firms. If we use quality as a proxy for differentiation, we can visualize the relationship between differentiation and cost leadership as shown in Figure 6.3a. A firm using a differentiated strategy seeks to maximize quality (differentiation) while keeping its cost below the ceiling set by the "sustainable premium," that is, the additional price the buyer is willing to pay for superior quality. The cost leader, on the other hand, seeks to minimize its costs while keeping its quality above the minimum acceptable level. Assuming that both firms have similar margins, the differentiated producer's prices will be higher than those of the cost leader.

The relationship between quality and product cost holds for a given type of technology or approach to operations. By changing the technology, the differentiated player can lower its costs near the level of the cost leader, *provided the latter is still using the older technology* (see Figure 6.3b). Under these circumstances, the differentiated firm can lower its prices without affecting its profitability. This shrinks the sustainable premium, considerably reducing the cost leader's freedom of maneuver in pricing.

In theory, the cost leader can also adopt the new technology, lower its costs similarly, and restore the status quo. However, in real life, there may be a significant lag before this occurs. In the meantime, the cost-oriented firm is under pressure to reduce its prices or else lose share.

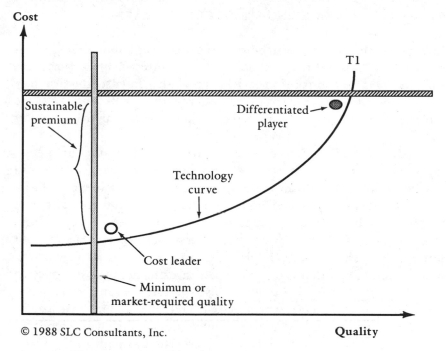

Figure 6.3a Differentiation vs. cost leadership.

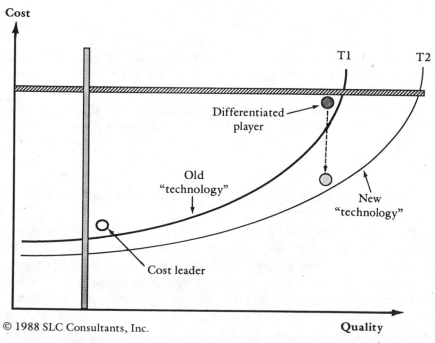

Figure 6.3b Is pure cost leadership sustainable?

Either way, the firm's profitability suffers, further handicapping its efforts to adapt to the new technology. If the investments required are sufficiently large and/or if the pricing pressure is intense, the firm may never recover its earlier market position, as witness Volkswagen's futile efforts to regain its position as the leading import car manufacturer against Japanese competition.[16]

In addition to the lag in adopting the new technology, the firm pursuing a cost leadership strategy runs the risk that its existing investments in cost reduction will be made obsolete by the new approach. General Motors found this out with its investments in factory automation; its joint venture with Toyota was showing lower costs than those it expected from the retooling of its other plants.[17] This considerably weakens the cost leader's competitive position. Now the firm must finance new investments while it continues to pay for past investments in cost reduction that have been rendered obsolete. It also increases organizational resistance to change. Executives will be reluctant to abandon what may be substantial investments in existing technologies and will have a tendency to invest more funds in (futile) efforts to remain competitive.[18]

To summarize, the returns for investing in a cost leadership strategy decline as the industry matures and companies that already have established brand identities lower their costs and prices. Under these conditions, the cost leader's choices are few and mostly unpalatable: The company can cut prices, but risks initiating a price war and, at the very least, lowers its profits. Changing product design or quality is difficult and offers little return. Such changes take time and, given that other firms have already established their positioning, do not significantly improve the company's perception in customers' eyes. The company cannot narrow its focus to a niche without losing its position as one of the leaders. Finally, the returns for changing channels or promotion are usually low, even assuming such changes are feasible without jeopardizing the company's leading position.

Under What Conditions Will a Focus Strategy Succeed?

In any market, there will be only two or three successful, differentiated competitors and usually only one firm will be able to establish and defend a cost leadership strategy. By elimination, the other participants must choose focus or "niche" strategies to remain viable players. Thus, for most companies, the issue is not "Should we choose a differentiation (or cost leadership) strategy?" Unless a firm is one of the early entrants or has unique resources/skills, it is (usually) futile to try to implement a differentiation or a cost leadership strategy; the odds are against the firm. Rather, the real question is, "Which niches offer the most returns, and which one(s) should we select?"

Unfortunately, companies all too often choose a focus strategy without carefully considering whether their choice is viable. Only later do they discover that the niche was not profitable or that they could not protect themselves from attacks by firms following differentiated or cost leadership strategies. The U.S. domestic airline industry is replete with examples of firms (Air Atlanta, Regent Air, and MGM Grand Air) that have tried to establish niche or focus strategies and have failed.

For a focus strategy to be viable, a firm must be confident that the needs of customers in that niche are distinct, that there are enough of them, and that it will not lose these customers to firms following a differentiated or a cost leadership strategy. More formally, the proposed focus strategy will be successful if (and only if) the following three conditions hold.

Customer needs must be unique or different. Satisfying customer needs in this segment must require definite changes in product design, packaging, distribution, or pricing, that is, the segment must offer some tangible returns for making these changes. Modifications in advertising, per se, are not sufficient evidence of truly unique/different needs. Left-handed golfers are an example of unique needs; on the other hand, the requirements of female (right-handed) golfers might not be unique if they can use clubs designed for shorter, lighter males without undue inconvenience. The acid test is, "Are customer needs so different that they cannot use existing products without major changes in their usage, work patterns, or behavior?"

In addition to customers with unique needs, there must be mobility barriers that keep the major firms *out* of the market. Viable mobility barriers—as opposed to merely perceived ones—represent cost disadvantages of the major firms as compared with a focused competitor. We can classify these mobility barriers according to these cost disadvantages:

- Direct costs of entry, such as product design change costs, incremental manufacturing costs, costs associated with separate channels of distribution, and additional promotional expenses
- Indirect costs of entry, such as the costs imposed on the overall product line due to the need to rationalize prices and prevent arbitrage
- Special conditions favoring niche players, such as local regulations (especially in international markets), superior efficiency in understanding and adapting to customer needs, or proprietary design/ technology.

If the market is lucrative enough, mobility barriers won't keep the majors out, while conversely, if the market is not very attractive, the major players will not be interested. Thus, the strength of the mobility barrier must be considered in relation to the attractiveness of the market, that is, market size as compared with the economies of production or operation.

Last but not least, there must be enough customers as compared with the MOS—minimum operating scale—required by the underlying technology. What's more, the number must be "just right." If it is too small, the focus strategy will not be profitable. If the number of customers with these unique needs is too large, the major players will be tempted to enter the market. Determining whether a particular focus strategy will attract the right number of customers is complicated by the difficulty of estimating the minimum optimal size of the plant,[19] and by pricing issues. All too often, firms adopting a focus strategy underestimate the ability of the major players to compete economically. They also tend to overestimate the customers' willingness to pay for specialized products or services.

Relationship to Return—Leverage

These three conditions are closely tied to the marketing mix. Figure 6.4 summarizes the interrelationships between these three conditions and the 4Ps. Product and place are crucial in determining the degree of uniqueness of customer needs, while price is only moderately important, and promotion is relatively unimportant. This suggests that, other things equal, market segments requiring significant changes to product and/or place are to be preferred over those demanding changes in promotion or price alone.

Product and place also provide better protection as mobility barriers, as they impose direct costs on new entrants. Promotion alone usually provides a relatively weak mobility barrier. Price is a moderately effective

	Product	Place	Promotion	Price
Determine uniqueness of needs	—Very important—		Little effect	Moderate
Provide mobility barriers	—Very effective—		Limited impact	Moderate
"Right" number of customers	Very important	—Secondary importance—		Very important

Figure 6.4   Focus strategies and the marketing mix.

mobility barrier, particularly if it imposes indirect costs by upsetting or distorting the would-be entrant's existing pricing patterns.

Finally, product and price are key in determining whether a particular focus strategy will attract the "right" number of customers. Place and promotion, on the other hand, have much less effect.

Why Zenith Succeeded . . . and Regent Air Failed

The very different experiences of two companies, Zenith and Regent Air, illustrate the importance of these conditions in determining returns to and the viability of a focus strategy. In personal computers, Zenith succeeded by concentrating on government and educational markets to the virtual exclusion of others. Regent Air (along with Midway Airlines and several other startups) failed to establish a viable niche in providing first-class travel at coach prices.[20]

The reasons for Zenith's success and Regent's failure become evident when we analyze the two strategies in terms of (1) the uniqueness of customer needs, (2) the presence or absence of viable mobility barriers, and (3) the "right" number of customers (see Figure 6.5).

Zenith's strategy met all three conditions satisfactorily. Customer needs were unique, primarily with regard to distribution and pricing. Educational and government buyers wanted to deal directly and were not particularly interested in local service or a large dealer network. Low price was a key criterion in the purchase decision. These requirements created viable mobility barriers, primarily through indirect costs. Other manufacturers, notably IBM, were at a cost disadvantage owing to their need to keep prices higher in other segments and, consequently, wanted to prevent arbitrage. Therefore, they could not match Zenith's prices without risking a backlash from dissatisfied customers in other

Condition	Zenith	Regent Air
• Unique customer needs	• Direct shipments • Lower prices	• More space, luxury
• Viable mobility barriers	• Direct costs of separate sales organization • Indirect costs of preventing price arbitrage	• None
• "Right" number of customers	• Sufficient volume	• Not enough "first-class only" passengers

Figure 6.5   Why Zenith succeeded . . . and Regent Air failed.

segments.[21] Finally, the number of customers was adequate. In fact, Zenith's only weakness lay in this area; the volume of government and educational purchases has become so large as to attract the major players.

Regent Air's strategy, on the other hand, met only the requirement that customer needs be unique. There were no viable mobility barriers; the major airlines could (and did) counter Regent's services by offering upgrades to first class for a large segment of the target market, namely business travelers. The majors could afford to do so because of their larger size, which enabled them to reconfigure aircraft and add more first-class seats at low cost. Last, as became obvious in a few months, there were not enough customers willing to forgo the other amenities offered by the trunk airlines—convenient connections, frequent flier programs—to make the concept economically feasible.

Braniff provides perhaps the most spectacular example of what happens when a firm chooses the wrong strategy—twice. First, Braniff erred in trying to become a major player immediately after deregulation; it disregarded the fundamental axiom that only two or three firms can be successful in implementing a differentiation strategy. After the inevitable result—bankruptcy—Braniff was purchased by the Pritzker group, which decided on a "first-class at coach prices" strategy, believing that it could leverage the high quality reputation of its Hyatt hotel chain. This, too, failed and Braniff is again in bankruptcy court.

Summary

Individual companies' strategies are one or some combination of these three generic approaches. We can therefore use the criteria developed in this chapter to evaluate the likely returns for adopting a particular approach. These criteria will also provide insight into the possible returns for various tactics, for example, the returns for lowering prices, widening the product line, or making operational investments to lower costs.

In the next chapter we will synthesize these various themes—the effects of the various competitive forces, freedom of maneuver, and returns—into strategic prescriptions for the different players as industries evolve from growth into maturity and, ultimately, decline.

7

How Strategic Leverage and Company Choices Change as Industries Evolve

Up to this point, we have analyzed the relationships between structure, position, and leverage and their implications for a company's strategic choices under *static* conditions, implicitly assuming that industry structure does not change. In this chapter, we will relax this assumption and study how leverage and strategic choices change as industries evolve over time.

For this purpose, we will use the familiar framework of the industry (product) life cycle,[1] which classifies industries into four stages of evolution—infancy (or emerging), growth, maturity, and decline. We begin by summarizing the results of empirical research that describes how the five forces of competition change as industries evolve.[2] This provides the foundation for analyzing how the nature of the industry conflict changes over time. In turn, this enables us to define how strategic objectives are affected by these changes and detail the implications for a firm's overall business strategy.

Next, we describe how a company's leverage changes as the industry evolves.[3] This allows us to examine how the constraints on maneuver change over time and identify the crucial tactical concerns at different stages of industry evolution. Finally, we review how strategic issues and decisions shift during industry transitions—from emerging to growth, from growth to maturity, and from maturity to decline.

In broad terms, we can summarize the effects of changes in industry structure on company strategy as:

- As industries evolve, the nature of the conflict changes, from the win/win situation typical of emerging or early growth stage, to either win/lose or limited warfare during the late growth and maturity stages, and to win/lose or even lose/lose during decline.
- These changes are predictable and arise out of the very forces that create industry growth or consolidation.
- The net effect is to steadily narrow individual firms' strategic choices.
- Freedom of maneuver and return also change in a predictable fashion.[4]
- Industry transitions are particularly important as they often require firms to make major changes in long-term objectives and/or overall strategies.

We must stress that the process isn't entirely one-sided; individual firms' strategies can (and do) affect industry structure profoundly. For example, a market leader can cause an industry to consolidate by increasing capacity and lowering costs, thereby forcing weaker participants to exit or be acquired. Similarly, a new entrant can change an industry competition from limited warfare with almost no price competition, to a win/lose situation with intense price discounting. However, as the industry ages, such changes (1) become more difficult, (2) require greater financial and technological resources, and (3) pose considerably higher risks.

How Structure Changes as Industries Evolve

Industries typically evolve through four distinct stages (Figure 7.1). First, there is an introductory or *emerging* stage in which industry sales are low (in relation to the subsequent peak) and industry growth is slow. At some point, the industry enters a *growth* phase in which sales explode and new entrants rush into the market. This growth phase can continue for a prolonged period or it can be quite short. As overall sales slow down, the number of participants, the terms of competition, industry technology, and so on, stabilize and the industry enters *maturity*. Finally, industry growth stops altogether and many firms start to exit, marking the beginning of the *decline* of the industry.

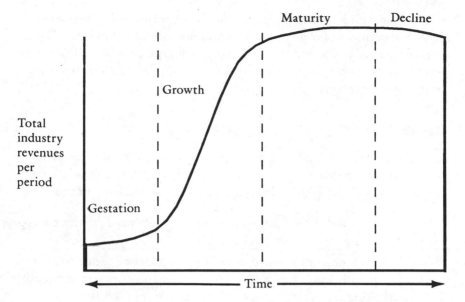

Figure 7.1   The S-shaped curve of industry evolution.

While the industry (or product) life cycle model is widely accepted, it also has been widely criticized.[5] The major concerns about the model are:

- It is hard to distinguish between the industry life cycle and individual product life cycles, especially when the industry is large and includes several major innovations.[6]
- We cannot predict the duration of individual stages or the total life cycle with any accuracy.
- Some industries may even "skip" a stage, going from growth abruptly into decline.
- Structural changes do not always follow the same pattern; for example, some industries may consolidate rapidly quite early in their life cycle, while others stay fragmented late into maturity or even decline.

The model does not account for industrial renewal, the rejuvenation of a mature or declining industry by new technology, and/or new entrants.

A major concern underlying these objections is that, applied mechanically, the industry life cycle concept could become a self-fulfilling prophecy. For example, emphasizing price because the industry is regarded as being in late maturity will guarantee that competition will intensify. At the same time, it could cause firms to overlook opportunities to differentiate the product or the firm.

These are valid objections; nevertheless, we believe that there are fundamental patterns of change that are common across industries and that, used judiciously, the industry life cycle concept provides valuable insights into changes in industry structure and their implications for a company's objectives and strategies.

Key Drivers

While there are few hard and fast rules about what creates the dynamic for growth in a particular industry, three factors appear to play a significant role in explaining the S-shaped pattern of the industry life cycle:

- The emergence of a "dominant design"[7] that speeds market acceptance of a new product/technology
- The development of new production processes or techniques[8] that dramatically lower the cost of the product and/or raise the quality levels, thereby greatly expanding the potential market
- Actual or perceived economies of scale in manufacturing, logistics, or marketing[9] that provide the incentive to invest capital and stimulate industry growth.

Not surprisingly, these three factors are often interrelated, for example, the emergence of a dominant design is facilitated by new production processes or techniques, which lead to economies of scale in manufacturing. In the U.S. automobile industry, the standard design (the Ford Model T) and the introduction of the paced assembly line were virtually simultaneous; further, it was the combination of the standard design and mass production that led to tremendous economies of scale, first in production and later in distribution and in marketing, creating the first mass market car.[10]

To the extent that these factors have their roots in technological innovation, they also provide an intuitive explanation for the S-shaped[11] pattern of industry evolution (see Figure 7.2). This curve has four stages, (1) an introductory phase where performance improvements are slow despite sizable R&D expenditures, (2) an explosive growth phase where performance skyrockets with very little additional investment in development, (3) a maturity stage, where technological developments start to settle down, and (4) a final decline stage, where there is very little performance improvement despite sizable R&D investments. These four stages correspond approximately to the four phases of the industry life cycle, particularly in the case of major innovations (such as the large-scale integrated chip) that create new industries virtually singlehandedly.

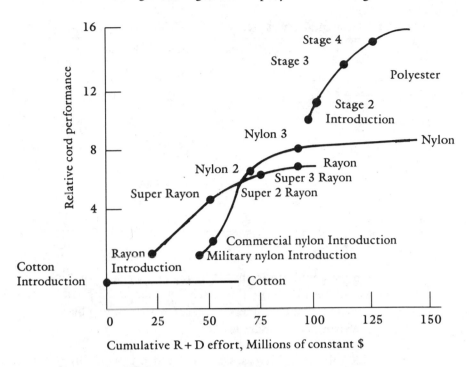

From Richard N. Foster, *Innovation: The Attacker's Advantage.* Copyright © 1986 by McKinsey & Co. Inc. Reprinted by permission of Summit Books, a division of Simon & Schuster, Inc.

Figure 7.2   A technology S-curve.

Implications for the Forces of Competition

How industry structure changes as an industry evolves through the various stages is summarized in Table 7.1.

Barriers to Market Entry.   Overall, the cost of entry tends to increase as the industry evolves. If economies of scale are a driver of industry growth, their significance will increase as industry sales grow, reaching very high levels in late maturity. Similarly, product differentiation advantages become more significant as growth slows and technological diffusion reduces the headstart of early entrants.[12] Access to channels of distribution becomes more difficult—and thus more important as an entry barrier—in the later stages of the life cycle due to lack of "shelf space," that is, channels tend to be quite satisfied with established brands and not very receptive to new entrants even when they offer significant advantages. On the other hand, we cannot draw any *a priori* conclusions about switching costs or cost disadvantages independent of

Table 7.1   How industry structure affects the forces of competition.

	Stages of Industry Evolution			
	Emerging	Growth	Maturity	Decline
Barriers to Market Entry				
Scale	Low			High
Differentiation	Low			High
Access	Low			High
Switching Costs	—	—	—	—
Rivalry	Low			High
Substitution	Nil	Low	Low/Medium	High
Buyer Power	—	—	—	—
Supplier Power	—	—	—	—

scale, although we could argue that, to the extent that switching costs exist, they would be higher in the maturity than during the growth phase, due to the fact that customers' investments are higher because they have been purchasing the product longer.

Rivalry.   Rivalry also increases as the industry ages. Other things being equal, the diffusion of technology tends to reduce the feature or performance differences between various firms' offerings in the later stages of the life cycle, increasing the tendency towards greater competition. At the same time, diffusion of technology increases customers' knowledge of, and familiarity with, the technology. This tends to increase buyer pressures and intensify competition among industry participants. Finally, the slowdown and eventual decline in total industry sales also tends to intensify competition.

Substitution.   The threat of substitutes typically becomes significant only in the late maturity or decline stages. We can explain this intuitively in terms of technology S-curves when we recognize that during periods of high performance growth for a given investment in R&D, the expected return from investing in substitutes isn't attractive. It is only when the return on investments in the existing technology slows down that the market starts paying attention to alternative technologies. Consequently, only in late maturity or decline is substitution likely to emerge as a significant competitive threat.

Buyer and Supplier Power.   Regarding the two remaining forces of competition—buyer and supplier power respectively—we cannot draw any such general conclusions. We could argue that, other things being

Table 7.2   Empirical results from PIMS data.

Variable	Growth	Growth Maturity	Maturity	Declining Maturity	Decline
Avg. real market growth (%)	10.5	12.3	0.3	−10.5	−1.7
New entrants (% of markets)	43	25	21	18	—
Share instability (index)	5.7	4.4	3.7	3.7	3.8
New products (% of sales)	10.2	5.4	3.5	3.7	2.8
Product differentiation (index)	51	43	42	40	32
Price differentiation (index)	7	6.3	6.2	6	5.4
Gross margin (%)	30.5	26.2	26	23.8	21.8
ROS (%)	10.1	9.4	9.1	8.7	7.2

Source: Buzzell and Gale, *The PIMS Principles: Linking Strategy to Performance,* New York: The Free Press, 1987. Reprinted with permission.

equal, buyer power increases in the later stages of the industry life cycle due to the increased knowledge of buyers and reduced product/service differentiation due to the diffusion of technology. While this might be true, we do not believe it materially alters the situation; if buyers were powerful during the growth stage of the industry, they would be powerful during maturity. If buyers are weak during the growth stage, it is unlikely that they would become powerful during maturity or decline. It is useful to distinguish between intermediaries/channels and end users. We conjecture that the power of intermediaries increases as the industry matures. Limits on "shelf space" inevitably increase intermediary power in late growth and maturity as more suppliers are competing for the attention of a few key channels. In theory, manufacturers could create new channels; however, we would argue that the expected cost of creating the additional channels is prohibitive, effectively neutralizing the manufacturers' ability to reduce intermediary power.

Quantitative analyses using the PIMS database broadly support these conclusions.[13] Table 7.2 summarizes the key conclusions.

How Industry Evolution Affects the Industry Conflict

The nature of industry conflict changes as the industry evolves from emerging to growth, maturity, and ultimately, decline. At different stages of the industry life cycle, the number of firms participating in the industry varies considerably as do their perceptions of current and future industry prospects. In the early stages of growth, the number of participants is usually large, and collective expectations regarding sales growth and profitability are high; consequently, the nature of the conflict tends to be win/win. As industry growth slows, the number of active players typically declines along with expectations regarding future sales and profit growth. This changes the payoff to either win/lose or limited warfare. Finally, during the decline stage, the nature of the conflict shifts to lose/lose as overall industry prospects shrink.

Emerging Industries

Early in the life of an industry there is very little conflict or even perception of conflict. Instead, at this stage there is usually considerable camaraderie and a sense of a need for collective action. This was evident, for example, in the personal computer industry's words and actions in the late 1970s and early 1980s (prior to IBM's entry); a similar spirit is visible today in the emerging U.S. home videotext industry.

Thus, we must classify the nature of the payoffs as win/win for the following reasons:

- *The overall market is undefined,* with the result that firms have no clear idea of industry growth rate; indeed, it may be very difficult to make any sensible estimates of growth rates.
- *Technology is still evolving,* adding to the uncertainty regarding likely growth and profitability.
- *The number of industry participants is large* and includes participants with very diverse backgrounds, such as start-ups funded by individual investors or venture capital, subsidiaries of larger, established firms, individual inventors and entrepreneurs, and even potential buyers looking for substitutes or opportunities in backward integration.

Consequently, there is little perception that an individual firm's gains occur at the expense of another competitor. Furthermore, given the embryonic state of technology, players stand to gain more by sharing information than by withholding it.

Growth Stage

Industry conflict can be categorized as win/win during the early and middle stages of growth, changing towards win/lose or limited warfare in late growth/early maturity. Three factors contribute to this outcome:

- Extremely rapid market growth, enabling individual firms to grow almost despite themselves
- Lack of information, which prevents the various players from clearly identifying their gains and losses—20 percent growth in revenues appears very satisfactory so long as managers (and investors) are unaware that the industry as a whole grew 50 percent in the same period
- High turnover among industry participants, which makes identifying competitors difficult and obscures "who gains at whose expense."

Maturity

The situation changes as overall market growth slows and the number of participants stabilizes with a few firms emerging as leaders in terms of share and industry patterns regarding innovation and competition. At this point, the nature of the conflict shifts from win/win to win/lose or limited warfare. These changes may occur relatively gradually, as in the case of the personal computer industry. Or they may be quite abrupt, as in the U.S. long-distance telecommunications market and the CAD/CAM (computer-assisted design/manufacturing) industry.[14]

This shift in the nature of the payoffs, from win/win to win/lose or limited warfare occurs because

- Overall industry growth rate has slowed dramatically.
- Technology has matured, reducing product differentiation and increasing price competition.
- Firms increasingly have the same breadth of product lines, serve the same segments and the same number of customers.

This overlap—in products, segments, and customers—naturally increases the perception, created by the slowdown in overall growth, that "firm A's gains can occur only at firm B's expense."

The exact nature of the outcome—win/lose or limited warfare—depends on (1) the underlying cost structure, especially the relative proportion of fixed and variable costs, (2) the height of any exit barriers, (3) the relative market share of the leader(s), (4) the perceived/actual objectives of the leader(s), and (5) the speed with which the transition to industry maturity has occurred. If fixed costs and exit barriers are relatively high, the industry leader does not have high *relative* share, and industry growth has slowed abruptly, the most probable outcome is win/lose. This is especially likely if, as was the case in the CAD/CAM industry, historically high sales growth rates have conditioned expectations; in such cases, it appears highly likely that firms will try to maintain their growth patterns even at the expense of their competitors. Under such conditions, limited warfare is very difficult to enforce; individual firms' objectives will not permit such cooperative equilibrium.[15]

If the transition to industry maturity occurs over a sufficiently long time period and/or the industry leader has the ability (and the foresight) to contain industry competition within certain limits, then limited warfare is possible, other things—particularly industry cost structures—being equal. Examples of such situations are the ready-to-eat cereals industry, the beer industry, and the (deregulated) long-distance telecommunications industry.[16] In the long term, this industry consensus may be stable, as it has been for more than 25 years in the case of the ready-to-eat cereal industry. Or else it may be temporary, either because the equilibrium was inherently unstable, or because one of the participants (or, as is often the case, a new entrant) destroyed the tacit consensus by acting out of step with the rest of the industry. Philip Morris did this in the beer industry when it bought Miller Brewing and proceeded to dramatically increase advertising expenditures, forcing Anheuser-Busch to counterattack and, in the process, significantly increasing industry consolidation as regional brands dropped by the wayside.[17]

Decline

Finally, as the industry enters the decline phase, the nature of the conflict changes to a lose/lose, as all the participants try to protect their own positions. If exit barriers and fixed costs are high, industry conflict is likely to be particularly intense as smaller players (and their bankers) resort to increasingly desperate price-cutting in vain attempts to increase revenues and cash flow. Larger players are forced to follow in order to protect market shares, and the entire industry is locked in a vicious downward spiral.

Occasionally there may be a truce or an attempt to limit industry conflict. In general, such standoffs are short-lived, especially if the cost of exiting the industry is high. If exit barriers are relatively low, then one or two firms may be able to force the weaker players out and remain profitable. Motorola has followed this strategy successfully in the discrete transistor market. While total industry sales have fallen steadily as discrete transistors have been almost totally replaced by integrated circuits in most applications, Motorola has apparently increased its share of the market to considerably more than 60 percent and, by all accounts, is profitable.

Finally, a word about the nature of conflict in cyclical industries such as many capital goods industries and air transportation. These tend to be win/win on the upswings and lose/lose on the downsides; however, over the long run, they tend to be win/lose as the industry consolidates. The cyclical nature of the industry—which is usually the result of the cyclical nature of the demand for the product—almost always ensures that there will be considerable excess capacity during the downswings. This makes limited warfare difficult; regardless of their intentions, the financially weaker firms find it almost impossible to restrain their output in the downturns, due to their need for cash. Air transportation is a typical cyclical industry where the nature of the competition, after deregulation in 1980, has alternated between win/win and lose/lose, but where the basic trend is towards industry consolidation.[18]

How Industry Evolution Affects Strategic Leverage

Along with changes to industry structure, industry evolution also affects a company's leverage along product, place, promotion, and price. As we did earlier, we will first qualitatively examine the relationships between the various phases of industry evolution and the 4Ps.[19] Subsequently, we will discuss empirical evidence confirming these intuitive conclusions.

Typically, in the emerging stage of the industry, the technology is still evolving. Therefore, intuitively we would expect product-related issues to dominate, first, as the various participants each try to create *the* dominant design, and, after the dominant design emerges, as other firms (with different designs) react by changing their designs, counterattacking or improving on the evolving industry standard.

Once the dominant design becomes relatively well established and industry growth takes off, we would expect selecting and developing suitable channels to become key concerns as firms try to segment markets and build efficiencies in production and marketing. We would also expect promotion to gain in importance as buyer awareness increases and firms start establishing their identities.

As the technology and the industry mature, we would expect promotion and sales efforts to move to center stage. With increasingly mature technologies, feature/performance differences become less pronounced; consequently, companies will have to increase their promotional and sales expenditures to attract and retain customers. Finally, in the late maturity and decline stages, with increased industry rivalry, pressure from substitutes, and buyer pressures, we would expect to see pricing become the central marketing concern.

These qualitative conclusions are summarized in Table 7.3. On the basis of this very rudimentary examination, we would expect that

- Product decisions would have the most impact (offer the most leverage) on profitability and market performance in the emerging and growth stages of the industry life cycle
- Place or channel decisions would become significant in terms of leverage during growth and, possibly, maturity
- Promotion decisions would be important during maturity
- Pricing decisions would have the most leverage (again in terms of profitability and market performance) during decline.

Empirical studies using the PIMS database provide broad support for these conclusions.[20] The results of one study using a sample of 1,234 industrial products manufacturing businesses, analyzed over the time

Table 7.3 How industry evolution affects the 4Ps.

	Product	Place	Promotion	Price
Emerging	Dominant design has not emerged Technology in flux Product is key	Wide variation in types, number of channels Very little power undefined Roles not clear	Not very important Media, messages, expenditures— all	Not very important Wide variations in levels, conditions
Growth	Dominant design is being established New product introduction rates are very high	Channel roles becoming clearer Key channels are emerging	Industry patterns are still evolving	Not yet significant –price points vague –little/no emphasis
Maturity	Well-defined offerings, features Rapid emulation of flankers, specialties	A few, well-defined channels "Shelf space" battles beginning	Promotion and sales activities becoming key to share	Pricing patterns well established Price competition emerging
Declining	Little or no product innovation	Channels consolidating Channel margins under severe pressure	Promotion and sales activities intensifying	Price competition intense

period 1970 to 1980, are summarized in Table 7.4. The sample included 323 cases of businesses in the growth stage, 857 in the mature stage, and 54 cases of businesses in declining industries. Businesses in the introductory or emerging stage of the life cycle were not analyzed due to insufficient data. The study analyzed the relative importance of different variables such as technological change, new products as percent of total sales, promotional expenditures as a percent of sales on *return on investment,* defined as net income/average investment, and *relative average market share,* defined as the percentage market share of the business/the percentage market share of its three largest competitors.

As Table 7.4 shows, the PIMS data support the overall patterns described in Table 7.3. Technological change and R&D expenditures do peak during the growth phase. Relative product quality declines as expected throughout the life cycle, suggesting that relative price also declines (the study could not provide specific confirmation of this point due to multicollinearity). Advertising and promotional expenditures peak during maturity.

Having reviewed how the nature of the payoffs and the relationship between industry structure and the 4Ps change over the industry life cycle, we will now analyze the implications for a company's objectives, for strategy selection, and for various tactical issues. Throughout, it is important not to lose sight of the underlying causal chain, namely:

- External forces (technological opportunities, customer requirements) are the major drivers of industry evolution.

Table 7.4 How different factors influence ROI, relative market share over the industry life cycle (regression coefficients).*

	Industry Growth Phase					
	Growth		Maturity		Decline	
Policy Variable	ROI	Share	ROI	Share	ROI	Share
Product customization	−0.134	—	−0.066	—	—	−0.384
Product line breadth	—	0.221	—	0.242	—	—
Relative product quality	0.093	0.287	0.107	0.178	—	—
Product R&D/revenue	−0.194	0.106	−0.111	—	—	—
Sales force/revenue	−0.174	—	—	—	—	0.411
Relative advtg. exp.	—	0.119	—	0.126	—	−0.273

(—) denotes that the relationship was not statistically significant.

*Adapted from Anderson, Carl R. and Zeithaml, Carl P., "Stage of the Product Life Cycle, Business Strategy and Business Performance," *Academy of Management Journal,* V.27, N1, 1984.

- Industry evolution causes changes in industry structure.
- Changes in industry structure cause changes in industry payoffs.
- Changes in the payoffs require that firms participating in the industry change their objectives.
- Changes in objectives demand corresponding changes in strategies and tactics.

Implications for Strategic Objectives: Overview

We can now examine the implications of industry evolution for a firm's long-term objectives and strategies. As we shall see, a firm has considerable freedom of choice during the growth phase, when industry structure and payoffs create relatively few restrictions. As the industry ages, however, a company's leverage becomes more restricted and major strategic changes carry significant risks. Finally, in the decline phase, the options narrow to basically two, namely, either stay and drive out the other participants or decide to exit early on favorable terms.[21]

We will proceed in two steps. First, we will study how industry structure and payoffs define the available alternatives. We will then categorize key issues that are likely to affect which specific objectives and strategies are chosen and summarize the primary factors underlying these issues. We will omit the first or emerging stage of industry evolution in this analysis. During this phase, industry technology, customer needs, and company capabilities are in such a state of flux that it is very difficult to draw any broad, categorical conclusions.

Implications for Growing Industries

Table 7.5 summarizes the potential choices, key issues, and implications for a firm's objectives during the early and middle growth stages of an industry. We will first discuss how they vary for the industry leaders, other participants, and new entrants and then show how this framework can be applied in practice.

The Leaders

At this stage of industry evolution, there are typically three to five firms that are potential contenders for industry leadership. These players' choices are related to long-term positioning. While the win/win nature

Table 7.5   Implications for company objectives.

| | Growth Phase | |
Participants	Alternatives	Key Factors
Leaders	Capture/remain No. 1 Capture/remain No. 2 Become *the* cost leader Find/create profitable niches and dominate them	*Company-specific* role to-date capabilities resources commitment *Industry-specific* rate of technological evolution patterns of market development *External* new entrants
Other Players	Sell out or stay into maturity Find/create profitable niches and dominate them	*Company-specific* technology/marketing strengths *Industry-specific* Duration of technology "window"
New Entrants	Be No. 1 or No. 2 Become *the* cost leader Find/create profitable niches and dominate them	*Company-specific* Opportunistic vs. competitive entry *Industry-specific* Resources required for entry

of the conflict means they can choose their strategies without undue concern about retaliation from competitors, fundamentally each firm should be looking down the road towards industry consolidation and anticipating how it would ideally like to be positioned as sales growth slows and the industry matures.

The first question is, "Can we maintain our position as the industry leader?" If the answer is no, the next logical question is, "Can we be number two—the 'other guy'—Pepsi to the industry's Coke?" Another possibility is, "Can we become *the* cost leader?" Failing all of these, "Can we find a defensible niche?"

These choices are based on the observations that (1) there are usually no more than two differentiated, across-the-board competitors in an industry and that (2) only one firm can successfully be the lowest cost producer. What this implies is that, in a growing industry with, say, five firms closely grouped in terms of market share and product differentiation, competitors number four and number five must either beat out competitors one, two, and three to successfully establish either a differentiation or a cost leadership strategy, or start focusing on niches early in order to find defensible ones that are also profitable, or else use the remainder of the growth period to build defenses, for example, by customizing their products or processes, creating switching costs for users.

Edging out the top three players (in terms of market share) requires a firm to grow faster than the leaders are growing. This may be possible during the early stages of industry growth, especially if one of the leaders is slowing down. However, it becomes increasingly difficult in the middle stages of growth as the technology stabilizes and the dominant design becomes widely accepted. Consequently, at this stage of industry growth, players number four and five should concentrate on finding/creating defensible, profitable niches and avoid committing resources in futile efforts to participate across the board as differentiated producers or cost leaders.

For the top two or three firms, there is more room for maneuver but correspondingly greater risks. Two traps to avoid are *hubris,* or technological/marketing arrogance, a company's over-confident assumption that *its* approach is the only possible one and that its position is secure, and/or *strategic myopia,* an inability or unwillingness to confront these critical strategic issues regarding long-term positioning and make difficult choices.

The two often go together; hubris creates and reinforces strategic myopia. Ford's success with Model T created an attitude best summarized by the famous quote, "any color you want so long as it's black." This hubris made Henry Ford extremely reluctant to abandon an aging design and slowed the changeover to the Model A. It also bred strategic myopia; because Ford had controlled the market in the past, he couldn't visualize that his company might *not* control the market in the future.

In order to choose among the available alternatives, firms must first answer the following questions that are fundamental to setting long-term objectives:

- What in our track record to date will convince the industry that we can become/remain industry leaders?
- Do we have the financial resources, technological and managerial capabilities, and above all, the organizational commitment to achieve differentiation or cost leadership?
- How much time do we have to design and implement a differentiation or cost leadership strategy?

- Will technological superiority be sufficient or will customers (especially channels) play an important role in determining who will emerge as industry leaders?
- Which potential entrants are likely to have the capabilities and the commitment to be serious challengers for industry leadership?

The answers to these questions can be determined by analyzing several factors, which can be organized according to whether they are (1) company-specific, (2) industry-specific, or (3) external to the industry as a whole.

Company-specific factors relate primarily to company capabilities, intentions, and commitment, namely, its role in industry to date, capabilities and resources—technical, managerial, and financial—and competitive position, as well as the ability to define and concentrate organizational resources on a specified objective ("strategic intent"). The last is an important but intangible factor and one that is difficult to assess. In the personal computer industry, for example, Compaq was able to concentrate clearly on the objective of being "a credible alternative to IBM," while AT&T could not, despite its substantially greater resources.

Industry-specific factors of importance are (1) the rate of technological evolution and (2) the manner in which the market is developing. How technology is evolving determines to a considerable degree how long the growth stage will last and how rapidly consolidation might occur. How the market develops determines whether buyers (especially channels) will be important in determining which firms are likely to emerge as the leaders, and how soon rivalry will change the conflict from win/win to win/lose, thereby hastening industry consolidation.

External factors that should be considered relate to the possibility of entrants posing a significant threat to the leaders. In particular, firms should carefully examine which industries are threatened by the new technology and the capabilities and traditional strategies of potential entrants from these industries. Our rationale is that logical entrants into a new industry are existing producers of substitutes or existing suppliers to the same group of customers. Further, it is likely that a firm competing on the basis of differentiation in that industry will seek to compete in the same fashion in the new one, provided it has the technological, managerial, and financial resources.

A careful examination of these three factors will answer the basic questions listed previously, in turn, these answers will point out the most feasible strategic alternative. For example, analysis may show that, while the company has the capabilities and the commitment, the market leader's market share advantage is large and that the technology appears to be maturing. In this case, the objective of industry leadership should be abandoned as it has a low probability of success, that is, the expected return—more precisely the risk-adjusted return—from any investments in trying to capture leadership is low. The expected return could be even lower if we include opportunity costs, for example, the potential profits that a firm would have obtained by concentrating its resources on developing and strengthening a particular niche.

Other Players

Just as there are several firms vying for industry leadership at this stage of industry evolution, there are numerous smaller participants. Their choices are more limited; indeed the fundamental decision they must make is whether to stay or sell out. Selling out—to a new entrant or to one of the industry leaders—is often a particularly attractive alternative as the combination of past and prospective rapid sales growth drives up the prices firms are willing to pay.

The basic choice is, "Should we stay in the industry (as an independent entity) into maturity or should we sell out during the growth phase?" If a firm chooses to stay independent, then the logical question is, "Can we find or create niches that are both defensible and profitable, and in which we have a chance of being number one or two?" The largest of these firms may have the opportunity to dislodge one of the weaker industry leaders, but for the vast majority of the players in this category, the expected return from such efforts is extremely poor.[22]

If a firm cannot find suitable niches (and sometimes even when they can), then the best course might well be to sell out. In this case the only question is, "How can we position the firm to maximize its value (and hence raise the price) to a prospective purchaser?" One possibility is to sell to an unsuspecting entrant, preferably one that is large and decentralized! Alternatively, a firm could concentrate on products/customers in areas complementary to the industry leader and position itself to be acquired either for its capabilities or to eliminate a threat to the leader's own efforts in the same areas.

The key consideration is similar to the ones outlined earlier during our discussion of the leaders. Some differences:

- An important, company-specific factor is a firm's ability—technological and/or marketing—to identify and capitalize on emerging specialty needs. If the conclusion is that the firm has few *competitive* advantages in this area then, quite frankly, its prospects are bleak. In this case, it may be best to sell out quickly.

- The rate at which technology is maturing is important in deciding the timing of the "sell" decision. Early in the growth stage is likely to be too early, whereas waiting till the technology and the industry are close to maturing may be too late, as buyers will most probably recognize that future prospects are not too attractive.

- Likely entrants should be analyzed not only for the threats they may pose to the firm but also in terms of their propensity to enter new markets by acquisition.

As before, an examination of the three sets of factors will help a firm either choose a specific niche or focus area or decide that its investors are best served by selling out. The two are not necessarily antithetical, in fact, quite the contrary. In most cases, a well-designed and executed niche strategy also increases a firm's attractiveness to potential buyers.

New Entrants

The high growth rates at this stage of industry evolution also attract many potential and actual entrants. Entry strategies also vary, from direct entry with significant R&D and production investments, to entry via acquisition of an existing player, to joint ventures, to venture capital for promising entrepreneurs. However, a basic question in determining objectives, entry strategies, specific tactics, etc., is, "Why should we commit our recourses—capital, technology, and managerial—to this new market?" This issue of motivation or rationale for entering often gets overlooked in the early flush of growth that is typical of the industry at this stage, inevitably leading to loss of direction and, often, disillusionment and withdrawal from the market.

Like the industry leaders, new entrants have the full range of options open before them. Their choices can be expressed as, "Can we capture industry leadership? Can we capture the number two slot? Can we be *the* cost leader? or Can we find a defensible niche?"

The responses to these questions will vary depending on whether the entrants' motivations for entering the industry are *opportunistic* or *competitive*. Opportunistic entrants view the new industry purely as a chance to increase revenues or profits and not as a potential threat or a direct adjunct to their current businesses. Competitive entrants, by contrast, are firms that believe the new industry threatens their existing products, their ability to control their markets, or both.

These differences in motivations place potential limits on the alternatives available and on entry strategies (see Figure 7.3). Opportunistic entrants, firms who view their entry into the industry purely as an investment, albeit one made in pursuit of a diversification strategy, do not have the same strategic imperatives that drive competitive entrants. Competitive entrants face definite adverse consequences that opportunistic entrants do not, namely, loss of customer control, lower revenues, or even total substitution by the products and services offered by the new industry.

As a result, we believe that competitive entrants should not dissipate their resources in seeking profitable niches. Specifically, if either (1) the industry is not strategic enough to justify the investment required to capture a leadership position or (2) a firm does not possess the necessary resources to become a leader in the new market, then it should not enter the market. The reason is that, in either case, the firm risks draining resources from other, strategically important areas to fund what will become dead-end investments, *even if they are eventually profitable.*

Two considerations of particular importance are the *feasibility of differentiation* and the *resources required.* Certain positions, for example, technical leadership or mainstream brand positioning, may already have been preempted; in this case, the resources required increase sharply, while the probability of success declines. Resources required depend on the mode of entry—direct, by acquisition(s), through joint ventures, or participation in the form of venture capital. The costs of direct entry, in turn, depend on the nature of the technology, barriers to entry related to differentiation, and in the late growth stage, the costs of overcoming access barriers.

Opportunistic Entry	Competitive Entry
• *Don't* have restrictions on entry strategies	• *Do* have restrictions on entry strategies
• Don't *have* to be industry/niche leaders	• *Do* have to be industry/niche leaders
• Can afford to "skim"	• Can't afford to "skim"
• Opportunity costs not measurable	• Opportunity costs are measurable
• Expect "market-based" returns	• May accept "below-market" returns to protect other interests
• May be quicker to exit	• May be very slow to exit
• Identities, timing of entry are not predictable	• Identities, timing of entry are predictable

Figure 7.3 Opportunistic versus competitive entry strategic implications.

Implications for Mature Industries

As the industry matures, the payoff changes from win/win to either limited warfare or win/lose. This transition narrows the choices available to industry participants considerably (see Table 7.6). If the industry becomes embroiled in a win/lose conflict, the choices are basically to try to limit conflict, continue fighting, or exit the industry. If warfare is limited, the choices are similar: maintain status quo, violate tacit agreements, escalate the conflict, or exit. Entrants too have few alternatives. First and foremost, they must decide whether to enter the industry at all at such a late stage in the evolution of the industry. It is difficult to conceive of situations where firms would *willingly* enter an industry engaged in extensive competitive warfare. Assuming then that entrants are likely to choose only industries where warfare is limited, the remaining question is which would be more profitable, joining the status quo or breaking it.

Table 7.6   Implications for company objectives.

Participants	Maturity Phase	
	Alternatives	Key Factors
Leaders	Establish limited warfare Maintain limited warfare Initiate price wars or concentrate on defending share	*Company-specific* relative share position relative cost position resources available *Industry-specific* height of exit barriers switching costs rivals' intentions, capabilities *External* regulatory climate
Other Players	Defend my position against larger firms To whom should I sell Attack—or accept status quo	*Industry-specific* mobility barriers intensity of competition
New Entrants	*Should* we enter at all Join status quo—or intensify industry rivalry Acquire—or build-up	*Company-specific* financial resources technological capabilities familiarity with industry *Industry-specific* terms of competition nature, speed of response

The Leaders

Our underlying hypothesis is that, in most cases, firms (and managers) will prefer limited (nonprice) warfare to explicit price-based competition. Our reasoning is:

- At this stage of industry evolution, the product design, manufacturing technology, and so on have matured.
- The number and types of channels have stabilized.
- The emerging dimensions of industry conflict are likely to be *promotion* and *price*.
- Companies realize that price-based competition tends to lower overall prices and further, that prices once lowered are difficult to raise again, especially if buyer power is high, unless there are external forces, for example, overall inflation.[23]
- For this reason, other things being equal, companies will prefer to restrict competition to *discretionary* nonprice activities such as increased customer service, higher advertising expenditures, etc., thereby avoiding downward pressure on margins.
- Finally, the leaders have the most to lose in any price-based warfare, being the firms with the most market share and the largest margins.[24]

Thus in our opinion, *at this stage of industry evolution,* the market leader's basic goal should be to establish and maintain a state of limited warfare.[25] Consequently, if the conflict is win/lose, the leader's first objective should be to determine if it can change the conflict to limited warfare. If the industry is engaged in limited warfare, the leader's first priority should be maintaining this state of affairs.

As discussed above, the leader's alternatives are few and related to maintaining or restoring limited warfare (see Table 7.6):

- *Win/lose.* The first question the leader must ask is, "Can we limit the dimensions of the conflict, especially in the area of pricing?" If that does not appear feasible, the only question that remains is, "Should we initiate price competition or should we focus primarily on defending our share?"
- *Limited warfare.* The only issue here is, "Can we maintain the status quo (limited warfare)?" If this is not feasible, then the only question that remains is, "Should we initiate price competition or should we focus primarily on defending our share?"

We can classify the key considerations as company-specific, industry-specific, and those external to the industry:

Company-specific factors of particular importance are (1) a firm's relative share position, (2) its relative cost position, and (3) resources available. Relative share and cost position decide whether a firm's threats will be credible to the other players, while its resources will dictate the ability to carry out a sustained campaign of relentless price-cutting or punitive actions against players who violate industry norms.

Industry-specific variables of concern are (1) the overall cost characteristics, (2) the height of any exit barriers, (3) the presence or absence of any switching costs, and (4) the intentions and capabilities of the various key competitors. Overall cost characteristics will help decide whether limited (nonprice) warfare will be stable and/or if it is possible to limit price competition at all.[26] If exit barriers are too high, attempts to force competitors out of the industry are likely to prove ruinous. High switching costs make it difficult to capture market share from current participants, making price attacks less attractive. Finally, the leader must understand the likely responses of the other competitors to any major moves. For example, a policy of aggressive price warfare to "rationalize" the industry by forcing some players to leave could be doomed to failure if one of the firms turns stubborn and refuses to cooperate in its own demise! Another common error is underestimating opponents' relative cost positions. This is particularly dangerous when pursuing a cost leadership strategy.

External factors of importance are those related to the regulatory/antitrust climate, which plays a major role in choosing among these alternatives. The greater the latitude permitted by government, the easier it will be to successfully execute preemptive price competition, and vice versa.

Industry-specific factors are particularly important for two reasons. First and foremost, they define the feasibility of establishing stable, limited competition. In some cases, it may be virtually impossible to restrict price competition due to high fixed or storage costs, strong exit barriers that make it difficult for the smaller players to leave the industry, the perception that the industry is strategically important, or because there are numerous equally balanced competitors. In such situations, trying to achieve or maintain stable, limited warfare is almost certainly an exercise in futility and the leader must concentrate his attention on whether to choose long-term goals that are *offensive,* for example, "eliminate major competitors," or *defensive,* for example, "maintain current market share."[27]

Second, industry-specific factors also define the potential risks and rewards of aggressive moves. Evaluating such risks and rewards is particularly important in industries where conflict is limited. The danger in such cases is that a thoughtless or hasty move by the leader may be misinterpreted by the other players, causing a chain reaction that destroys industry consensus.

Other Players

The strategic choices available to the secondary participants are also limited. If they have the resources and the capabilities, they can choose to attack the leader's weaknesses in the hope of changing industry structure to their advantage. However, doing this successfully requires nerve, in addition to deep pockets. Alternatively they can try to adapt to industry conditions or, failing that, they can exit.

The smaller firm's position is particularly difficult if it has failed to locate and establish a defensible niche. It is then vulnerable to attack by larger competitors seeking to maintain their growth or seeking to increase market share. In such cases, the best choice might be to seek out a prospective purchaser while it still has the initiative.

Alternatives vary depending on whether the terms of competition are win/lose or limited warfare:

- *Win/lose.* The only question is, "Can we successfully defend our position/niche against attacks by larger competitors?" If the answer is no, then the objective should be to identify who is most likely to be interested in purchasing the firm and position it so as to maximize the price.

- *Limited warfare.* The choices here are "Should we attack, or should we accept the status quo?" The firm can opt to escalate the conflict by introducing new products or technologies, raising the levels of promotional and/or advertising activities, or developing new channels of distribution. Price competition should only be a last recourse. If the firm accepts the status quo, then the question is, "How much latitude do we have in terms of pricing, share objectives, promotional activities, and so forth?"

In an industry facing a win/lose payoff, the primary variables of concern are industry cost structure, the presence or absence of any mobility barriers, and the intensity of competition. In addition, we must consider any changes in technology or buyer behavior that may reduce the intensity of competition. If competition is limited, the central issues are (1) whether any of the leaders is vulnerable to attack, (2) along which dimensions—new technology, product design/flanking, new channels, increased promotional expenditures, or limited price competition—and (3) how do the resources required compare with those available to the firm. Table 7.6 summarizes the various factors in terms of the three categories used earlier.

New Entrants

While it is conceivable that a firm will enter an industry where the competition is already win/lose, it is difficult to see why it would want to do so. It would be paying the costs of entry, it would be handicapped by lack of information, and it would not have the advantage of tactical surprise. Therefore, we will restrict our analysis to the situation where an outsider decides to enter an industry where competition is limited.

In this case, the firm may choose to support the status quo, or it may decide to increase industry rivalry. If it chooses to intensify industry competition, it may do so by introducing new products/technologies, using new channels, raising advertising and promotional expenditures dramatically, changing the existing pricing structure, or a combination of these moves. The ultimate goal of such moves is to change industry structure and the terms of competition in *its* favor.

The first question is, "*Should* we enter this industry at all at this late stage of industry evolution?" The answer to this question decides whether the firm should maintain the status quo or change it through aggressive moves. We can categorize motives for wanting to enter a mature or maturing market as follows:

- *Pure investment.* We can expect firms to enter mature markets if the expected return is perceived to be higher than in their own industries. This can occur, for example, if the returns from further investments in their own industries are seen to be limited due to technological obsolescence, environmental or health-related pressures, or long-term shifts in buyers' preferences. An example of such entry is the acquisition of packaged foods companies by tobacco firms (e.g., Nabisco Brands by R. J. Reynolds).

- *Leverage core competencies.* Entering a mature industry may be attractive if it allows the entrant to achieve above-market returns by leveraging its core competencies or its common resources in manufacturing, distribution, or marketing.

- *Exploit opportunities.* Finally, firms may enter a mature industry to exploit perceived or actual weaknesses or to capitalize on inefficiencies. Existing players may be using outmoded technology, may be neglecting emerging segments, or may have become complacent due to a long period of successful oligopoly. Federal Express' entry into the overnight package industry and Philip Morris' acquisition of Miller Brewing are classic examples.

If a firm's entry into a market is purely an investment, we believe that it will tend to support the status quo, and that the possibility that it will deliberately choose to intensify rivalry is remote. If the purpose of entry is to exploit opportunities, almost definitely the firm will intensify rivalry in the industry. Maintaining the status quo in this case is virtually impossible; the whole reason for entry was to exploit weaknesses—weaknesses that are inherent in the current status quo. Entry to leverage common resources falls between these two extremes. On balance, however, we conjecture that here, too, a firm will prefer to join the status quo rather than incur the risks inherent in intensifying industry rivalry.

Successful entry at this stage depends on a firm's resources and likely reactions of existing participants (see Table 7.6). If the entrant wishes to maintain the state of limited warfare, it must demonstrate its familiarity with the terms of competition and signal its peaceful intentions (see Chapter 9). If the entrant intends to change the terms of competition in its favor, then it must carefully analyze how key competitors will respond, how long it will take them to respond, and what the intensity of the counterattack will be. Competitive reactions are affected by such factors as the degree of industry concentration, the ownership structure of existing firms, the extent to which they have diversified into other industries, their internal resources, and so forth. The nature of the threat also influences how fast competitors will retaliate. Other things being equal, firms are likely to be slower to respond to a new technology, while increases in advertising and promotional expenditures will be matched relatively quickly.

Implications for Declining Industries

As industry revenues and profits start to decline, participants must choose between staying and exiting. Firms will choose to stay in the industry only if they perceive that they can maintain their profitability by forcing other firms to leave, or if they anticipate a renewal of industry growth through new technologies/markets. Our analysis covers only leaders and other players; at this stage of industry evolution, it is reasonable to assume that there will be few entrants.

The Leaders

The leaders' primary objective must be to reverse the decline in industry growth through new innovations or by finding hitherto untapped markets, such as exports. Failing this, leaders must choose between increasing/maintaining their sales and profits by forcing weaker players to leave, and keeping conflict limited even as the industry declines (see Table 7.7).

In choosing between these alternatives, firms must take into account (1) the height of any exit barriers, (2) the presence or absence of switching costs, and (3) the ownership structure and intentions of the other players. High exit barriers and switching costs may effectively preclude forcing other participants out. In such cases, attempts to consolidate the industry will merely reduce overall price levels and profitability, leaving the total number of players unchanged. Similarly, management intentions and alternatives affect the costs and feasibility of such an end-game strategy. Privately owned firms that derive the majority of their revenues from the industry can be expected to fight hard for survival. Therefore, it may be cheaper in the long run to buy out such firms. Firms whose revenue base is diversified may be more prone to exit, particularly if industry sales account for only a small portion of total revenues.

Table 7.7 Implications for company objectives.

Participants	Decline Phase	
	Alternatives	Key Factors
Leaders	Reverse the decline Play "win/lose" and force others to exit Can I keep conflict limited in decline	*Company-specific* management intentions technology, marketing skills *Industry-specific* height of exit barriers switching costs ownership structure
Other Players	When—and how—do I exit the industry	*Company-specific* alternative investment opportunities *Industry-specific* intensity of competition exit barriers

Other Players

For the smaller players, the issue boils down to "When (and how) should we exit the industry?" In principle, they can aim to renew industry growth, but the expected returns of such a strategy are low because other things being equal, developing new markets offers greater returns to leaders while imposing substantial costs on the smaller firm (which is least able to afford them), and developing new technologies to restore industry growth is both expensive and extremely risky.

Staying on makes economic sense only if competition is limited and a firm has few or no other investment alternatives offering comparable returns.

Summary

We have completely developed our central theme of leverage, together with the two subthemes of maneuver and return. The next step is to show how to apply our conclusions to designing specific company strategies, using the structure-position map presented in the beginning. However, before we leave the topic of analyzing leverage, we will discuss two related topics. First, we will demonstrate the value of strategic mapping in visualizing and thereby gaining an *intuitive* understanding of strategic leverage. Separately, we will discuss how companies can use market signals to adapt or change their strategic leverage.

Strategic Mapping: A Tool for Visualizing Leverage

Strategic mapping is a particularly valuable analytical tool that provides insights into strategic leverage. It is an essential prerequisite for any manager who is serious about developing an intuitive understanding about the freedom of maneuver and the likely returns in any markets in which his or her firm competes. A well-constructed strategic map shows how industry participants cluster into specific groups, highlights the economic forces (if any) separating the different groups, helps identify any barriers that could restrict maneuver or influence return, and provides insight into the essential choices facing a company.

In this chapter we describe how to create and use such strategic maps. First, we outline a systematic approach for mapping an industry's environment. Using this approach, we generate a map of the overnight package delivery industry. We use this map to analyze the nature of competition before Federal Express entered the market, how Federal Express' entry changed the situation, and the strategic leverage choices of industry participants today. An important feature of many industry maps is the presence of "mobility barriers"—internal barriers to entry separating different groups of competitors within an industry.[1] The presence or absence of such mobility barriers directly affects a firm's ability to pursue focus or "niche" strategies. We discuss how mobility barriers are created by the underlying economic forces within the industry and their implications for leverage and strategy selection. Finally, we create a map of the U.S. domestic airline industry and use it to illustrate the importance of mobility barriers in understanding leverage and designing strategies.

131

Why Use Strategic Mapping?

Industry mapping is a tool for understanding the structure of a given industry and analyzing and anticipating competitive actions within the industry. Specifically:

- It categorizes markets into various areas or groups, which may vary considerably in terms of the leverage available.

- It identifies the reasons why some market areas[2] are better protected from internal (and external) competitors and relates these reasons to the underlying economic forces.

- It categorizes industry participants in terms of the various groups/market areas and helps identify where individual firms may be vulnerable.

- It helps determine which areas/groups offer the most leverage and whether to enter/exit certain groups or market areas.

- It provides insight into which areas leverage is concentrated and what factors constrain maneuver or limit return.

An industry map is particularly useful when there are a number of firms following divergent strategies, all competing in the same market, as is often the case in markets that are growing rapidly. (See Chapter 7.) In this situation, a well-constructed map helps categorize the various firms into groups or clusters. We can then analyze each of the clusters and determine how they differ from one another in terms of the underlying industry structure, their strategies, and overall group profitability. Further, we can evaluate the long-term prospects of each group, that is, will companies concentrating on a particular niche or market area remain successful in the future, or will their positions be usurped by entrants from other areas. We can then decide whether to maintain our existing market position, whether it is feasible and worthwhile to build defenses against would-be entrants, and whether we should abandon our current positions and/or enter new areas.

Creating an Industry Map

A good industry map is a formidable strategic tool, providing considerable insight into industry structure and a firm's market position. Developing a good map ultimately depends on a strategist's ability to select the most appropriate aspects of the industry and to close his or her mind to other factors. Thus, it is heavily influenced by the strategist's knowledge of the industry and the underlying economic forces. We can define a general procedure for creating industry maps as follows:

- *Define the coverage of the industry map.* This depends critically on what is viewed as the "relevant market."[3] In general, it is better to take a broader view of the market, for example, to look at the total package delivery market—same day, next day, and two-plus day delivery—instead of restricting ourselves to the overnight delivery segment alone. A broader definition ensures that we will focus on the market as defined by customer needs, as opposed to industry products or capabilities.[4] On the other hand, an overly broad scope for the market tends to confuse key issues. For example, we could view the overnight package industry as being the "information distribution industry," in which case the number of competitors increases dramatically and includes the major telecommunications firms, the regional telephone companies, the long-distance carriers, and so forth. Striking the right balance between an overly restricted definition and one that is cosmic in scope requires careful thought.

- *Identify principal dimensions along which participants may be classified.* Companies vary in their degree of specialization, brand identification, emphasis on "push" versus "pull," channel selection, service quality, service focus, technological leadership, degree of vertical integration, and so forth. In addition, areas of the market may differ in terms of the relative strength and importance of the five forces of competition. We have found it useful to identify a handful of *dissimilar* players—firms that are polar opposites in their strategies, market focus, profitability—and compare them along these dimensions. In many cases, this process quickly identifies factors that are most likely to be significant in explaining the differences among the firms.

- *"Cluster" participants using various combinations of key dimensions.* The goal should be to obtain a few—three to five—distinct groups of firms. Within each group (or cluster) the firms should, ideally, be very similar in their strategies, market focus, financial results, growth rates, and so on. Market segments, per se, may or may not be relevant; therefore we suggest that little attention be paid to them initially. Patience and imagination are essential; typically, several alternatives might be tested before the "best" set of key dimensions are found. Often the axes will be correlated with the various clusters arranged linearly. Sometimes this is the result of choosing two interdependent variables; in which case, try again. Conversely, a map that does not cluster the firms into groups but has them scattered uniformly provides little insight.

- *Choose the dimensions that provide strategic insight.* This is the final step; from the various alternatives, choose the one(s) providing the most insight into the industry situation. Typically, the result is a two-dimensional map (three-dimensional maps are even more difficult to work with) highlighting the different groups of firms and indicating any mobility barriers preventing new entrants or transfers from one group to another.

- *Analyze individual clusters/groups.* The first question to ask is, "How stable is this group—today and in the future?" All too often, industry groupings are historical accidents, with nothing except tradition or competitive inertia preventing other firms from entering that particular market area. Where this is the case, the logical questions for an incumbent are, "What can we do to create mobility barriers to prevent other firms from entering this area (assuming, of course, that the group has above-average profits)? What role can the 4Ps play? Which approach is likely to be most effective?" Conversely, firms outside this group must ask themselves, "Is this market area worth entering? What approaches should we use? Will entering this market area destabilize the status quo and reduce everyone's profits? What tactics are the incumbents likely to use to repel new entrants? How can we counter their efforts?"

- *Analyze intergroup rivalry and identify any mobility barriers.* If firms within two different groups do not compete, it is usually because there are some "mobility" barriers that prevent one or the other or sometimes both from competing effectively. In turn, these mobility barriers are related to cost disadvantages facing the would-be entrant. Therefore, we can identify potential or actual mobility barriers by analyzing the degree and the nature of competition between firms in different groups. Next, we need to study each of these barriers to identify the underlying cost disadvantages, if any. We can then analyze if and how these barriers can be avoided or overcome, and then determine the implications for marketing strategy.

Of necessity, this process is iterative. Usually, we start with a candidate map and then proceed to analyze the various groups, as well as intergroup rivalry. These analyses suggest modifications to the original diagram, including possibly the use of new or different dimensions along which to cluster the various participants and so forth. The key is not completeness but *strategic insight;* in most cases, an industry map that is complete is so detailed as to be virtually useless.

The Overnight Package Delivery Industry

To fully understand the value of industry mapping, let us analyze the overnight package delivery industry both before and after the entry of Federal Express with its Courier Pak™ service. To create this industry map, we will consider the entire *intercity* package delivery market, namely, same-day delivery, overnight delivery, and two-plus day delivery. This eliminates the international and intracity markets as well as the markets for electronic mail and facsimile services/equipment from our analysis.[5] The various participants in this market are

- *Airlines,* providing same-day package service
- *Freight forwarders,* a major category in the mid-1970s, they provided both next-day and two-plus day service
- *Overnight package delivery firms,* such as Federal Express and Airborne, the bulk of whose business was overnight service, with some two-plus day volume as well
- *Package delivery firms,* a category dominated by United Parcel Service (UPS), providing primarily two-plus day service in the mid- to late 1970s
- *The United States Postal Service (USPS),* which provided overnight service (ExpressMail™) and regular or two-plus day service.

In 1973, there were five firms competing in this market, and by 1981, the number had increased to 10.[6] The services and strategies of the different participants varied considerably. Airline package delivery services were not aggressively marketed and concentrated almost exclusively on same-day delivery. As a rule, packages were delivered to the airport by the sender and were picked up at the other end by the recipient. In the 1970s, package delivery firms such as UPS as well as the Postal Service concentrated almost exclusively on the two-plus day market, where the volumes and revenues were much higher. They offered pick-up and/or delivery and marketed their services primarily through print media and point-of-sale promotions (especially the USPS).

Before Federal Express introduced its Courier Pak service, air freight forwarders were the only players in the overnight package delivery market.

These firms booked air freight space with various airlines in advance and filled the capacity with a variety of packages of all sizes, from overnight letters to large cartons/crates. Very few firms had national pick-up and delivery networks, relying for the most part on contracts/informal arrangements with local firms. The industry was highly fragmented with the largest player—Emery Air Freight—having less than 20 percent market share.

To prepare a map of this industry, it is convenient to use *speed of response*—same-day, overnight, and two-plus day—and *cost*—low, medium, or high—as the two dimensions along which to cluster the various participants. We can then cluster the players into three groups as shown in Figure 8.1. At one end are the airline package delivery services; UPS and USPS are at the other extreme, with the air freight forwarders and ExpressMail in the middle.

The situation was static, and with good reason. To the airlines, package delivery was a low marginal cost, extremely profitable business. The

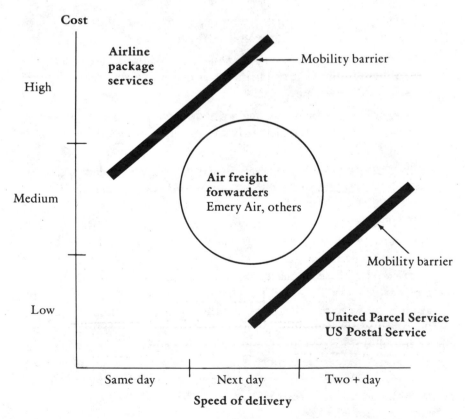

Figure 8.1 Overnight package delivery industry map.

planes and routes were already in operation, and there were no local pick-up/delivery costs. The only direct expense they incurred was advertising. To UPS and USPS, overnight package delivery was a distraction, not worth the investment. USPS did provide a form of overnight delivery with its ExpressMail service, but it was a low marginal cost operation, using pre-existing air freight and delivery networks.

Mobility Barriers. The overnight package delivery market was protected from attack by the airlines or UPS/USPS by two factors. First, both the airlines and UPS/USPS faced significant cost disadvantages when competing with the freight forwarders who composed this market (see Figure 8.1).

- *Airlines.* If they entered the overnight package delivery business, the airlines faced the prospect of alienating an important group of cargo customers—the air freight forwarders. In addition, they would need to schedule many night flights in order to ensure that packages reached their destinations on time. Most probably, they would also have to maintain a large fleet of delivery trucks and people to drive those trucks; they could not very well rely on the air freight forwarders to deliver their packages after having taken away their livelihood.

- *UPS/USPS.* The major factor preventing this group from entering into the overnight package delivery market was the need for a fleet of cargo planes more or less dedicated to this operation. Their strategic focus was also very different; they were oriented to moving large packages at (relatively) low cost and were not geared to handling the needs of this group of customers.

A second reason was the lack of incentive. The airlines were making enough money from their package services and by selling cargo space to the air freight forwarders, so they had no incentive to integrate forward. By the same token, UPS/USPS' view was that overnight package delivery was a small drop in the bucket and, as such, not worth the effort or investment.

As a result of these mobility barriers and the lack of incentive, Emery Air Freight and the other air freight forwarders were in a very protected area of the market. Furthermore, none of the participants had any incentives to make substantial investments and change the situation. Competition within the overnight package group was limited, and the various firms were making virtually monopoly profits without major capital requirements. Thus, the middle group in our map was stable, had relatively high profits, and was protected from attack by existing participants by significant mobility barriers. The major threat (which nobody anticipated at the time) was that a new entrant would come in and upset the status quo.

The Situation after Federal Express

In 1973, Federal Express changed the entire overnight package industry by creating a hub-and-spoke system, based in Memphis, Tennessee, which allowed the firm total control over the movement of a package, from pick-up to delivery. This changed the economics of the industry dramatically, virtually overnight!

Once the initial investment in planes and trucks was made, Federal Express enjoyed a far higher contribution margin as compared with Emery, the leading air freight forwarder. On every overnight package averaging one pound in weight and approximately 1/10th of a cubic foot in size, Federal Express' contribution—revenues net of direct, out-of-pocket costs for pick-up and delivery—was $75 per cubic foot or 66 percent of revenues.[7] By contrast, Emery's fixed costs were much lower but its variable costs were higher and its cash flow and profitability correspondingly more modest. The two firms' marketing strategies were also radically different, as can be seen from Figure 8.2. Emery, along with the other air freight forwarders had focused on the corporate traffic

	Federal Express	Emery
Target Market	Executive/secretary	Traffic clerks & traffic managers
Product	Speed & reliability	Freight pickup & delivery
Pricing	Value based	Weight & volume based
Promotion	• Extensive TV & print advertising • High budget	• Primarily print • Low budget
Place	• Direct salesforce • Extensive control over atmospherics	• Direct & local freight • Consolidators with little or no control over atmospherics

Figure 8.2 Differences in marketing strategies Federal Express versus Emery.

manager/clerk. Its promotional expenditures were limited and confined to print media. Federal Express, on the other hand, bypassed the traffic department and concentrated on the executive/secretary, using television heavily to create brand recognition and a direct "pull."

Implications for Industry Structure.   The net result was that, in the space of 10 years, the overnight package business changed from a stable, highly fragmented industry with little competition and no vertically integrated players, to a rapidly consolidating one with a handful of totally integrated participants. In part, this evolution was inevitable; once Federal Express showed that there were significant economies of scale in a fully integrated operation, it was only a matter of time before the poorly capitalized players were driven out (or bought up) by firms with greater resources.

Entry and mobility barriers facing potential entrants into the overnight package business were also much higher due to the need for major promotional expenditures and to economies of scale:

- *Advertising expenditures.* In 1987, Federal Express spent over $58.7 million on advertising and raised it dramatically in 1988 to $82.6 million due to competitive pressures, with a large portion of that spent on television advertising. To create awareness, a would-be entrant would have to invest comparable sums over several years.
- *Economies of scale.* The leading players enjoyed significant economies of scale in the size of aircraft, the operation of the central sorting "hub," and to a lesser extent, the local pick-up and delivery.

But these barriers were not completely symmetrical, that is, Federal Express was not handicapped to the same degree if it chose to enter the same-day or two-plus day segments. In one segment of the overnight package market—document transmission—Federal Express could enter for very little cost, because it already had the local delivery network in place. Further, the demand for this service was likely to occur in the middle of the day, a slack period for the network. In part, this was the logic underlying ZapMail.[8]

Similarly, while UPS faced high mobility barriers in entering the overnight package market, Federal Express could enter selected segments of the two-plus day delivery market for almost no additional cost. Once again, the key capital items such as airplanes and delivery trucks were already in place, and their costs covered by the revenues from the overnight package operations. Therefore, so long as Federal Express did not have to add to its capacity, revenues from lower priority packages were nearly pure profit, since the firm incurred few incremental costs in providing the service.

Even if ZapMail had succeeded, it's unlikely that the airlines would have retaliated because package delivery was a tiny part of their total operations. On the other hand, the potential threat to UPS was more serious, particularly if Federal Express concentrated on the lucrative high value/weight shipments, as was to be expected. In that case, UPS faced the prospect of being "cream-skimmed" by the upstart. For this reason, once the concept had been proven successful, UPS had little choice but to enter the overnight package business.[9]

By the end of 1987, the overnight package delivery industry had become highly consolidated. Overall market growth had slowed, and prices were coming under pressure, especially from heavy users. Several firms had either left the business, had merged, or had been/were about to be acquired. The focus of competition had shifted to price and service.[10]

Strategic Implications

We can now appreciate the value of the technique of strategic mapping. Our map of the overnight package market would have alerted Emery and the other freight forwarders that new entrants—not existing participants—would be the major competitive threats. Subsequent to Federal Express' entry, it would have pointed out the critical importance of locating/creating defensible niches. When the market consolidated in 1988, it would have helped predict the focus and intensity of competitive warfare.

Prior to Federal Express' Entry.   The map would have immediately concentrated attention on new entrants and substitutes as the principal threats. Thus, it would have acted as a "screen" for competitive analysis; once the locus of future threats was defined, firms would have concentrated their attention on tracking costs/technological changes and the progress of potential and actual new entrants. This is a particularly valuable, if relatively unknown, benefit of such maps. Carefully constructed, strategic maps help direct scarce managerial resources effectively to the most likely (and often overlooked) threats, instead of spreading them so thin as to be virtually useless.

After Federal Express Entered the Market.   As is evident from Figure 8.1, the economic "terrain" is flat; there are no obvious mobility barriers protecting particular segments of the overnight package market. Thus, the strategic map would have shown Emery that its position was extremely vulnerable. Similarly, it would have alerted the other participants—Purolator, Airborne—to the necessity of creating defensible positions within segments of the market as soon as possible.

First, let us consider the implications for Emery, then the share leader. From the map it would have been evident to Emery that the nature of the conflict—and the terms of competition—within the overnight package industry had changed considerably, from limited or no competition to one in which a new player (with unknown values) would be setting the rules. Taken in conjunction with Federal Express' cost advantages and the general rule that typically only two or three firms manage to emerge as truly differentiated competitors, Emery would have concluded that maintaining its leadership position could be extremely expensive and possibly futile, and that it must move quickly if it wanted to maintain a differentiated position, before other participants—existing players and new entrants—took the initiative away from Emery in this new environment.

For the other firms such as Purolator and Airborne, the lack of protected niches, together with the Federal Express' overwhelming cost advantages, would have indicated the vital importance of identifying segments or market areas wherein they could *create* defenses. For example, they could concentrate on the corporate market and negotiate long-term, high-volume contracts with selected customers. Alternatively, they could specialize, for example, emergency parts shipments, medical shipments, and so forth. Speed was of the essence; they had to isolate likely segments early on, while Federal Express was busy coping with the demands of the major portion of the market. Once the market was fully developed it would be too late to carve out a defensible niche.

The Situation Today. The lack of natural mobility barriers within the overnight package market and the failure of individual participants to create defensible niches have led to the situation today, namely, intense price competition, heavy promotional expenditures, and limited share movements except through mergers or acquisitions.

Industry Terrain and the Importance of Mobility Barriers

The overnight package industry map also highlights the importance of mobility barriers, especially when the underlying economic terrain is flat. Mobility barriers help keep competitors out of specific niches, thereby enhancing group or industry stability. To be viable, these barriers must create cost disadvantages for potential entrants; they are therefore intimately related to industry technology and cost characteristics.

Further, these barriers are often asymmetrical; potential entrants into the niche face higher (lower) costs compared with incumbents seeking to expand out of it.

Why a "Flat" Terrain Is Dangerous

By a flat terrain, we mean markets or segments where there are no "natural" mobility barriers due to discontinuities in the cost characteristics of the industry. Such discontinuities arise from the nature of the technology, distribution requirements, or other industry or market characteristics. In many industries, we find that there are few (if any) such discontinuities, for example, the overnight package industry, the domestic U.S. airline market (discussed in the next section), and the U.S. long-distance telecommunications market. Such markets are dangerous for all participants for the following reasons:

- *Major players find it difficult to change share.* A flat terrain usually leads to static or "trench" warfare in which share positions fluctuate and can be maintained only through continually high expenditures in promotion and sales effort.[11] In such cases, none of the variables offer any leverage and market share gains are slow, uncertain, and require considerable effort at the tactical level, for example, larger salesforces, price concessions, frequent promotions. Major players find they can't maintain share against each other or against smaller niche participants except by "flanking"—regularly producing specialized offerings to counter competitive inroads, as seen in the overnight package industry. Typically, such flanking efforts consume substantial resources without significant returns.[12]

- *Focus or niche strategies are highly vulnerable to attacks by major players.* Without mobility barriers based on economic discontinuities, profitable niches are likely to be rapidly invaded and taken over by the majors. Other things being equal, the larger resources of firms following differentiation or cost leadership strategies will overwhelm existing participants, forcing them either to exit the market, be acquired, or settle for considerably lower profit and share levels. Of the eight regional airlines operating in the U.S. market in 1978 (when airline deregulation went into effect), only two or three are surviving as independent entities.[13]

- *Win/lose wars can be ruinous.* If the nature of the conflict becomes win/lose or a zero-sum game, the result can be extremely expensive as each participant spends ever-increasing amounts on gaining or regaining market shares lost to other players. The large PBX market

today is a good example; at present there are three major participants, and competition is intense. As a result, prices have fluctuated
rapidly over the last six years, without significant share changes.

Strategic Implications.   For the major players, the strategic implications of a flat terrain vary depending on the feasibility and long-term
stability of limited warfare. If limited warfare is feasible and likely to be
stable, they should quickly define the limits on pricing and promotion
and determine how to send market "signals" to other key participants to
help minimize price competition. Major efforts to significantly expand
share are likely to destabilize the industry; therefore, any such moves
should be weighed very carefully. If limited warfare is not feasible or not
likely to be stable, the major players must prepare for a long slogging
match that could be very expensive, depending on the perceived strategic
stakes.

For smaller firms, a flat terrain means they must concentrate their
energies on *creating* mobility barriers early on during the growth stage of
the industry, while the major players are still consolidating their hold on
the overall market. Their tools for creating these defenses are technological and marketing investments that lower their costs relative to those of
the larger players, for the niche in question. Specifically:

- *Technological investments.* They should endeavor to (1) lower the
  minimum operating scale (MOS) for the niche, and/or (2) lower the
  costs in the niche below those of the major players. As we discussed
  earlier, for a niche strategy to be viable, there must be an adequate
  number of customers in the niche in relation to the MOS. One way
  of creating viable niches, therefore, is to lower the MOS by investing
  in product and process technology. Similarly, by reducing their costs
  below those of likely entrants following either differentiation or
  cost leadership strategies, the smaller firms can make the segment
  less attractive to such entrants.

- *Marketing investments.* Technological investments typically concentrate on product design and production costs. Firms can also erect
  mobility barriers through investments in specialized, unique channels of distribution, superior customer satisfaction, long-term volume contracts, intensive sales coverage, and other marketing
  investments. Specialized channels of distribution create entry barriers by blocking access. Superior customer satisfaction and volume
  contracts create switching costs. Intensive sales coverage increases a
  new entrant's marketing costs, making the market potentially less
  inviting.

Firms generally use a combination of these techniques, as the experience of Subaru of America demonstrates.[14] Subaru has been a pioneer in all-wheel drive vehicles, making substantial technological investments in this area. It has concentrated on developing superior customer satisfaction, with the result that more than 50 percent of its sales are generated through word-of-mouth, and its advertising costs per vehicle are the among lowest in the industry. Finally, high customer satisfaction has led to high repeat purchase rates, giving additional protection from competition.

The Role of Mobility Barriers

As defined earlier, mobility barriers are constraints that keep firms in one group from entering another group within the same industry. They are key features of the market's economic terrain, somewhat analogous to the ridges and valleys of a military map. Other things being equal, market areas surrounded by significant mobility barriers are more attractive as they provide natural defenses against competitors. Particularly when user needs are not highly differentiated, mobility barriers are essential for the success of focus strategies. Without such barriers, large firms following differentiation or cost leadership strategies will enter a niche once it proves attractive, that is, has above-average profitability, and will dominate their smaller counterparts.

Their Relation to Cost Characteristics.   Conceptually, mobility barriers are similar to barriers to market entry. The main difference is that mobility barriers separate firms already participating in the market. These firms have made some investments and, in many cases, are producing comparable products and services.

To analyze mobility barriers, we must concentrate on the incremental cost differences between the two groups. Consider the situation shown in Figure 8.3, which shows two industry groups, A and B. We show that a mobility barrier exists if firms in group A face cost disadvantages if they try to serve group B's customers, with the result that their prices would be higher (or their profits lower) than those of incumbents. Thus mobility barriers have their roots in the factors that create these cost disadvantages, such as the following:

- *Uniqueness of customer needs.* The more unique the needs of group B's customers, the greater the difference ($C_E - C_B$), where C_E denotes the costs faced by prospective entrants and C_B stands for the costs faced by firms in group B. If customer needs are unique and

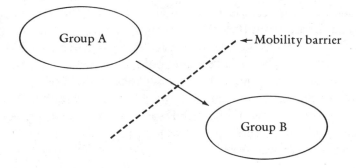

A's entry costs $= C_E = C_B + \Delta$ where $C_E > 0$ and $\Delta > 0$

Figure 8.3 Mobility barriers and cost characteristics.

constitute an entirely different market altogether, then the mobility barrier becomes an entry barrier. In the overnight package industry, customer needs were fairly distinct from those of the same-day or two-plus day segments. On the other hand, in the domestic U.S. air travel market, the needs of regional travelers are not significantly different from those of national travelers (apart from destination); consequently, the mobility barriers are lower.

*   *Learning/specialization effects.* Sometimes incumbents have competitive advantages because of (1) learning curve effects in their market niche, and/or (2) specialized investments by incumbents in product or process technologies. Learning and specialization effects are particularly important sources of mobility barriers when customer needs are not highly differentiated, that is, when group B's customers will readily accept group A's products.[15]

*   *Selling costs.* Intensive sales efforts often act as significant mobility barriers, particularly if product costs are comparable, that is, $C_A \approx C_B$, and entrants are not accustomed to high sales expenditures in their own market area. Intensive sales efforts often create extremely high expectations regarding customer service, effectively raising the cost of entry.

Other factors such as access costs, switching costs, and other cost disadvantages independent of scale (for example, proprietary technology, access to raw materials or skilled labor) can also create mobility barriers.

Asymmetrical Mobility Barriers. The cost differentials between two groups can be asymmetrical, that is, the differential $(C_E - C_B)$ is substantially greater than (or less than) the corresponding differential

$(C_E - C_A)$. This was the case, for example, in the mobility barrier separating Federal Express and the other overnight package carriers from UPS, USPS, and others in the two-plus day segment. Given slack airplane capacity, the overnight package firms could carry two-plus delivery packages for almost no incremental cost. Thus they could enter UPS' market area at very little cost, while UPS, on the other hand, would have to make sizable investments in equipment and planes to enter the overnight package delivery business. In such cases, the group encountering the higher mobility barrier (group A in Figure 8.4) is vulnerable to attack from the outside and, in the long run, may be less profitable and possibly unstable.

Asymmetrical mobility barriers can restrict strategic and pricing flexibility considerably depending on the relative sizes of firms in the two groups. For example, if group B is vulnerable because firms in group B face higher costs when entering group A (see Figure 8.4), we have two possibilities:

- *Defending firms are larger than potential attackers.* In this case, entrants may be deterred by the relatively larger resources of incumbents, despite the formers' cost advantages. However, if firms from group A can compete in group B on the basis of low or even zero marginal costs, then defenders have few alternatives except to counterattack by entering group A, despite the higher entry costs. Failure to do so will allow attackers to "cream skim," that is, concentrate on the most lucrative customers or segments, as we discussed in the case of UPS versus Federal Express. Pricing tactics to discourage attackers won't work due to their extremely low costs;

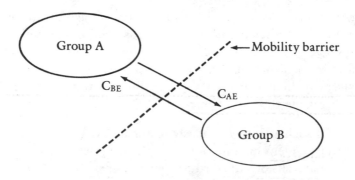

A's entry costs $= C_{AE} = C_B + \Delta_1$
B's entry costs $= C_{BE} = C_A + \Delta_2$ and $\Delta_1 > \Delta_2$

Figure 8.4   Asymmetrical barriers.

defenders will be severely hurt well before prices are low enough to discourage entrants from group A.

- *Entrants are larger than incumbents.* In this case, group B is highly vulnerable to being overrun by entrants from group A. Strategically, firms in group B have essentially three choices: merge, exit, or coexist. Merger may be attractive, especially in the early stages when entrants may pay high premiums. Exit becomes the only choice when management fails to adapt to the changed competitive environment. Finally, coexistence requires either that firms in group B (1) erect mobility barriers, or (2) avoid direct confrontations with the entrants. As we discussed earlier, erecting mobility barriers is easiest in the early stages of industry evolution, before potential entrants discover the attractions of group B. Direct confrontations can be avoided by refocusing on target markets of secondary interest to firms in group A or minimizing price competition or both. Obviously, a nonconfrontation strategy places distinct limits on the firms' growth and profitability.

The above example also shows why mobility barriers are essential to the long-term feasibility of focus strategies.[16] Firms following focus strategies are almost always significantly smaller than competitors following differentiation or cost leadership strategies. If larger firms also have the mobility barriers working in their favor, then a focus strategy is not viable in the long run. As soon as the larger firms find out how profitable the niche is, they will enter and capture the bulk of the profit.

The U.S. Airline Industry

The U.S. domestic airline situation provides another example of how valuable industry mapping is in gaining insight into strategic leverage and a company's choices. Our industry map will demonstrate the role of asymmetrical mobility barriers in the demise of the regional airlines. It will also enable us to study how industry structure affects a firm's marketing strategy and tactical freedom.

Industry Evolution

In 1982, the U.S. airline industry contained nine national or "trunk" airlines, five regional airlines serving selected markets, and numerous small commuter airlines (see Table 8.1). United Airlines was the leader in total revenue, while Eastern carried the most passengers. In the period

Table 8.1 Summary statistics of the U.S. airline industry as of 1982–1983.

Airlines	Sales ($000s)	Total Departures	Passengers (000s)	Revenue Share (%)
United	4,613,850	399,874	32,777	12.76
American	3,977,774	317,611	27,670	10.92
Eastern	3,769,237	500,800	35,138	10.35
Delta	3,361,792	493,246	33,678	9.98
Pan Am	3,471,376	137,734	12,255	9.53
Trans World	3,236,178	194,914	17,699	8.89
Northwest	1,888,247	152,351	11,356	5.19
Republic	1,530,668	460,215	18,022	4.20
Continental	1,415,206	216,126	13,071	3.89
USAir	1,273,012	291,524	14,639	3.50
Western	1,065,270	139,120	10,022	2.93
Piedmont	655,341	187,966	8,511	1.80
Frontier	537,736	141,120	5,850	1.48
Ozark	—	104,293	44,286	—
Air Cal	—	58,338	3,409	—
PeoplesExpress	—	—	2,857	—

1982 to 1987, the industry consolidated considerably. Continental purchased Eastern and PeopleExpress and merged them along with the routes of New York Air and Frontier (which had been bought by People-Express earlier). Western Airlines, Air California, and PSA, three large Western regional carriers, were acquired by major airlines (Delta, American, and USAir). In the Midwest, Republic and Ozark, with large regional route structures, were acquired by or merged with TWA and Northwest, respectively. Further, many commuter operations were acquired or merged with the large trunks—Air Wisconsin with United, Britt with PeopleExpress/Continental, and so forth.

In part, this consolidation occurred due to the use of "hub-and-spoke" networks that emphasized the importance of controlling traffic originating/terminating into major gateways such as Chicago, Atlanta, and Denver. However, an industry map shows that the consolidation was inevitable, given the cost characteristics of the industry and the asymmetrical nature of the mobility barriers separating the regional carriers from other groups.

Creating an Industry Map

As the first step, we can cluster the airlines participating in the market in 1982 into three groups—national or "trunk" airlines, regionals, and commuter airlines. We can then summarize the differences among the three groups as shown in Table 8.2.[18] The barriers to entry into the group of national airlines are extremely high, both in terms of capital and differentiation. Barriers to entry into the regional airline market are moderate and low in the case of commuter carriers. Other factors, such as brand identification, promotional strategies, and horizontal integration, vary considerably among the three groups.

Thus, one dimension for the industry map could be the *characteristics of the served (or target) market*. A useful second dimension is the *average stage length*—the distance between successive takeoffs and landings—which is intimately related to the cost characteristics of an airline. Using these two dimensions, we obtain the industry map shown in Figure 8.5.

Table 8.2　Differences among the three groups.

	Industry Structure		
	United	Frontier	Air Wisconsin
Entry			
Economies of Scale	High	Moderate	Low
Differentiation	High		Low
Capital Requirements	Very high		Low
Buyer Power			
Intermediaries	Moderate to weak	Moderate to powerful	Weak
Suppliers	— —	Not powerful	— —
Substitutes		Nil	Bus/automobile/ rail
Rivalry	Moderate/ high	Very high	Low

	Strategic Groupings		
	United	Frontier	Air Wisconsin
Dimension			
Brand Identity	Very important		Not important
Push/Pull	Pull	?	Push
Service Quality	Important		Not important
Technology Leadership	Important		Not important
Price Policy	Moderately important	Very important	Not important

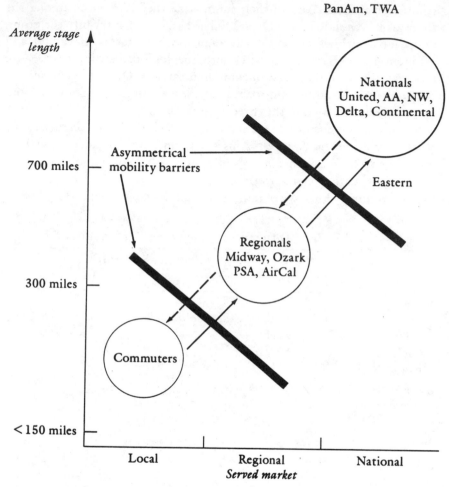

Figure 8.5 Industry map for the airline industry.

In terms of this map, most of the airlines are part of three strategic groups. This industry map immediately reveals some interesting features:

- Eastern has significantly shorter average stage lengths as compared with its national competitors. This portends trouble for Eastern, since it suggests that, while its costs are similar to those of other competitors, its revenue per passenger may be similar to the regionals. (Eastern, in fact, did not survive.)

- USAir's average stage length (and therefore its cost characteristics) places it midway between the regionals and the nationals.

- In 1982, Delta was (relatively) on the periphery of the national group, having many of the characteristics of a large regional.

- In 1988, there were six large trunk airlines—United, American, Delta, USAir, Northwest, and Continental/Eastern. The last two pursued cost leadership strategies. United traditionally had been *the* differentiated competitor, while American moved up rapidly using the same strategy. This placed Delta in an awkward position as industry growth slowed down, given that there are typically only two truly differentiated competitors in an industry. This also suggested USAir was "stuck in the middle," that is, neither differentiated nor a cost leader.

- Mobility barriers between commuter and regional airlines are related to equipment cost and performance characteristics and are symmetrical.

- Mobility barriers between the regionals and the large nationals are not symmetrical. Regional airlines wishing to serve national markets have to either lease or purchase suitable larger aircraft or else operate existing equipment inefficiently, assuming it is feasible, which is not the case with transcontinental routes. The larger airlines, on the other hand, can adjust their fleet allocations and enter regional markets with relative ease and at lower cost, especially in the short run.[19]

Regional Airlines: Endangered Species

The map also suggests that regional airlines are vulnerable to attack from both sides. At the low end, while mobility barriers are symmetrical, they are not particularly high and, therefore, provide little protection from attack by the commuter carriers. At the other end, asymmetrical mobility barriers make the regionals vulnerable to national airlines. The nationals can crossover whenever a regional market appears profitable, but the regionals cannot enter lucrative national markets, for example, the transcontinental routes.

As a result, the industry group of regional airlines is inherently unstable. Individual firms, therefore, must either (1) merge with a large trunk carrier, (2) exit the industry, or (3) survive as independent carriers by creating mobility barriers or learning how to coexist. In theory, the regionals could also survive by becoming trunk carriers through internal expansion or horizontal mergers. However, this strategy is not likely to succeed, as the experiences of Braniff and PeopleExpress demonstrate. The existing players simply are not going to allow a regional carrier to enter their group without counterattacking in force.

Furthermore, airlines that wish to remain independent regional carriers have few options. As the successive experiences of Air One, Regent Air, and McClain demonstrated,[20] a premium or luxury strategy is not viable; the target market for such premium services is too small in relation to the minimum operating scale required. On the other hand, a no-frills niche strategy is also vulnerable if it is too successful, that is, if it draws away significant revenues from the majors, as PeopleExpress learned to its cost.[21] The reasons are the high strategic stakes that force the majors to compete in all potential niches and the cost structure of the industry that makes erecting mobility barriers extremely difficult. Thus, survival as an independent regional carrier requires that a firm learn the art of "peaceful coexistence," avoiding direct competition with the large national carriers by concentrating on secondary routes/market segments, minimizing price competition, and in general, maintaining a low profile.

Midway Airlines

To fully appreciate the implications of peaceful coexistence, let us consider the situation of Midway Airlines, a regional carrier that uses Chicago's Midway Airport as its hub. Midway competes directly or indirectly with all the major airlines, particularly United, whose hub is at Chicago's O'Hare Airport. The requirement that it avoid/minimize direct confrontation with the major airlines affects Midway's freedom of maneuver and strategic leverage as follows:

- *Pricing.* Midway's room for maneuver in setting prices is limited. First, it cannot set its prices *higher* than the major airlines on comparable routes; given its limited route structure and the difficulty of making connections with other airlines in Chicago, it simply cannot obtain any premium over the large nationals. At the other end, if it sets fares substantially below the nationals, it would force them to retaliate, triggering a war that Midway is almost certain to lose, given its limited resources. Midway must keep its fares within a narrow band

$$Price_{National} \geq Price_{Midway} \geq Reservation\ Price_{National}$$

where the "reservation price" is the fare level below which the nationals will feel obliged to retaliate by entering Midway's routes, lowering their own prices, and so forth. Because this reservation price is unknown to Midway, it must estimate what the lower limit is likely to be. Further, at the upper end, the airline cannot quite set its prices equal to those charged by the majors; it has to provide some incentive to passengers to fly on Midway.

- *Product.* The constraints on pricing impose corresponding constraints on product strategy. Midway can survive and prosper if (and only if) there is a significant gap between $Price_{National}$ and Reservation $Price_{National}$, otherwise the nationals will attack regardless of the prices Midway sets. For this gap to exist, the majors must perceive Midway's product to be inferior to their own, thereby justifying some price premium for the national carriers' offerings. Obviously, the greater the perceived differential, the lower the majors' reservation price and the greater Midway's freedom to price. On the other hand, if passengers perceive Midway's services as distinctly inferior, they are not likely to fly on the airline. Thus, its service offering must be below that of the large nationals and yet attractive enough to induce passengers to fly Midway.

- *Promotion.* This is constrained by financial limitations and by the need to avoid direct confrontations with United, American, and other nationals. Advertising messages should not stress Midway's price advantages; a strong play on price merely invites retaliation. Instead, advertising and promotional focus has to be on the non-price benefits of flying Midway.

- *Target markets.* Both in terms of routes and with regard to passenger segments, Midway must avoid competing head-on with the larger carriers; the returns are very low in such head-on competition. Ideally, it should "nibble" at the routes and target markets of several major carriers trusting to the difficulty (and illegality!) of concerted action by the major players. It should not target too obviously on the business travelers, the heart of the nationals' profits. Nor should it rely too heavily on vacation travel, because it is too seasonal and extremely price sensitive.

- *Place.* This is the one dimension where Midway has the greatest leverage. The primary channel—travel agents—tend to block access to customers due to their more lucrative ties to the trunk airlines. Increasing Midway's presence with agents by increasing commissions paid is likely (a) to be futile, given the small percentage that Midway represents of any agent's volume, and (b) could be destabilizing if viewed as a threat by the major airlines. In fact, Midway has much to gain and relatively little to lose in bypassing travel agents wherever appropriate by selling directly to large accounts, using in-office ticket booths, and so forth.

In practice, Midway Airlines' strategic focus shifted considerably before adopting its present strategy, which appears to be similar to the "minimal confrontation" approach outlined above. The airline began life as a low-cost, low-fare carrier along the lines of PeopleExpress—in terms of our framework—a low-end focus strategy. Subsequently, in 1983, it tried to launch Midway Metrolink, a service offering first-class amenities at coach prices. Like all other high-end focus strategies, this, too, foundered for lack of customers and retaliation by the majors.[22] (A final note: In late 1991, Midway Airlines was purchased by Northwest.)

Summary

In this chapter we presented a technique for visualizing a company's leverage in a given market. This provides insights that conventional analysis alone may not; it can also be a useful tool for creative thinking about the company's long-term positioning. In the final chapter of Part Two, we will explore how companies can use market signals to adapt or change their strategic leverage.

9

Using Market Signals to Create or Modify Leverage

The primary purpose of market signaling is to (legally) control the intensity of competition in an industry and thereby retain some freedom of maneuver and leverage, especially with regard to pricing. Without such coordination, an industry may plunge into all-out war, depressing prices and profits. Signals may be directly related to price, for example, retail and wholesale price levels, discount structures, and price "points." Or they may deal with other variables that affect prices, such as promotional terms and conditions (especially any coupons or offers), trade allowances and terms, financing, capacity expansion plans, and so forth. A number of techniques are used, including speeches to industry associations, preemptive announcements, appeals for "responsible" behavior, and the need for "industry leadership."

Market signals are tactical tools that help managers maintain or change their freedom of maneuver and strategic leverage. They are used in support of strategic objectives such as limiting industry warfare, deterring entry, and defining acceptable terms of competition. Before using these tools, managers must be aware of the following limitations:

- *Market signals are only effective in mature and declining industries and when the number of players is limited.* The purpose of signals is to establish an oligopoly and limit/avoid destructive price competition, which is of concern only in the mature and declining stages of industry evolution, as we discussed in Chapter 7.[1] Further, signals are messages from one player (for example, the industry leader) to another (would-be entrant, offender) regarding past or prospective actions. However, antitrust laws require that these messages be sent through overt, public channels, such as trade and general publications and industry forums. If the number of players is large, the sheer volume and ambiguity of such messages tend to make them ineffective.

- *Market signals are effective only if the structure of the industry permits stable cooperative solutions.* Before using signals, it is essential to analyze industry structure and see if, in fact, limited warfare is feasible and stable. Destabilizing forces such as high fixed or exit costs may make a cooperative solution impossible. Typically, this occurs when the short-term expected costs of *not* reducing prices unilaterally exceed the long-term benefits of maintaining price discipline. In such situations, *it is extremely unlikely that market signals will impose price discipline.*

- *Market signals cannot be interpreted in a vacuum.* To understand and profit from signals, managers must fully appreciate (1) industry structure, (2) the nature of strategic leverage, (3) the relative competitive position of the firm sending the signal, and (4) the profile of the firm and its management.

- *Market signals can be misleading.* Competitors sometimes signal to distract or confuse, using them as bluffs or feints. Or isolated actions of one participant may be misinterpreted as signals. Therefore, there is a real danger of reading too much into signals and/or believing that it is possible to predict competitor behavior with accuracy.[2]

Two Industry Examples

We will begin our discussion of market signaling by briefly reviewing examples of the use of signals in two different industries. The first situation describes industry responses to a leader's attempt at changing the terms of competition in its favor, while the second details the signals sent by an acquirer whose actions were consolidating the industry.

Airlines

In mid-January 1985, American Airlines reduced fares drastically across the board. American's ostensible purpose was to increase passenger volume and to change the habits of the traveling public by making passengers book trips much earlier. As Thomas Plaskett, American's then senior vice-president for marketing, said, "The response has been extraordinary. For the first four days of the promotion, we averaged over 300,000 calls a day, up from the usual 130,000 calls." He went on to add that he expected volume to level off to about 200,000 calls daily by the summer, still a hefty 35 percent more than American's previous activity. American's move set off a flurry of matching fare reductions and public statements from the other carriers, as follows:

- All the major trunk airlines matched American's fares and terms immediately, with the exception of PeopleExpress, which *raised* its fares, and Continental, which *did not* match the new fares.

- Various competitors' public comments were extremely revealing:

  "It [American] is not doing any favors for business."—*Delta*

  "Bookings may be soaring, but profits aren't."—*Northwest*

  "We don't see it as a threat."—*PeopleExpress*

  "AT&T said we're overloading the system."—*United*

  "[May not] be able to keep 30-day advance booking rules—may have to switch to 14 day-advance booking."—*Anonymous*

The rest of the industry was sending very direct signals to American to the effect that (1) it would match any price moves by American, (2) the price cut was not likely to change the status quo, and (3) price warfare might escalate more than American or anyone else would like.

Farm Equipment

On November 26, 1984, Tenneco announced that it would acquire the farm machinery operations and the name of International Harvester. The acquisition led to a series of exchanges between Case/IH (the new combination) and the other players—Deere, Massey Ferguson, and Allis-Chalmers. To fully understand the significance of these signals, we must review the state of the farm equipment industry in the mid-1980s:

- The industry was in the middle of a five-year slump, the worst since the Depression of the 1930s.
- Deere was the industry leader, with approximately 40-plus percent share of the market; it was marginally profitable.
- The new Case/IH combination would, in theory, rival Deere in size and market share.

- Allis-Chalmers had been losing money, while Massey Ferguson was all but bankrupt, dependent on Canadian government guarantees for its survival.

Tenneco's Words.   Shortly after the merger, Tenneco made a series of public statements:[3]

- "We're not a company that retreats . . . and Jim Ketelsen [CEO of Tenneco] doesn't retreat."—*Senior Tenneco executive*
- "We have just an excellent chance of bringing [Case/IH] up to our profitability goals in a very short time. In my eyes, the [IH] dealer organization is worth more than we paid for the whole thing."— *Jim Ketelsen, CEO of Tenneco*
- "Streamlining has to be done in order to make the industry healthy." —*Anonymous Tenneco executive*

Tenneco's Actions.   At the same time, Tenneco was making major changes. It eliminated as much as 35 percent of industry capacity by shutting down IH's nearly century-old plant in Moline, Illinois. The old familiar red IH brand was phased out. It also started trimming the 2,600-strong dealer organization, with company stores and more cooperative dealers being preferred.

Competitors' Words.   Deere's public reaction was muted: "We don't know if this is good or bad for the industry—we'll wait and see." Massey and Allis-Chalmers appeared more concerned with their own situations. Massey Ferguson commented, "Everybody in the industry has been talking to everybody else for at least the last three years. A lot of these conversations will continue." Allis-Chalmers addressed the same theme when its spokesperson said, "An Allis-Massey merger is *not* on; we're forecasting a return to profitability in two years."

Competitors' Actions.   Public statements not withstanding, Allis-Chalmers started actively looking for a buyer for its farm equipment operations. Massey continued to retrench. Deere was the most active, in contrast to its public stance. Deere sales representatives called on anxious Case and IH dealers and customers, encouraging them to switch. At the same time, Deere closed one of its nine U.S. sales branches and cut 1,000 white-collar jobs.

The main dialogue was between Deere, the leader, and Case/IH, the potential challenger. Case and its parent, Tenneco, were signaling that they would compete vigorously for market share. At the same time, their actions to reduce excess manufacturing capacity and trim the number of dealers offered some hope that the ruinous price wars of the early 1980s would not be repeated, that is, they were signaling to raise their (and Deere's) freedom of maneuver regarding pricing. This conclusion was bolstered by Tenneco's deep pockets, which meant that Case/IH would not have to cut prices merely to stay afloat. Deere's actions indicated that it was prepared for a long struggle and would not give up share without a fight. On the other hand, by not attacking Case/IH more vigorously through price cuts, promotions, and so forth, Deere was indicating that it recognized that leverage in these areas was nonexistent and that it desired limited warfare; it wasn't going to initiate "all-out" conflict in an effort to force Case/IH to exit the industry.

Given the financial and marketing weaknesses of the other players— Massey was nearly bankrupt and Allis-Chalmers was suffering heavy losses—their responses were important only as distress signals. Massey was trying (unsuccessfully) to find a buyer, while Allis-Chalmers was indicating which buyer(s) it did *not* want.

The Objectives of Market Signals

As these two examples indicate, we must fully understand the structure of the industry, the nature of the conflict, the relative position of the firm sending the signal, and the likely responses before we can interpret signals or decide which actions to use in signaling our intentions. We can, however, draw some general conclusions about the objectives of market signaling in different industry situations, that is, possible motives for using signals. These inferences will then assist in anticipating potential signals as well as provide insight into which actions will most effectively signal our own intentions.

Firms' reasons for using market signals will vary depending on whether the industry is mature, declining, or cyclical. The messages will also vary depending on the relative position of a firm—whether it is the industry leader, a significant competitor, or a new entrant. Table 9.1 categorizes potential objectives along these dimensions for mature and declining/cyclical industries. We will discuss each of these in turn.

Mature Industries

Industry conflict here is either win/lose or limited warfare; for this reason there are no entries under the heading lose/lose. We can classify the reasons for using market signals as follows (see also Table 9.1):

Table 9.1 Objectives of market signals.

	Nature of Conflict	
	Win/Lose or Limited War	Lose/Lose
Mature		

Leaders	Entry deterrence
	Setting, enforcing terms
	  of competition
	Limits of "permissible"
	  acts
		N/A

2nd/3d Players	Negotiate with leader Support of status quo Warning/retaliation Impending exit	
Entrants	War/peace	
Declining/Cyclical		
Leaders	Domination Terms of competition Limits of "permissible" acts	Terms of competition Retaliation
2nd/3d Players	Acceptance of status quo Desperation Willingness to be purchased	Acceptance of status quo Desire to be purchased

- *Leaders.* In the late growth, early maturity stages of industry evolution, leaders can use signals to deter entry. They should definitely use signals to set the terms of competition, such as defining leverage, as either limited warfare or win/lose. Signaling can also be used to signify their commitment to the industry and to their strategy, as well as to establish the limits of "permissible" behavior, the limits of maneuver.

- *Other players.* We are primarily concerned with firms who are second or third (occasionally fourth) in terms of market share; signals from other players tend to be ignored or drowned out. Second or third players in the industry should use signals to (1) "negotiate" with the leader regarding the terms of competition, (2) indicate their acceptance and support of industry norms, (3) convey warnings to deter the leader and others from hostile acts, or (4) alert potential buyers to their impending exit from the industry.

- *Entrants.* These firms should communicate whether they will abide by industry norms or aggressively change the status quo.

The U.S. residential long-distance telephone market provides an excellent example of how market signals can be used to establish and demonstrate support for limited competition. AT&T, the leader with more than 60 percent of the market, has effectively established and communicated to its leading competitors, Sprint and MCI, the limits of acceptable behavior in terms of pricing differentials, market share, and promotional expenditures. During the critical period 1985–1987, when residential customers were choosing their long-distance carriers, AT&T demonstrated its commitment and determination through sizable increases in advertising expenditures.[4] Last but not least, it has also deterred entry by the regional Bell companies through legislative and regulatory proceedings and, perhaps more effectively, by demonstrating a "linkage" between its willingness to bypass the local companies and their entry into the market.

For their part, both MCI and Sprint have demonstrated their acceptance of and support for the status quo:

- They have minimized price comparisons in advertising.
- They have generally maintained price differentials within the informal limits set by AT&T.
- They supported AT&T's petition for relief from regulatory limits on its rate of return.[5]

Philip Morris' entry into the domestic beer market with its acquisition of Miller Brewing was accompanied by (1) a repositioning of Miller as a mass market beer, and (2) substantial increases in advertising. Both these actions were overt, direct signals of Philip Morris' intention to break up the prior state of low-key, low-intensity competition.[6]

Declining/Cyclical Industries

Here the terms of competition can be limited warfare, win/lose, or lose/lose. Signals should be used extensively to stabilize the situation, warn other participants of a firm's willingness to use desperate, almost suicidally short-sighted pricing tactics, or hoist the "For Sale" sign:

- *Leaders.* In a declining industry, these firms should use signals to declare their intention to dominate the industry and, by playing win/lose, to drive other players out of the game. Alternatively, they may decide to try to maintain limits on price warfare; in that event they should use signals to clarify the terms of competition. If the nature of industry warfare is lose/lose, as may happen in late decline or during a downturn in a cyclical industry, leaders can use signals to modify the terms of competition. When maintaining limits on price competition becomes difficult, as is often happens in these industry situations, leaders should use signals to communicate their territorial limits and their commitment to the industry.

- *Other players.* Here, too, we are primarily concerned with firms who are second, third, or at most, fourth in market share. In declining industries, these firms should use signals to declare their support for limited warfare. In both declining and cyclical industries, they can use signals to communicate their willingness to use desperate measures that could precipitate an industry-wide price war.[7] Finally, they can use signals to indicate their willingness—or desire—to be purchased.

The U.S. discrete transistor industry has been declining since the mid-1960s, when the commercial development of integrated chip made discrete transistors obsolete. The number of active players has dropped from a peak of 14 in 1979 to 3 today. Throughout this period, Motorola has consistently signaled its intention to dominate the industry through pricing tactics, investments in capacity and R&D, and manufacturing techniques.

In the farm equipment example discussed earlier, Case/IH's actions signified an acceptance of the industry status quo in a cyclical industry. Furthermore, by reference pricing, that is, basing its list prices on Deere's published list prices and maintaining a tacitly accepted differential, Case/IH (and its parent, Tenneco) signaled its acceptance of Deere's price leadership. As we mentioned earlier, Massey and Allis-Chalmers, correctly, hung out "For Sale" signs, hoping that one of the two majors or a new entrant would purchase them, as Allis-Chalmers subsequently was by Klöckner-Humboldt-Deutz.

In the airlines, another cyclical industry, the various responses to American's fare reductions revealed the competitors' determination to retaliate and vigorously defend their market shares. Note that, in this case, American concentrated on United's and Continental's reactions, as they were its primary competitors. The responses of the other airlines, for example, PeopleExpress, were irrelevant because American did not compete directly against them and, more importantly, because United (as the largest carrier) and Continental (as a major, price-oriented competitor) were key to the success or failure of American's strategy. When United immediately countered with a similar program and Continental started to publicize that American had raised *business* fares,[8] this restored the status quo but at lower overall fare levels.

Variables Used in Signaling

Companies can signal their intentions in a number of different ways, not all price-related. Plant expansions/additions, announcements of R&D expenditures, the rate and timing of new product introductions, responses to pricing changes—all of these activities are used to communicate with competitors to establish, maintain, or change a state of limited price competition.

Table 9.2 summarizes some of the commonly used techniques of market signaling. For convenience we have separated them into specific actions and public relations/media communications. It is important to separate routine or normal actions in these areas from *deliberate* market signals. For this purpose, we need to know the context in which these actions/statements are made.

- *Acquisitions* may be a definite signal, particularly if they follow a pattern or if individual acquisitions are accompanied by statements indicating further purchases in pursuit of some overall corporate objective.

- *Plant expansions or additions* acquire special significance only if they are announced during a period of general industry overcapacity or they represent capacity far in excess of industry projections. They may also be feints or bluffs, designed to scare other competitors from similar additions of their own.

Table 9.2   Variables used in signaling.

Mature Industries	
Actions	Plant additions/expansions
	R&D spending
	Rate, timing of new product introductions
	Acquisition plans, activities
	Pricing changes
Media	Talks to industry and general business press
	Advertising, especially tactical responses
Declining/Cyclical Industries	
Actions	Plant expansions, consolidations
	Maintenance of full line
	Channel consolidation
	Sales force changes
	Pricing patterns
Media	Speeches to trade and business audiences
	Comments to common customers

- *R&D spending* can be a deliberate signal if it is accompanied by considerable publicity, for example, announcements of a new R&D center, expanded/accelerated hiring plans.

- *New products* are sometimes used to signal commitment or deter entry. For example, in late summer 1988, Apple Computer announced its Macintosh IIx in part to pre-empt a pending new product introduction from NeXT; Apple was thereby signaling its determination to contest the university market.

- *Media* activities are particularly popular in signaling. These can take the form of speeches to industry or dealer/distributor associations, interviews in the trade press, specific tactical advertisements, and so on. Sometimes the message is fairly obvious, for example, general exhortations to "maintain customer services" or "the importance of a full line" can be translated fairly easily into "let's avoid price cutting."

Naturally, some actions carry more significance than others. Acquisitions and additions to capacity (in an industry that already has excess capacity) are very tangible statements of competitive intent. At the other end of the scale, media activities unaccompanied by more definitive actions such as price changes, increases in promotional spending lack credibility as signals.

Why Firms Use Signals

We can obtain considerable insight into the issues involved in market signaling by analyzing the classic "Prisoner's Dilemma."[9] In one variation of this game, there are two players, A and B, who cannot communicate directly. Every time the game is played, each player has to decide either to cooperate or defect; furthermore, their choices must be made independently and simultaneously. The payoffs for each of the four possible combinations of choices are shown in Figure 9.1. If they both cooperate, they receive a payoff of $5 apiece, if they both defect, they each lose $5, and if A defects while B cooperates, A gains $10, while B loses the same amount.

If the game is played only once, the "best" strategy for player A is to defect; it is his best choice against player B's decision to cooperate and also against B's decision to defect. Similarly, defecting is also the best choice for player B. Thus, the net result of playing the "best" strategies is that both parties lose $5 each. This is the dilemma!

If the two parties could communicate overtly with each other, they would agree to cooperate. Even when such overt communication is not

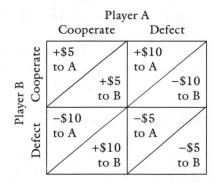

Figure 9.1   Prisoner's dilemma—payoff matrix.

permitted, they will try to communicate through indirect means (or signals), provided that the incentives are high enough and/or the game is played over several rounds.[10] Achieving this tacit collusion is the main objective of market signaling. Whether the signals will be effective depends on

- *Availability and symmetry of information* regarding the payoffs for the various choices
- *Participants' value functions,* what they are and whether they are the same for both players
- *Payoff structure,* that is, the perceived returns and risks of cooperative behavior
- *Signaling tactics* that each player can use without being guilty of overt (in the context of antitrust) collusive behavior
- *Enforceability,* that is, the degree to which cheating can be/will be detected, the probability of retaliation, and the expected costs of such retaliation to the guilty party.

In the simple example described in Figure 9.1, both players have complete information regarding the payoffs, which are symmetrical. In addition, it is safe to assume that both players want to maximize their returns (or minimize their losses); their value functions (or utilities) are one-dimensional and easy to measure. The expected returns of cooperative behavior are higher than those of noncooperative strategies, and cheating is easily detected by either player. While the choice of signaling tactics is limited to the strategies used in successive rounds of the game, it is still possible for them to achieve tacit collusion and cooperate when the game is played over several rounds.

When there are several players in the game, the payoffs are either not known or else not understood equally well by the various participants and different players have different objectives (for example, some participants want to maximize market share, while others are focused on near-term profits), it will be difficult to achieve tacit collusion through signaling. This suggests that signaling will be most effective in mature and declining industries and when the number of participants is limited.[11]

Relationship to the Structure of the Payoff.   The two-player example is also useful in analyzing how changes in the payoff structure affect the outcome. Consider the game shown in Figure 9.2. In this case, the returns for defecting are very high for both players, in fact much higher than the profits to be made through cooperative behavior. Further, the risks of defection are low—a loss of $5 versus a potential gain of $100. There is little incentive to communicate (at least initially), and the two players may never reach a cooperative agreement. This example describes likely behavior in industries where the (perceived) short-term revenue gains of defecting—by cutting prices, offering promotions or incentives, and so on—are high and the long-term costs of noncooperation are relatively low.

We find additional insights into the role and the effectiveness of market signals when we recognize that, in real life, the payoffs are uncertain. In other words, the players must not only consider the *expected* returns from cooperating or defecting, but they must also take into account the *uncertainty* or *variance* in these returns. There are several possibilities, depending on the relative expected returns and risks of cooperating and defecting; here we will consider only the following:

- The expected returns to cooperation are much greater than expected returns from defection, and the variances of the returns are

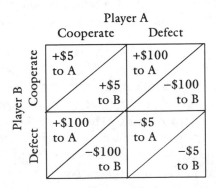

Figure 9.2   Prisoner's dilemma—changed payoff matrix.

Adapted from Raiffa, *The Art and Science of Negotiation,* Belknap/Harvard, 1982.

the same for both choices. In this case, there is every incentive to try to achieve tacit agreement, and signals will be effective. The RTE cereals industry, discussed in Chapter 2, falls into this category.

- The risks in defecting are much greater than expected returns, in which case most managers, being risk averse, will be reluctant to defect from any tacit agreement. (We are assuming that the risks in defecting are higher relative to cooperation.) Risks in defecting can be higher than the expected returns if, for example, the leader has a considerable share and cost advantage and has shown its willingness to retaliate. A good example of the risks being higher than the expected returns from defecting (or one-sided play) is the U.S. automotive industry in the 1950s and 1960s. For Ford and Chrysler, the expected returns from abandoning General Motors' price leadership were not worth the (perceived) risk of increased price competition and other retaliatory actions.

- The risks are asymmetrical, or the variability of the return to cooperation is much greater than (or much less than) the variability of the returns to defection or one-sided play. In this case, we hypothesize that the industry situation will always be unstable (or stable), possibly regardless of the relative magnitude of the expected returns. The U.S. airline industry, discussed in greater detail below, is an example of the perceived variability of the return to cooperation being much higher than that due to defection. Airlines believe that if they stay with cooperative strategies when a competitor defects, that is, cuts fares, they incur far greater risks than they would if they followed suit.

In some cases, the structure of the payoff matrix leads to an "escalation game,"[12] where both players find themselves unable to cooperate, *despite the obvious benefits of tacit collusion*. A simple example of this is a bidding contest in which two players, A and B, bid alternately for a fixed amount, say, $10. The winning bidder pays the auctioneer the amount of his bid and collects the $10. However, the *losing* bidder has to pay the amount of *his* highest bid to the auctioneer! As a result, both parties tend to keep on bidding well past the value of the prize. Further, once the bidding has exceeded $10, *both* parties have an incentive not to quit; the psychological investment is too high.

The best strategy for both players is to agree that the first person will bid $1 (or the minimum bid amount), the second will pass, and they will divide the profits equally. However, such explicit collusion is not permitted by law. Even if it were permitted, would the players trust one another, that is, how would the nonbidder be able to enforce the agreement after the fact or, vice versa, how could the bidder be certain that the other player would pass? And when explicit collusion is not allowed, what signals could they use and how effective would they be?

Escalation games can and do occur in industries where the fixed costs and/or exit barriers are high. In such cases, the basic structure of the marketing conflict is unstable, and signals are not effective in maintaining a cooperative equilibrium for reasons similar to the simple auction game just described.

Signaling Tactics.   In a game, players can send signals by their successive bidding patterns or through such nonverbal means as are allowed. In real life, firms have a number of tools available for use in signaling, ranging from overt pricing actions (similar to bidding patterns) to indirect communications such as speeches, articles, messages through third parties such as dealers/distributors, and so forth.

Enforceability.   Finally, in analyzing the effectiveness of signals in achieving tacit coalitions or collusions, we must consider whether and how quickly competitors can detect any violations or defections, together with the likely/expected consequences. In the game shown in Figure 9.1, for example, any cheating is immediately apparent and can be punished in the next move at relatively low cost. In the case of the second game shown in Figure 9.2, the penalty for cheating is much smaller than the potential gain; consequently, cheating is much more likely.

Summary

Sending, receiving, and interpreting market signals is an art. To use signals effectively, managers must have an intuitive "feel" for the industry's current state of play, which actions should be considered significant and which can be ignored, and insight into the motivations and thoughts of the other key players. The last is particularly important; unless a manager has a thorough understanding of the other parties' motivations and concerns, as well as an intuitive appreciation of the strategic leverage in the industry, he will have difficulty accurately anticipating their reactions. Consequently, when using market signals, it is essential that the manager be personally familiar with the backgrounds, mores, and values of his counterparts at other firms, or else work with someone who has "grown up" with the industry to help him obtain the necessary intuition and insight.

PART
THREE

EXPLOITING STRATEGIC LEVERAGE

10

Selecting Strategies That Exploit Leverage

Having fully analyzed a company's strategic leverage, we will now discuss the implications for the firm's objectives, strategies, and tactics. For this purpose, we will introduce a new tool: the Structure-Position map. We will use this map to organize our analysis of how a company's leverage influences its long-term objectives and strategy choices. Next, we will describe how tactical decisions can affect the success of a strategy. Finally, we will analyze how a company can improve its strategic leverage, that is, how it can change the terms of competition (the rules of the game) or even the overall structure of the industry (the game itself).

The Structure-Position Map

To enable managers to translate their understanding of their company's leverage into specific objectives, strategies, and tactics, we have developed a framework called the Structure-Position map. As the name indicates, this framework has two dimensions—*industry structure* and *company competitive position* (see Figure 10.1). We use the nature of the conflict as a proxy for structure. Further, we organize this in a sequence that parallels the manner in which payoffs change as an industry evolves. In this fashion, we incorporate industry dynamics into our framework. We subdivide company competitive position into four categories, namely:

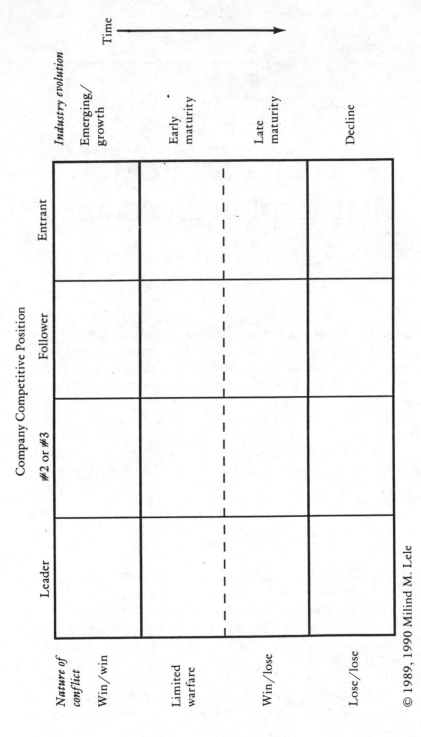

Figure 10.1 The Structure-Position map.

© 1989, 1990 Milind M. Lele

- *The leader* of the segment or industry as appropriate
- *The second/third players,* that is, the companies closest to the leader in size, capabilities, and market share
- *Followers,* being all other players including niche players or specialty firms, but excluding entrants
- *Entrants,* namely firms entering the market for the first time, either by creating new capacity or through acquisition.[1]

We can then summarize our conclusions regarding the various players' choices in terms of the Structure-Position map as shown in Figure 10.2.

Leaders.   During the growth stage the leading firm must try to define the game and set the overall pattern of competition. As the industry settles down into a period of slower growth, the leader's objective should be to limit price warfare.[2] When that becomes infeasible, the leaders should move aggressively to consolidate the industry as an "end-game" strategy. During decline, the leader must try and change the game and, hopefully, re-ignite growth.

Second/Third Players.   During the growth period, these firms must make every effort to define/modify the game and the overall terms of competition in their favor. As industry growth slows, they have two choices: Play within the rules or try to change the rules. If they elect to play within the rules, they can use them to nibble away at an unsuspecting (or lazy) leader's market share. Or they can exploit the rules by "sawing the floor" around the leader, possibly even displacing him. As the industry starts to decline, they have to decide their end-game strategies, that is, whether and when to exit, how to position themselves if they choose to stay, and whether to change the game itself.

Followers.   Early on during the emerging or growth phases of the industry, followers or would-be niche players must understand how the industry is likely to evolve (learn the game) and how to exploit industry structure to create a niche (anticipate the rules). As industry growth slows, followers must create strong defenses (raise the barricades) to deter the major players from entering their market segment. During decline, these players are well entrenched, they can survive for a long time, as shown by Rolls Royce in automobiles and Leica in 35 mm cameras. Alternatively, they may prefer to sell out, timing their exit for maximum gain.[3]

Entrants.   Opportunistic entrants' objective should be to skim the cream rapidly (exploit the game), exiting when industry growth slows to

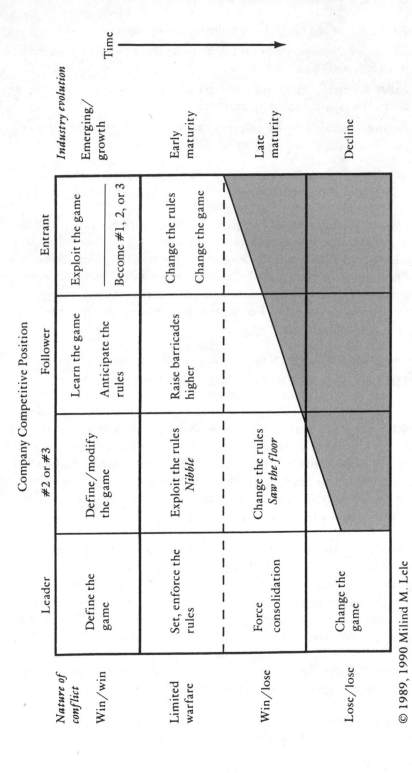

Figure 10.2 The various players' choices summarized.

© 1989, 1990 Milind M. Lele

174

a crawl. As the name implies, their goal is quick profits; consequently, they should avoid making any investments that raise their exit costs. Strategic entrants—companies who believe the emerging industry threatens their existing market or who possess core competencies that are central to the new industry—should aim at becoming key players (capture one, two, or three). Otherwise, they are well advised to stay out; better no entry at all than a poorly funded, half-hearted effort.

Rationale

Before examining the individual players/choices in greater detail, we will summarize our reasoning. From our earlier discussions, it will be evident that (1) these choices are logical consequences of the nature of industry payoffs and the company's competitive position, (2) industry evolution is the underlying driving force, and (3) a company's freedom to select its long-term objectives depends on industry structure, dynamics, and the firm's prior decisions.

Choices Are Logical Consequences of Payoffs, Position. Consider the different players' choices when the nature of the game is limited warfare and all participants realize that it is in their common interest to avoid extensive price warfare.[4] Beginning with the leading player, in theory, he or she can do anything: attack competing firms, raise prices, lower prices, change products, increase promotional intensity, or other actions. In reality, leverage is constrained by the fact that the total payoff is constant, by the perception that cooperation is more profitable than one-sided, or "competitive" play, and by the self-interest of the leader. Because payoffs are constant, any significant increase in sales or profits must come at the expense of the other players.[5] But seeking such increases will destroy the cooperative equilibrium as other participants, seeing their revenues or profits threatened, counter attack. *Raising* prices is also risky; competitors may not follow. Thus, the leader's choices are limited to maintaining margins or maintaining its competitive position, or to some combination of both.

The second or third player's alternatives are also similarly affected by the payoffs and their own position. They too stand to gain more by playing cooperatively—within limits—as opposed to trying overtly to improve their position. Thus their fundamental choice is whether to merely maintain their position in the industry status quo, or to *covertly* attack the leader.

When total returns are constant and the major players have tacitly agreed not to attack each other, their logical next target in pursuit of revenue or profit growth is smaller, niche participants. Faced with this situation, the niche player has few choices. Counterattacking is expensive, risky, and the larger players simply have more resources. Nor can niche players control price competition once the majors enter their niche. The alternative is to entrench the firm in its niche by tactics that raise the (perceived) costs of entry, create switching costs for customers, or both, in other words, by increasing its leverage relative to that of entrants.

Last but not least, potential entrants also find their alternatives limited. First, because total payoffs are constant, incumbents are likely to view any entrant as a potential threat to their own revenues and profits. Second, entry barriers are likely to be high,[6] consequently a purely opportunistic or "cream-skimming" entry is not attractive. This leaves entrants with only two choices: They can join the existing status quo, or they can try and displace one or more of the leading incumbents.[7]

Industry Evolution Drives the Sequence.   This is most clearly illustrated by the firms' choices when the payoffs are increasing (win/win or growth). Absent an underlying industry dynamic, there is no particular pressure to decide their long-term positioning. These choices become relevant only in the context of industry evolution. It is the dynamics of industry evolution and consolidation with its corollaries, namely,

- The virtual certainty that, at some point, industry growth will slow down
- Typically only two or three players are successful in differentiating themselves across the board, and only one firm can be the cost leader
- Unless the firm is among the leaders in the market or in a segment, its profitability will be poor, making the choice of positioning important.

Absent such pressures, it is very difficult to argue that one positioning is more important than any other.

Flexibility Depends on Structure, Dynamics, and Prior Decisions. For example, while a follower's ability to find or create a secure, profitable niche is ultimately determined by the industry economics, its ability to defend that niche is considerably influenced by the manner in which the industry has evolved as well as by the firm's actions (or lack of them) in building defenses around its position. The U.S. airline industry after deregulation provides two contrasting examples, PeopleExpress and Piedmont. PeopleExpress virtually created the niche for low-cost travel.

However, it did not create any defenses against entry by the majors, for example, dedicated channels of distribution, switching costs for key customer segments. Further, it threatened the major airlines when it started to target their business customers. These two actions, when coupled with the industry's lack of significant built-in mobility barriers, virtually ensured PeopleExpress's demise when industry competition intensified. By contrast Piedmont Airlines, another niche player, had created a strong defensible niche for itself, by providing superior service and concentrating steadily on its regional markets. As a result, Piedmont survived the early price wars, despite a similar lack of built-in mobility barriers, and was able to command an attractive price when it was ultimately purchased by USAir.

Restrictions on Flexibility Are Due to Evolution, Changes in Payoffs. Consider the second/third player's choices (Figure 10.3): During the growth stage, a firm can choose among four options: Capture number one, maintain two/three, find or create a secure niche, or sell out to an entrant. But beyond this initial stage, however, the firm's choices are increasingly restricted by industry evolution and the corresponding changes in payoffs. Assume that the firm has decided to maintain its position as the second/third player. As the industry enters maturity and the payoffs change from win/win to limited warfare, the firm's leverage and therefore its strategic choices become more limited. At this stage, for instance, capturing number one is usually not a viable option; the incumbent can be expected to counterattack vigorously, precipitating widespread industry warfare.[8] Nor is overt price competition desirable. Thus, if the firm wishes to play within the existing terms of competition, its only choices are two: strategic and tactical defensive (maintain status quo) or strategic defensive and tactical offensive (saw the floor).[9]

How Leaders Can Exploit Leverage

The manner in which a leader's choices change vividly illustrates the interplay between structure, position, and industry evolution. As we saw, early on industry structure is not a major driver except indirectly, through the ease or difficulty of entry into the market. Strategic choices are governed more by industry evolution—the rate at which the industry is growing and how and when it is likely to mature—and a firm's competitive position—whether it was an industry innovator/pioneer, the degree to which it is perceived as a trendsetter, and its resources in relation to existing competitors and anticipated entrants.

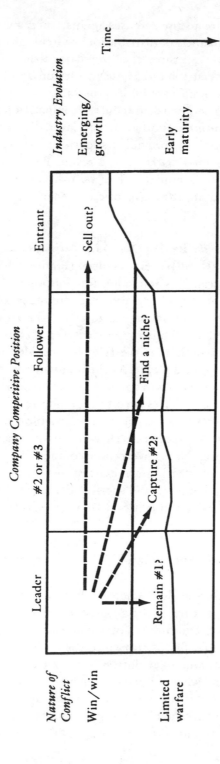

Figure 10.3 The leader's choices during the growth stage.

As the industry matures, structure and position move to the fore, overshadowing evolution. Structure determines whether limiting price competition is even feasible, while relative position dictates the degree to which a leader can set and enforce limits on price warfare. Later on, structural constraints such as high exit barriers may prevent a leader from forcing out other participants; under suitable circumstances, this can create highly destructive and debilitating price competition.[10]

Growth or Win/Win. In the growth stage of industry evolution, the nature of the conflict is win/win; industry sales and profits are exploding, and there is little or no rivalry. Industry leaders are difficult to identify as market shares are changing rapidly, and different firms are trying to establish control over technology or market evolution. Therefore, in this context, the term "leader" refers to the half-dozen or so firms that are at the forefront of industry evolution in terms of technological changes, sales, and market development.

At this point, a company can choose among four basic objectives (see Figure 10.3): (1) It can try to maintain its leadership position as the industry evolves; (2) it can opt to be a strong number two, the "alternative choice"; (3) it can use the profits from its temporary leadership position to find or create lucrative, defensible product or market niches; or (4) it can decide to sell out to a would-be entrant at an attractive price.

These objectives, in turn, decide a firm's strategies and tactics (see Table 10.1). If a firm wants to remain the leader or be a strong second, its

Table 10.1 Objectives, strategies, and tactics—leaders.

	Objectives	Strategies	Tactical Issues
Win-Win	Maintain 1 Capture 2 Find/create niche	Differentiation (rarely cost leadership) Differentiated focus	Control of product/market evolution Control of shelf space
Limited Warfare	Minimize price warfare	Entrenchment Consolidation	Flankers Price leadership Signaling
Win/Lose	End price wars Dominate	Consolidation Differentiation and cost leadership	Signaling Aggressive price and promotion tactics
Lose-Lose	Divest Dominate	—	—

overall strategy must be differentiation;[11] it must create a uniqueness about its products or services in most major segments of the market. In turn, the firm's tactics must focus on controlling/influencing (1) technological or market evolution and (2) "shelf space," that is, the number, types, and presence in channels of distribution. If the firm wants to find or create lucrative, secure niches, its strategy should be towards the differentiated end of focus.

The central issue is long-term positioning. As the industry matures, only two (at most three) players are likely to be successful in establishing an unique, differentiated identity across-the-board,[12] and only one firm can become the cost leader. Thus, unless they can find or create a niche, other front-runners risk being neither industry nor segment leaders and, therefore, earning substantially lower profits.[13] Consequently, a firm that is at the forefront during the growth stage must realistically assess its chances of being either first or second in the long run. If, as is likely, its prospects of remaining first or second are remote, then it should concentrate its energies on finding a secure niche that it *can* dominate. Alternatively, its interests may be better served by selling out to a potential entrant; prices are likely to be very attractive, and the new owner may have the necessary financial and managerial resources.

The speed of industry evolution—whether anticipated or actual—determines the importance and the urgency of making these choices. As we discussed earlier, without an underlying industry dynamic, there is no particular pressure to choose a particular long-term positioning. Thus, in an industry that is growing relatively slowly, as was the case with the U.S. black-and-white television industry of the 1950s and early 1960s, leaders have little pressure to select a particular positioning early on. In rapidly growing ("high tech") industries, he who hesitates is lost. Leaders must quickly identify and capture the most suitable positioning early, otherwise they risk losing control over industry evolution. Consequently, managers should concentrate the bulk of their efforts on this issue and balance the importance of technological leadership and market control.

Strategic decisions made during the growth stage have long-lasting effects. Typical mistakes are (1) the belief that a firm will maintain its initial technological/innovative leadership, despite the near-certain entry of larger players with sizable vested interests, (2) the failure to recognize how industry forces—especially buyer (channel) power—change and adapt their strategies to these new realities; (3) the lack of clear, realistic long-term objectives. For example:

- California Cooler was the original innovator in the category of fruit juice mixed with wine beverages, yet it failed to realize that larger players with far deeper pockets would soon move in. As a result, it did not establish a beachhead in a secure niche. Today it is languishing far behind the leaders.

- PeopleExpress failed to recognize how the formation of giant "hub-and-spoke" systems had changed the economics of the airline industry since the early days of deregulation. As result, it abandoned its hitherto successful, low-end niche strategy by trying to attract business passengers, with disastrous results.

- Allis-Chalmers lacked a clear, long-term objective for its farm equipment operations. Faced with competition from much larger rivals, Allis-Chalmers seesawed between wanting to be full-line producer and niche player.

The early participants in the U.S. microwave oven industry—Amana and Litton in particular—made all three mistakes.

Maturity: Limited Warfare on Win/Lose.   As growth slows and the industry starts to mature, a leader must determine whether limited price competition is feasible, given the structure of the industry and the company's position and resources (see Table 10.1). If price warfare is containable, the leader's objective must be to establish and maintain the terms of competition, i.e., the price differentials it will permit, price leadership, the types and intensity of promotion, and intermediaries' margins and pricing patterns. Its strategy should be *entrenchment;* tightening its hold on major customers and intermediaries. The leader should not hesitate to use acquisitions[14] either to capture and control key market segments or to further consolidate the industry and limit price competition. Tactical areas of primary concern are (1) introducing/countering with appropriate flankers to ensure that competitors do not increase their share and (2) maintaining price leadership, while ensuring that the price umbrella is not so generous as to allow other players to "nibble" away at its share.[15]

Kellogg in the ready-to-eat cereals industry is a classic example of how a leader's tactical choices are constrained by objectives and strategic leverage. As Table 10.1 suggests, Kellogg's long-term goal should be to limit price warfare; as the leader, it is hurt most by price competition. Furthermore, Kellogg's leverage is also quite limited due to (1) the structure of the industry, (2) industry payoffs, and (3) Kellogg's competitive position. Specifically (see Figure 10.4):

- Kellogg's leverage in place and price is limited. The buying power of supermarkets makes it impossible to switch to other outlets. Nor

Variable	Maneuver (M)	Return (R)	Leverage = M × R
Target Market	Must address all major segments	Low to moderate	Low
Product	Quality, width & positioning constrained	Variable	Low to moderate
Place	Very limited— buyer power is very high		Low
Promotion	Δ Promotion limited by need to control industry warfare	Moderate	Low to moderate
Price	Δ Price limited by need to control price warfare	Low	Low

Figure 10.4   Kellogg's strategic leverage in RTE cereal industry.

can Kellogg change prices at will. If it raises wholesale or retail prices too high, the company risks losing share. Wholesale price cuts could trigger an industry-wide war as other players try and maintain their share. Finally, since demand for RTE cereals is price-inelastic, retail price cuts serve little purpose.[16]

- The need to compete in all major segments also restricts Kellogg's ability to choose its target markets or pursue niches; excessive focus on a niche such as health food cereals, for example, would distract its attention from the mass market. Thus, Kellogg's leverage in this area is also low.

- Product and promotion are the two dimensions in which Kellogg has some leverage. However, even here, its freedom to change is constrained by position (product) and by its objective of limiting price (or promotional) warfare.

Thus, as long as Kellogg wants to (1) retain leadership and (2) limit price warfare, its tactical choices are limited. It must avoid radical changes to price (including channel terms and conditions) and promotional levels, using them primarily to signal its intentions and to discipline any violations. Occasionally, it may raise promotional levels to limit the profits of numbers two and three, thereby preventing them from using the price umbrella to fund any share gains; this would reduce the other players' profits without creating price warfare. With regard to product and target market, Kellogg should let niche players be the innovators. Given the lack of significant mobility barriers and Kellogg's economies of scale in promotion and distribution, it can use "second but better" tactics without risking its market share. For Kellogg, the downside risks of diverting resources on an unsuccessful first entry are much higher than the share it could lose by being slow to enter. (Contrast this with the GE versus Whirlpool situation described later in Chapter 12.)

If limited price warfare is unlikely because of industry structure or the leader's position, weak management must decide whether to impose price discipline, through consolidations if necessary; to dominate the industry by driving out weaker players through relentless price and product competition; or to exit the industry. The first two choices pose substantial risks: reimposing price discipline may not be feasible without extensive (and expensive) consolidation, while high exit barriers or the understandable reluctance of competitors to "leave quietly" may make domination difficult, time-consuming, and expensive. Finally, at this stage of industry evolution, it may be difficult to find buyers offering attractive prices.

Decline or Lose/Lose.   During decline, essentially two choices exist: divest or dominate and harvest.[17] Divesting businesses may be difficult, in which case a firm may divest selectively, "milking" the existing investment. If a firm chooses to remain in the industry, it should move aggressively to consolidate the industry if at all possible, that is, if exit barriers are not too high. It should purchase smaller players or simply force them out by aggressively lowering its costs and prices, adding capacity, or taking other actions.

Becton Dickinson (BD) has followed the latter approach in the U.S. market for disposable plastic syringes. Since 1983, it has systematically invested in this business, increasing its total manufacturing capacity, improving quality, and maintaining sustained sales pressure through rapid service and heavy promotional activities. Largely as a result of this strategy, several major producers have left the industry, thereby increasing BD's share and profitability in a market where usage is growing slowly and prices are declining due to intense pressure from powerful buyers (the hospital purchasing groups).[18]

BD again illustrates the relationships between leverage, company objectives, tactical requirements, and investment decisions. Early on BD appears to have recognized that

- Price warfare could not be controlled without consolidating the industry

- There were few or no exit barriers preventing such consolidation
- The only dimension offering any leverage was price
- Sustained pricing pressure was essential
- To apply pricing pressure successfully, it needed to greatly reduce product costs.

Consequently, over several years BD became *the* low-cost producer, establishing world-scale plants in key locations. These low costs, coupled with the high quality (differentiated) image established earlier, allowed BD to become aggressive in pricing without precipitating widespread price warfare.

How Second/Third Players Can Exploit Leverage

During the growth phase, the second/third players' choices are the same as those faced by the (eventual) leader, particularly if, as is often the case, there are several potential contenders for leadership (see Figure 10.5). However, the second/third players' choices become particularly interesting as the industry matures. At this point, a firm can make significant gains. If the nominal industry leader is weak, complacent, or preoccupied by other activities such as diversification efforts, a determined number two or a clever number three can substantially narrow the gap. Occasionally it may even succeed in overtaking the leader.

The second/third players' options during industry maturity demonstrate the importance of strategic leverage. Only by thoroughly understanding where a company has any leverage and what industry forces shape its leverage, can a manager determine

- Whether it is feasible to improve/change his firm's competitive position
- Which *specific* tactics—low-profile attacks on neglected segments, changes to product quality/price ratios, bypassing existing channels—are most likely to succeed
- What are the potential risks of different approaches
- What should be the timing of such tactics.

Table 10.2 describes how second/third players' objectives, strategies, and tactics change in the four industry situations. As we mentioned earlier, during the growth stage, the choices are the same as that of the industry leader; consequently, we will restrict our discussion to

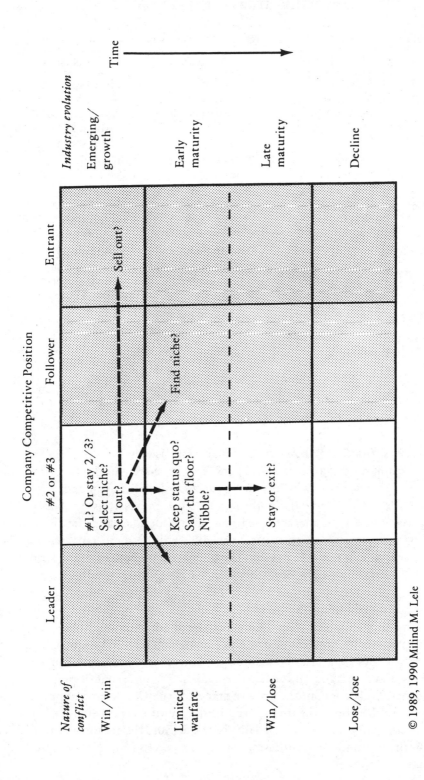

Figure 10.5 Choices facing second/third players in a market.

© 1989, 1990 Milind M. Lele

Table 10.2   Objectives, strategies, and tactics—second/third players.

	Objectives	Strategies	Tactical Issues

Win-Win	Capture 1
	Maintain 2/3
	Find/create niche
		Differentiation
		Differentiation or
		  cost leadership
		Focus
			How to accelerate
			  speed of
			  product/market
			  evolution
			Shelf space

Limited
  Warfare
	Maintain status
	  quo
	Increase share
	Capture 1
	Divest
		Follow/support
		  leader
		Nibble
		Saw the floor
			Signaling
			Flanking
			Attacking niches
			  or changing
			  performance/
			  price ratios

Win/Lose	Increase share/
	  strengthen
	  position
	Divest
		Selective attacks
		Acquisitions
		Changing terms
		  of game
			Target niches
			Acquisition of
			  niche players
			Channel changes

Lose-Lose	Minimize losses Divest	—	—

alternatives during maturity. When an industry is declining, second/ third players have virtually no options but to exit the industry under the most favorable terms possible.

Maturity: Limited Warfare.   The main issue is whether a firm should work to maintain the status quo or to increase its share without resorting to all-out price warfare, which is rarely successful. A firm can gain share on the leader either gradually (nibbling), or more aggressively by consolidating its hold on the market a segment at a time ("sawing the floor" around the leader).[19] Which tactical variables will be important depend on the structure of the industry and the long-term objectives of the firm. However, signaling will be necessary either to demonstrate adherence to implicit terms of competition or to lull the leader into continued complacency and lack of attention.

The manner in which John Deere surpassed International Harvester (IH) in the North American farm equipment market in the late 1950s and early 1960s is a classic example of how a second player can use structure and leverage to its advantage against a complacent or preoccupied leader.[20] Throughout the growth stages of the U.S. farm equipment industry, IH had been the undisputed leader, with Deere usually in second (occasionally third) position. But in the 1950s, IH became preoccupied with its nonfarm businesses, especially trucks, automobiles, and industrial equipment.

Deere seized this opportunity to make a series of moves that would enable it to dethrone IH. Its underlying strategy was to avoid direct price competition with IH. Instead, Deere "sawed the floor" around IH by

- Focusing its efforts on a core group of customers, namely, large, full-time farmers, to the virtual exclusion of other segments
- Developing a network of well-financed, aggressive dealers who could effectively meet the needs of this core segment, especially in the crucial area of service and parts
- Continuously improving the product quality/price ratio by investing in the parts and service infrastructure necessary to ensure rapid support all over North America.

Deere did not make any attempts to significantly change the product itself, increase promotional expenditures, or cut prices aggressively; there was no leverage in these areas.[21]

Maturity: Win/Lose. Here second/third players must decide whether to exit the industry, that is, sell out, or use industry warfare to increase share or otherwise strengthen position. If a firm chooses to stay in the industry and fight it out, then its strategy should be to increase its leverage by "changing the rules of the game" to its advantage. It can use a variety of tactics to change the rules, for example, consolidation by acquiring players in important niches, price attacks in selective segments, or changes to the channels of distribution. The last tactic can be particularly effective. The reason is that, as we show in Chapter 13, channel roles change as industries evolve. However, market leaders are often reluctant to change existing channel strategies, with the result that they are often inefficient and, consequently, vulnerable to price attacks by competitors using more efficient alternatives.

Japanese manufacturers of small office copiers used this tactic with devastating effectiveness against Xerox in the late 1970s and early 1980s. Xerox was committed to its in-house national sales and service organization and, therefore, at a serious cost disadvantage to Japanese imports who were marketing through local office equipment dealers. By the time Xerox widened its channels of distribution (and lowered product costs), the imports had obtained a very sizable share of the market.

Decline: Lose/Lose. Here second/third players have really only one choice: exit. The real issue is timing: Can a firm exit early enough so as to avoid distress-sale prices as and when the industry contracts violently?

What Followers Can and Cannot Do

As the example of Midway Airlines discussed previously shows, followers typically have very little leverage and must use it judiciously if they want to survive, let alone prosper.

A follower's strategic choices are summarized in Table 10.3. When the industry is growing, the primary consideration for a follower is, "Can we find or create a profitable, defensible niche, where we can be first, or at worst second, in market position?" If a firm cannot, it should sell out, preferably while industry growth is still high and potential entrants are numerous, thereby maximizing the returns to its shareholders. Exiting at this point is infinitely preferable to continuing until industry matures, when major players start to invade niche markets in search of continued growth.

While specific tactics will vary from industry to industry, product or market specialization is crucial to delay the entry of major players into niche markets. Particularly in the absence of natural entry barriers, a firm can use such specialized knowledge to create switching costs,[22] that is, making it expensive or unattractive for customers to change over to less specialized or customized products or services offered by larger competitors. Specialized channels can also make it more difficult for major players to enter a niche by raising their selling costs or requiring them to change their price structure.

As an industry nears maturity, a firm must decide whether it wishes to continue as an active participant or exit by selling out. There is a strong case for exiting; as industry growth slows and competition intensifies, the niche player often finds it difficult to protect its position without significant

Table 10.3 Objectives, strategies, and tactics—followers.

	Objectives	Strategies	Tactical Issues
Win-Win	Find/create defensible niche Be acquired	Focus	Product/market specialization Channel selection
Limited Warfare	Maintain status quo Entrench in niche Displace 2/3 Be acquired	Strengthen defenses	Price control Service intensity
Win/Lose	Minimize share loss Be acquired	Increase value Create nuisance value	—
Lose-Lose	—	—	—

investments. Conversely, buyers may be plentiful: current major players wanting to consolidate their hold on the market, firms looking for a secure niche, and late entrants wishing to enter the market. Under the right circumstances, bidding wars can raise prices to such a level that the alternative, staying in for the long-term, is no longer attractive.

If a firm chooses to continue in the market, its strategy must be to strengthen its defenses against the inevitable attempts by the larger players to increase their revenues and profits by entering lucrative niches. Two tactics play a particularly important role in achieving this objective. The first is close control over pricing, to ensure that unduly high prices do not tempt firms into entering the market. This is especially important in segments where exit barriers are high; in such situations, it is essential to prevent entry if at all possible. Once a firm enters, it is usually too expensive to drive it out. The other key tactic is service intensity; by increasing the levels of service offered, the niche player can make customers reluctant to switch except for really steep price differentials. When coupled with aggressive pricing, service intensity creates a major hurdle for potential entrants. They must lower prices in order to capture any revenues at all, while their costs are higher due to the special needs of the segment and the higher service levels provided by the established niche player(s). In other words, they have less freedom of maneuver and their returns are lower.

After price warfare becomes widespread, exit may be the niche player's only realistic choice, especially if the alternative is survival as a minor actor in a declining if not dying industry. The objective should be to extract as high a price as is feasible. This means that, other things being equal, the company should exit earlier rather than wait till the last possible moment. A potentially risky tactic is to raise prices by creating nuisance value, for example, aggressively attacking major players by lowering prices selectively in key markets, raising promotional expenditures, and increasing service requirements in areas the majors will feel obliged to match. The gamble is that leaders may prefer to buy out such nuisances rather than suffer the long-term consequences of forcing them out of the industry.

What Entrants Should Do

The objectives, strategies, and tactics for the two types of entrants—opportunistic and competitive—are summarized in Table 10.4. Two situations should be considered for entry—growing industries and mature industries with limited price competition. There is no reason to

Table 10.4 Objectives, strategies, and tactics—entrants.

	Objectives	Strategies	Tactics
Win-Win	Make short-term gains and cash out *Opportunistic entrant* Capture 1, 2, or 3 *Competitive entrant*	Find, attack targets of opportunity Differentiation or cost leadership	Rapid product roll-out Minimal investment in facilities Participate/control product evolution
Limited Warfare	Join Conquer	Maintain status quo Change the rules Change the game Consolidate/force exit	Signaling Changes in product/price relationships Attacking key/fringe segments
Win/Lose	—	—	—
Lose-Lose	—	—	—

(deliberately) enter declining industries or industries where price warfare is widespread.

The strategic choices facing entrants into a growing industry are evident; we will therefore discuss entering mature markets with limited price competition. Here, they have two alternatives: Should the firm join in the status quo? Or should it try to conquer the market by changing the terms of competition or the nature of the conflict itself? If a firm chooses to join the status quo, its strategy should be to maintain limited price conflict. Through carefully chosen market signals, it should reassure existing players that it does not intend to violate or significantly change the terms of competition within the industry.

More often, a firm enters a market with the intention of dominating or at least becoming a significant player. In this case, its strategy should be to "saw the floor" around the leader(s) and change the terms of competition or, in the long term, the structure of the industry itself. Typical tactics will be to attack fringe or secondary market segments, change the overall price/performance ratio, or use different channels of distribution.

The manner in which Japanese firms entered and subsequently dominated the U.S. television receiver market is a classic example of this approach.[23] At the time the Japanese entered, relatively limited price competition existed among the major manufacturers, and franchised dealers were the major channel of distribution. The Japanese manufacturers initially sold private-label TV sets through mass market chains such as Sears and J.C. Penney. Further, they intensified price competition by changing the relative performance/price ratio, offering higher reliability and quality for comparable or lower prices. The results are well known; within a decade, most U.S. TV manufacturers had been forced out of the market. Japanese firms have followed similar strategies with other consumer electronics, small appliances, and economy cars. They now appear ready to repeat this feat with mid-sized and luxury cars.

The Japanese strategy in consumer electronics is particularly interesting when contrasted with the approach of European manufacturers, which were the first entrants into the U.S. market. Without exception, these firms chose a niche strategies, often at the high price end. In terms of our framework, the European entrants were maintaining the status quo. By contrast, it is now clear that Japanese firms were intent on dominating the industry or at least sharing leadership; and were willing to change the prevailing rules, which were "no private-label sales to mass merchandisers, limited price competition, and adequate quality."

In the process, they also changed the game itself, from limited price warfare to extensive feature—and price-based competition.

The incumbents' freedom of maneuver and, therefore, their strategic leverage, were limited by their existing dealer networks and the desire to limit price warfare. As entrants, the Japanese firms were under no such compulsion; consequently, they could exploit the higher returns available by changing channels. Further, either by accident or by design, the Japanese firms realized that there was little leverage in increasing promotion, changing product standards (TV sizes), or competing aggressively over price. Consequently, they wasted little effort in these areas.

How to Change Strategic Leverage

Companies do not have to accept the limitations on strategic leverage imposed by structure or position. They can change the situation to their advantage in a number of ways. They can acquire other firms, thereby changing their competitive position. Or they can alter the competitive balance of the industry by creating strategic alliances. They can introduce new technology, which radically alters the structure of the industry. Alternatively, they can increase industry capacity substantially, thereby intensifying price competition within the industry and, possibly, forcing smaller players to exit.

We can group these different possibilities into two main categories according to whether they change (1) the terms of competition or (2) the structure of the industry itself. In this section, we will review some of the commonly used techniques in both categories.

Change the Rules

Managers can change the terms of competition in their industry in a number of ways, including:

- *They can attack pricing "gaps."* Mazda changed the upscale sports car market with its RX-7, which looked "just like a Porsche, at half the price!" Essentially Mazda was attacking an opening created by Porsche's continually increasing prices, which had stranded many buyers who wanted a Porsche but could not afford one.
- *They can change channels or channel roles.* In the late 1980s, Blockbuster Video consolidated the home video rental industry in a short four years by creating large, well-capitalized and well-managed outlets. Japanese entrants into the consumer electronics market displaced the traditional appliance dealers and increased the share of the mass merchandisers.
- *They can raise the intensity of competition.* By providing higher levels of service (Singapore Airlines), increasing advertising several-fold (Miller Brewing, Lotus), accelerating the rate of new product introductions (Sony in consumer electronics), or other tactical moves, firms can alter the tempo of competition. When this occurs, rivals who are lack financing or are not as nimble are left behind.
- *They can change the value/price ratio.* This is precisely what the Japanese did in so many markets and what Becton Dickinson did in hypodermic disposable syringes.

Change the Game Itself

Sometimes companies find it desirable to change the basic structure of the industry itself. For example, as we discussed earlier, when the industry is in late maturity, the leader may find it necessary to forcibly consolidate the industry. In other cases, a second or third player may find that changing the structure is the only way of overtaking the leader. These changes may be deliberate or, as often happens, they may be inadvertent. Some techniques include:

- *Introduce "new" technology.* A major discontinuous shift in the basic technology usually changes the make-up of an industry. But it does not always take a major technological innovation; industry structure can also be changed by marketing, logistical, or operational innovations. The Canon copier cartridge was an extension of the basic copier technology; because it changed the underlying economics of sales, distribution, and service support, it made a major change in the copier industry.

- *Consolidate channels.* This is the approach used by countless firms such as Blockbuster Video (described earlier), Toys R Us, Midas Muffler, American Hospital Supply, and others. Consolidation is particularly effective when an industry is fragmented and both buyers and suppliers are weak.

- *Consolidate the industry.* American Airlines's aggressive pricing and promotional tactics (1989–1990) appear to have had one aim: Consolidate the airline industry in order to keep price wars under control. Other examples are Motorola in discrete semiconductors (mentioned earlier) and Becton Dickinson in syringes.

Summary

In this chapter, we showed how managers can use the Structure-Position map, together with the knowledge of their company's leverage, to select their objectives and strategies and tactics. However, this framework is not intended to be applied mechanically, nor does it eliminate the manager's freedom of choice, that is, it is very decidedly not deterministic.[24] Nor does it reduce the need for managerial judgment. The chief value of our approach is that it helps managers identify and frame[25] the *right* issues, that is, it concentrates management attention on the areas of greatest concern and impact. Managerial skill and willingness to take calculated risks are still essential. Judgment is vital in determining which stage an industry is currently in and how rapidly it is evolving; in evaluating the firm's position relative to its competitors; and in assessing the likely risks and returns in altering the rules of the game, or even the game itself.

11

How Successful
New Products
Capitalize on Leverage

Managers must have an intimate, almost intuitive appreciation of their company's leverage when selecting new product tactics. Otherwise they will be severely handicapped when answering such questions as, "Upon which product/market areas should we concentrate our efforts? What *types* of new products and services should we be introducing? When? Should we support emerging industry standards, or should we challenge them? How should we use new products to strengthen our competitive position?"

Strategic leverage influences new product tactics through both maneuver and return. Different players' freedom to introduce products will vary depending on industry structure and their competitive position. For example, in the mainframe computers, IBM sets the standard. "Plug compatible" makers such as Amdahl and Fujitsu have little choice but to follow; given IBM's market position and the high cost to users of switching to a different make, plug compatible makers have little latitude to change product specifications. Their returns are also lower when compared with IBM.

Furthermore, a company's freedom to introduce new types of products and its returns for such introductions decrease as the underlying technology or product innovation evolves. IBM again provides an excellent illustration: In the mid-1980s, IBM could have set the standard for lap-top personal computers. Today, IBM must follow where Toshiba and Compaq lead; it has lost the initiative.

Understanding how leverage affects new product tactics and anticipating these shifts in leverage are therefore essential if managers are to successfully introduce the right products, at the right time, in the right position, and for the right price.

In this chapter, we show how companies can choose new product tactics that fully exploit their strategic leverage. We began by developing a tactical framework that uses two drivers, namely, technology or *innovation evolution* and *the diversity of customer needs*. With the help of these two factors, we show how new product choices change over time. Next, we examine new product tactics in the 16-bit personal computer industry to illustrate how this framework can be applied in practice. We then discuss the underlying rationale, that is, *why* the new product tactics suggested by our framework are the most appropriate for exploiting a company's strategic leverage. Finally, we analyze the implications for leaders, followers, and new entrants.

A Framework for New Product Tactics

The basic idea underlying our framework is that the manner in which new innovations evolve, in combination with the diversity of customer needs, makes one set of new product choices more likely to succeed than others.[1]

Innovation Evolution[2]

When we analyze successful product and service innovations, we find that they all evolve through the same pattern: an "emerging" or "gestation" period, a "growth" phase, a "maturity" phase, and finally, a "decline" phase (see Figure 11.1). The emerging phase is a period of indeterminate length during which the basic technological, infrastructural, or behavioral problems are solved. Until these basic issues are resolved, the innovation does not become widely accepted.[3] During the emerging phase, there are typically many, often small participants (low barriers to entry) with widely diverse product/service offerings, prices, and channels.

The emergence of a "dominant design"[4] triggers the growth phase of an innovation. The focus now shifts from product innovation to process innovation, while the market penetration of the innovation increases rapidly. Typically, technological changes peak in advance of market growth, which slows later. This phase is characterized by large numbers

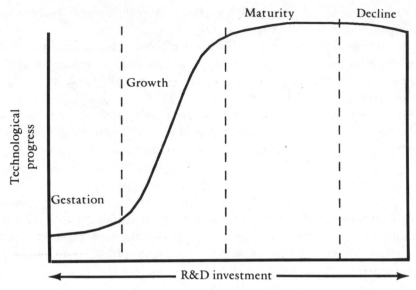

Figure 11.1   Phases of innovation evolution.

of entrants, especially in the early stages, and by extremely rapid market penetration.[5]

The maturity stage is typified by a slowing of market penetration and a consolidation in the number of suppliers. Returns on technological investments diminish rapidly, and there are no significant innovations regarding product/service features. Finally, decline sets in when the original innovation is superseded by a new innovation as, for example, when cotton tire cords were replaced successively by rayon, nylon, polyester, and steel.[6]

Understanding the stages of innovation evolution is important because the relative technological risks and costs change at each stage. For instance, in the emerging phase, the technological risks and costs of various different designs are similar; given that key technological or other issues have not yet been resolved, one design is as likely as another to emerge as the dominant design. Once there is a dominant design, however, the situation changes. The technological risks and costs of competing designs are now substantially higher, while the risks of products that work in conjunction with the dominant design are, relatively, much lower.[7]

Diversity of Customer Needs

New innovations diffuse through the market in distinct stages, with different groups of customers adopting an innovation at different times.[8]

There are different adopter categories, namely, innovators, early adopters, early majority, late majority, and laggards. Each has different user characteristics and requirements. Innovators are typically risk-oriented and will purchase even embryonic products; laggards are very slow to adopt new ideas and are likely to be price sensitive.[9]

These differences affect new product tactics because they determine (1) the relative attractiveness of a particular type of product to a given group of customers, and consequently, (2) the product's market potential, relative pricing, and likely penetration. Innovators, for example, typically form approximately 3 percent of the population but are not particularly price sensitive. Consequently, products aimed at this group have few restrictions on pricing, but their sales potential is quite small, especially when one considers the presence (at that stage of innovation evolution) of numerous competitors concentrating on the same market. Conversely, the early majority is a large group, approximately one-third of the total market. But their receptivity to innovations is lower; consequently, they are not likely to purchase innovations that are not compatible or consistent with the dominant design. This limits the market potential of competing designs once an industry standard emerges.

The Framework

We can now create the framework shown in Figure 11.2a. The Y-axis represents the individual product life cycle,[10] while the X-axis represents the various stages of innovation evolution. Note that we have omitted the emerging phase of innovation evolution. Given the various uncertainties, managers' choices are limited to either waiting until the environment stabilizes and a clear dominant design emerges or investing in the expectation that their products/innovations will become the dominant design.

Basic Heuristic.   To make this framework operational, we will concentrate on the *types* of product such as dominant designs, second standards, flankers, niche products, complements, second brands, and private labels, and how the sales growth rate of each type compares with the overall rate of innovation evolution, for example, the sales growth of flankers as compared with the rate at which the overall market for the innovation is growing. We can then fill in this framework if we recognize that the dominant design (and the second standard, if there is one) will grow, mature, and decline coincident with the innovation itself, and at each stage of innovation evolution, only those product introductions that can grow in the *next* stage are likely to be successful.

Innovation Evolution

		Growth	Maturity	Decline
Individual PLC	Introduction			
	Growing			
	Maturing			
	Declining			

Figure 11.2a   The basic framework.

The dominant design is the engine that drives the acceptance of the innovation in the marketplace; therefore, it must evolve in the same fashion as the market for the innovation itself. Similarly, the second standard, which is the alternative to the dominant design, also drives the growth of the innovation; therefore, it too must evolve in the same way as the total market (see Figure 11.2b). The second statement merely recognizes that product introductions that do not grow are considered failures.

The two statements together provide us with the basic heuristic or formula for completing the framework. If the dominant design evolves coincident with the innovation itself, the logical question regarding new product tactics is, "What types of new products should we be introducing as the dominant design is growing?" Our heuristic provides the answer: Products that will be growing when the sales of the dominant design slow down. We can determine the specific *types* of new products to introduce if we recognize that (1) initially, the dominant design will be purchased by the early adopters, (2) sales of the dominant design will start to slow as this category becomes saturated, and (3) the next adopter group, the early majority, being three times as large as the early adopters, will have more diverse needs, that is, they will want variations on the basic design. Thus, products that should be introduced when the dominant design is growing are flankers, niche

Innovation Evolution

		Growth	Maturity	Decline
	Introduction			
Individual PLC	Growing	Dominant design 2nd standard *High sales growth*		
	Maturing		Dominant design 2nd standard *Med. sales growth*	
	Declining			Dominant design 2nd standard *Low sales growth*

Figure 11.2b   How dominant designs evolve.

products, and complements—products that meet this diversity of needs[11] (see Figure 11.2c).

Similarly, when sales of the dominant design start to mature, the logical introductions are lower-priced products—second brands or private labels. As the dominant design (and the innovation) matures, any sales growth will likely occur in the last two adopter categories, namely, the late majority and the laggards. These groups are typically more price sensitive than earlier purchasers; thus, price-oriented product introductions are most likely to succeed (see Figure 11.2d).

Last, the answer to the question, "What types of products should we be introducing when the innovation enters the decline stage?" is "new" innovations. These can be aimed at extending the life of the current products/services, or they can be complete substitutes. As the current technology starts to reach its limits (and sometimes even before it reaches its limits), innovative users/customers will already be looking at new, alternative technologies or innovations to replace it. Therefore, rather than defend an indefensible status quo by spending more on R&D for the current innovation, firms should actively replace the current products with substitutes based on new technologies.[12]

The complete framework is shown in Figure 11.2e. To summarize, our framework suggests that new product tactics should change according to the following pattern:

Innovation Evolution

		Growth	Maturity	Decline
Individual PLC	Introduction	Flankers Niche products Complements *Low sales growth*		
	Growing	Dominant design 2nd standard *High sales growth*	Flankers Niche products Complements *High sales growth*	
	Maturing		Dominant design 2nd standard *Med. sales growth*	Flankers Niche products Complements *Med. sales growth*
	Declining			Dominant design 2nd standard *Low sales growth*

Figure 11.2c   What products should be introduced during the growth phase.

Innovation Evolution

		Growth	Maturity	Decline
Individual PLC	Introduction	Flankers Niche products Complements *Low sales growth*	2nd brands Private labels *Low sales growth*	
	Growing	Dominant design 2nd standard *High sales growth*	Flankers Niche products Complements *High sales growth*	2nd brands Private labels *High sales growth*
	Maturing		Dominant design 2nd standard *Med. sales growth*	Flankers Niche products Complements *Med. sales growth*
	Declining			Dominant design 2nd standard *Low sales growth*

Figure 11.2d   What products should be introduced during the maturity phase.

Innovation Evolution

		Growth	Maturity	Decline
	Introduction	Flankers Niche products Complements *Low sales growth*	2nd brands Private labels *Low sales growth*	New innovation
	Growing	Dominant design 2nd standard *High sales growth*	Flankers Niche products Complements *High sales growth*	2nd brands Private labels *High sales growth*
	Maturing		Dominant design 2nd standard *Med. sales growth*	Flankers Niche products Complements *Med. sales growth*
	Declining			Dominant design 2nd standard *Low sales growth*

Individual PLC

Figure 11.2e   The completed framework.

- During the innovation's growth phase, the emphasis should be on identifying the most likely and profitable product/market areas for introducing flankers, niche products, or complements.

- As the demand for the innovation starts to mature, the focus should shift to determining when and how to introduce lower-priced products—second brands or private labels.

- When the innovation enters the decline stage, the objective should be to identify how rapidly the decline might occur and determine which new innovations are likely to replace the current one.

Product introductions that are not consistent with this pattern are likely to be failures. In particular, this includes (1) products that fail to get accepted as dominant designs during the emerging phase of the innovation, (2) products introduced at the same time or after the dominant design that are not compatible with it, and (3) both premature and late introductions in other categories.

Before detailing our rationale, we will illustrate this framework by using it to analyze new product tactics in the 16-bit personal computer industry over the period 1981 to 1986.

The U.S. Personal Computer Industry

The U.S. personal computer industry grew extremely rapidly from 1981 to 1986. In 1981, approximately 1.5 million PCs were in use; by 1986, this had increased to more than 25 million. Industry shipments were averaging six million units a year, with total industry revenues exceeding $15 billion per year.[13]

   IBM was the major driving force in this industry; indeed, in the opinion of many industry analysts ". . . (T)he PC built the personal computer business."[14] IBM introduced the original IBM PC in August 1981. This was followed by the launch of the PC-XT in 1983 and the PC-AT in 1984. Shipments skyrocketed, from less than one million units in 1981 to an annual rate of six million units in 1983 where they stabilized (see Figure 11.3).

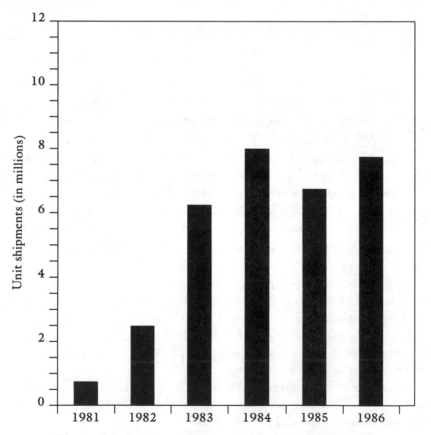

Figure 11.3 Personal computer industry shipments.

Innovation Evolution.   We can divide the time period into a *growth* phase lasting from 1981 through late 1983-early 1984, a *maturity* phase from 1984 to late 1985, and a *decline* phase thereafter. The operating systems and other technological features stayed essentially the same throughout this period, with the exception of computing speeds, which increased from the PC/PC-XT to the PC-AT.

The *dominant design* was the IBM PC with two floppy disk drives. This was the first model introduced in 1981 and accounted for the majority of PCs sold until late 1984–1985. The earlier versions had relatively small memories, while later units were shipped with 256 kilobytes of memory as standard. The IBM PC's sales growth paralleled the industry's during the growth and early maturity phases; however, in later years IBM's sales dropped faster than industry sales due to growing competition from lower-priced imports or "clones." Very rapidly, the IBM PC became the standard; with the sole exception of Apple, the previous industry leader, other manufacturers redesigned their equipment to be compatible with IBM or, failing that, they ceased making PCs altogether, for example, Digital Equipment Corporation.

Having defined the three stages of innovation evolution and identified the dominant design, we can now use our framework to predict the timing and growth rates of successful new product introductions and compare these predictions with what actually occurred. The results are summarized in Table 11.1:

Table 11.1   Summary of predictions vs. actual events—PC industry.

		Innovation Evolution		
		Growth	Maturity	Decline
Individual PLC	Introduction	PC—AT ('84) PC—AT ('83) COMPAQ ('83) ZENITH ('82)	Clones ('84)	Macintosh Plus ('86–'87) OS/2 ('88)
	Growing	Dominant design IBM PC (2 drive '82–'84)		
	Maturing		Late '84–late '85	
	Declining	Lisa ('84)		Terminated in '87

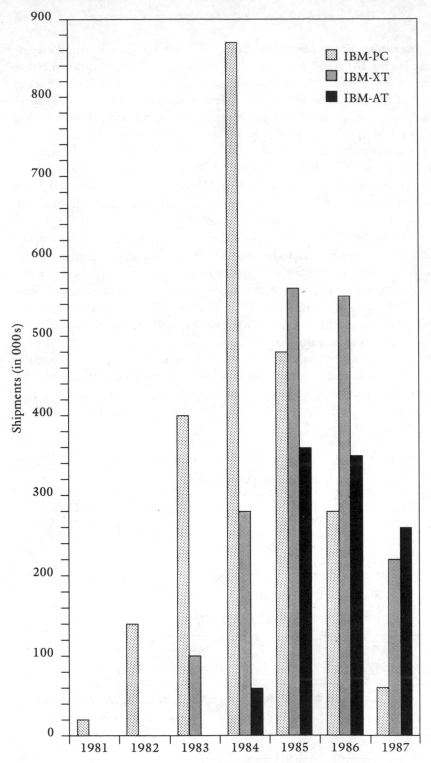

Figure 11.4a   Growth rates of XT and AT vs. basic PC.

- *Flankers*—products providing more capabilities or performance than the basic PC—should have been introduced in the period from 1981 to early 1984. Further, their sales should have grown from 1984 to late 1985-early 1986, when basic PC sales were maturing. This is exactly what occurred with the PC-XT and the PC-AT. They were introduced in 1983 and early 1984, respectively, and their sales grew from 1985 to early 1987 (see Figure 11.4a).

- *Complements* such as hard disk drives, modems, application software, and other accessories should also have been introduced in the growth stage (1981 to early 1984), and their sales should have been growing from 1984 to late 1985-early 1986. This is confirmed by the sales growth patterns of two important complements—hard disk drives and word-processing software (see Figure 11.4b).

- *Niche products* should have been identified and introduced during the middle and late growth stages (1982–1984) and should have been growing while the sales of the basic PC were maturing. Zenith introduced its products, targeted for educational and government purchasers in late 1982, and their sales grew at the rate of 64 percent per annum over the period 1983–1986. Compaq similarly introduced its portables—the Compaq, Compaq +, and Deskpro—in 1983 and their sales grew rapidly, from 53,000 units sold in 1983 to nearly 200,000 units in 1985.[15]

- *Second brands/complements* should have appeared in the mid-1980s, as basic PC sales were slowing down and should have grown rapidly in 1985–1986. Clones—machines compatible with the PC but priced lower—were introduced in 1984 and went from less than 10 percent of the market in early 1985 to more than a third of the market by mid-1986.[16]

- *New innovations* should have been evident by late 1986. By 1990 it was clear that the Apple Macintosh and its look-alikes (OS/2, Microsoft's Windows 3.0, Presentation Manager, Hewlett-Packard's New Wave) were the innovations replacing the earlier 16-bit, MS-DOS based PCs. For example, the Apple Macintosh, which was introduced in 1984, really took off in 1986 (with the appearance of the Plus), with 1987 sales of almost half a million units.[17]

In terms of our product evolution framework, these various product introductions are shown in Figure 11.5. Our framework also helps explain why certain firms succeeded in this industry while others did not. Specifically, we will use it to analyze the strategies of the following firms: IBM itself, AT&T, Digital Equipment Corporation (DEC), Texas Instruments, Compaq, Zenith, and Apple Computer.[18]

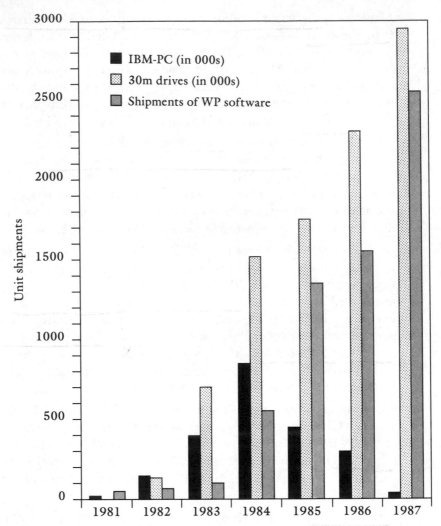

Figure 11.4b   Growth rates of hard disk drives, word-processing software and IBM-PCs.

IBM's product strategy in the growth and early maturity phases was virtually faultless. It concentrated its development resources on flanker products to maintain its control over the market. It also used third-party providers skillfully to control the evolution of complements. However, IBM failed to meet the need for a lower-priced product either through a "second brand" or private labels. This allowed the clones to first enter and, later, control the market.[19]

Based on our framework, the other (major) players' choices were either to (1) establish an alternative or "second standard," (2) embrace the IBM

	Growth	Maturity	Decline
Introduction	IBM-XT (1983) IBM-AT (1984) Zenith* (1983) Compaq* (1983) 30 M drives (1982–83)	Clones (1984)	Macintosh Plus
Growth	IBM-PC (1981–83)	IBM-XT (1984–85) IBM-AT Zenith Compaq* (1984–85) 30 M drives (1984–87)	
Maturity		IBM-PC (1984–85)	IBM-XT IBM-AT (1985–86) Zenith (1985–86) Compaq* (1985–86) 30 M drives (1986–87)
Decline			IBM-PC (1985–87)

* 16-bit processor models only

Figure 11.5   How 16-bit/MS-DOS PCs evolved over time.

PC design and compete head-on with IBM across the board, possibly as a "credible alternative," or (3) identify emerging product/market niches early on and concentrate on them. The first alternative, creating a "second standard" would require substantial investments with little likelihood of correspondingly high returns, especially in the growth and early maturity phases.[20] Competing head-on with IBM using a compatible design, while safer technologically, would require sizable financial and marketing resources. Finally, seeking out and concentrating on product/market niches that have not yet been "occupied" by IBM would most likely provide higher returns than competing with IBM for a slice of the main market; however, the technological and, to some extent, the marketing risks would be higher.

Viewed in this light, we must conclude that neither DEC nor AT&T used this strategy. DEC apparently tried to establish its designs (the "Rainbow") and operating systems as the standard or dominant design. The firm was, in many respects, ideally positioned to do just that; it had the credentials in smaller computers and among an important group of early users—engineers and scientists.[21] But it was slow to respond, not introducing its answer to the IBM PC for more than 10 months—May 1982 versus August 1981—and seriously underfunding its entry. Once these efforts failed, DEC essentially abandoned the PC market.

AT&T tried simultaneously to establish a new standard and position itself as a (compatible) credible alternative to IBM. The first attempt (based on the UNIX PC and the 6300 Plus) failed in the same fashion and for the same reason as DEC's; neither manufacturer could convince enough customers of the superiority of their respective designs. AT&T could have successfully positioned itself as the "credible alternative," especially because key channel members such as Computerland wanted a second source to reduce their dependence on IBM. However, AT&T's initial efforts along these lines were tentative, and by the time it committed sizable resources, Compaq was already established as the dealers' (and corporate buyers') preferred alternative to IBM.[22]

Texas Instruments (TI) was one of the early entrants into the PC market. Initially, TI had its own designs, like DEC; unlike DEC, it quickly shifted to a compatible design. However, TI made no other changes to its strategy; it made no visible efforts to identify and capture product/market niches. As a result, TI's positioning was weak, and it never made much headway in the market.

These three firms' failures in product tactics were repeated by many incumbents and entrants.[23] Zenith and Compaq, by contrast, succeeded because (1) they correctly identified the IBM PC as the dominant design, (2) they avoided competing with IBM for a portion of the main market, and (3) they focused their efforts on finding suitable product/market niches ahead of the competition.[24] Zenith recognized early on that (1) its own (CP/M-based) designs would not be competitive, (2) it did not have the financial or marketing resources to compete head-on with IBM, and (3) there would be demand from institutional buyers—government, defense, and educational institutions—for a credible supplier of compatible machines at prices lower than IBM. Further, this niche would be defensible only if it moved first and fast to develop suitable products and organized its salesforces and prices appropriately. On the other hand, Compaq was founded on the needs of a niche market, namely, users who wanted a degree of portability. Once Compaq established itself in this niche, it built on its strengths by producing what were essentially "upmarket clones," that is, PCs with more features and/or performance than offered by IBM, at comparable prices.

Apple Computer's experiences demonstrate the risks—and rewards—of establishing an alternative to the dominant design, as well as the importance of timing. The Apple II had been the dominant design among eight-bit microcomputers. Thus, when IBM introduced the PC,

Apple's choices were either to create a different, competing standard or produce compatible designs.

Apple first tried to enter the corporate/office market, hitherto IBM territory, with the Apple III, which was introduced in May 1980 and reintroduced in December 1981 (four months after the announcement of the PC).[25] The Apple III failed to establish itself because of reliability problems and lack of software.

Apple's next attempt to counter IBM was the Lisa, introduced in March 1983. While the Lisa attracted considerable attention, commercially it was a disaster; fewer than 20,000 Lisas were sold by the fall of 1983, and Apple's total losses on the Lisa approached $40 million. Largely as a result, Apple's stock price fell from a high of $63 to $17 per share.

Apple finally succeeded with the Macintosh, introduced in January 1984. Two aspects of the Macintosh deserve special attention: First, Apple established the University Consortium, a group of educational institutions that agreed to endorse/adopt the new machine in return for very substantial (50 percent in some cases) discounts. Second, the Macintosh did not start to make noticeable inroads into the corporate market until 1986. The University Consortium was vital to Apple because it created an installed base that, in turn, attracted the software developers and peripherals manufacturers that were essential if the Macintosh was to achieve wider commercial acceptance. In economic terms, Apple changed the "network benefits" of the PC by (1) targeting educational users who were less dependent on such network benefits (they could, and did, write their own software) and (2) changing the social and private incentives facing would-be adopters deciding between the IBM PC and the Macintosh.[26]

The reason why the Macintosh did not make noticeable inroads into the corporate and office markets until 1986 (with the introduction of the Macintosh Plus) is best understood in terms of our framework: The PC market was not ripe for a new innovation until the first innovation—the IBM PC—had matured and started to decline, that is, well into late 1985–1987. In our opinion, this fact, more than any other explanation such as the higher capabilities of the Macintosh Plus, greater availability of software, and so on, explains the Macintosh success.[27]

In financial terms, Apple has profited handsomely from its gamble to establish a different standard. In the past several years, Apple's gross profit margins and overall profitability have been higher than many other participants (see Table 11.2). What is more, Apple also appears to be gaining share in the corporate and office markets. Finally, the Macintosh approach to personal computers—icons, pull-down menus, a

Table 11.2　Gross margin comparison for Compaq and Apple.

	1989	1988	1987	1986	1985
Compaq					
Income	2876	2065	1224	625	503
Expense	1715	1233	717	360	325
Gross Margin	40%	40%	41%	42%	35%
Apple					
Income	5284	4071	2661	1901	1918
Expense	2589	2080	1364	1010	800
Gross Margin	51%	49%	49%	47%	58%

"mouse," and so forth—is becoming the de facto standard within the industry, with other participants trying to emulate it in different ways.[28]

Rationale: Capitalize on Leverage

Our basic contention is that, at each stage of innovation evolution, the product tactics described in the framework are the ones most likely to exploit a company's leverage to the fullest.

Our argument runs as follows: As innovations evolve, the likely returns of various new product tactics change. These changes in turn limit a company's strategic leverage and concentrate it among a few choices. The new product tactics suggested here most fully capitalize on a company's leverage and its expected return adjusted for risks. Other tactics either do not take full advantage of the returns and leverage available, or worse, they pursue alternatives virtually certain to fail.

The cumulative sales of an innovation grow, mature, and eventually flatten out (decline) in the S-shaped pattern shown in Figure 11.6. Further, the dominant design will account for a portion of the total sales and, by virtue of being the dominant design, these sales will also follow the overall S-shaped pattern (see the shaded area in Figure 11.6).

Thus, once the dominant design emerges, other participants and prospective entrants have choice of competing with the dominant design for a portion of *its* total lifetime sales, that is, trying to capture a portion of the shaded area in Figure 11.6; or identifying/anticipating emerging opportunities, that is, aiming at the unshaded area in Figure 11.6. However the market and technological risks, and therefore the likely returns, of these two alternatives are very different.

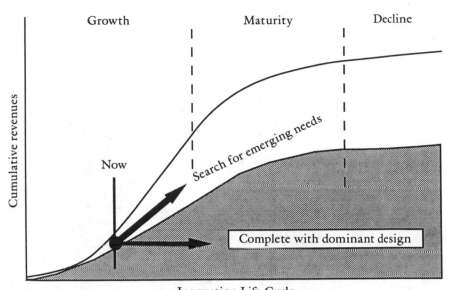

Figure 11.6   Product choices during the growth stage.

Risks.   Typically, the expected market for the dominant design and its direct competitors—the shaded area in Figure 11.6—is larger than the expected market size for flankers, niche products, and complements (the unshaded area in Figure 11.7). Further, the uncertainty surrounding the expected market for flankers, and so on, is higher as compared with the expected market for the dominant design. However, competition in the shaded area is likely to be high, whereas (especially in the early growth stages) competition for producing flankers or niche products is likely to be much less intense.

The technological risks and relative cost positions are also different in the two areas. In the segment served by the dominant design, the technological risks are low for emulators, firms offering compatible products. But for companies determined to establish a second standard, the technological risks are high. In the unshaded area where needs are emerging, the technological risks vary depending on the specific products. They are low for simple complements (for example, keyboards and accessories, in the case of the PC) and moderate to high for specialty or niche products (for example, the Compaq portable).

The relative cost positions and expected margins are also different. Firms competing with the dominant design will, in all probability, have

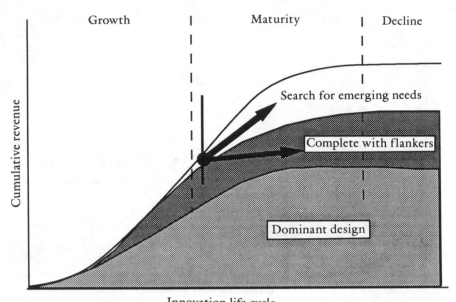

Figure 11.7   Product choices during the maturity stage.

higher relative costs, particularly if there are (1) patents and/or (2) experience curve effects.[29] Firms producing flankers, niche products, or complements have no such disadvantages. They also have fewer price disadvantages, especially for niche products and complements; in fact, in some cases they may even be able to charge a premium price for customers with specialized needs, for example, firms producing "ruggedized" PCs for special industrial or hazardous environments.

Finally, firms producing flankers, niche products, or complements may obtain the advantages of first entrants or pioneers. By definition, competitors to the dominant design have no such advantages; their freedom of maneuver is limited because they are reacting to moves by the standard setter (see Table 11.3).

In summary, should a firm choose to compete in the shaded area by emulating the dominant design or creating a second standard, it is likely to have many competitors, its costs will be higher and its margins lower than those of the dominant design, and it does not have the advantage of being first. Further, the firm trying to create a second standard faces the added disadvantage of user inertia. The second standard's technology must be compellingly better than the dominant design to induce new users to choose its offerings over the many advantages (for example, large software base, user experience) enjoyed by buyers of the dominant design.

Table 11.3 Opportunities and risks—niche players versus emulators.

	Niche Player	Emulator
Expected Market Size	Small	Large
Market Uncertainty	Medium—high	Low—medium
Likely Competitors	Few	Many
Technological Uncertainty	Low—emulators High—2nd standard	Varies
Relative Cost Position	—	Higher than dominant design
Relative Price Position	—	Lower than dominant design
First Entry Advantages	Feasible	Not possible

Returns.   Under these conditions, we must conclude that the returns are likely to be higher in the unshaded area (flankers, niche products, and so on) than in the shaded area unless

- The expected market for the dominant design is much larger than that for flankers, niche products, and so on (i.e., the unshaded area is small relative to the shaded area); or
- The limited capacity of the firm producing the dominant design enables other firms to capture at least the minimum market share needed for economic production; or
- There is considerable uncertainty about which flanker, niche, or complement needs will emerge and when they will emerge.

The choice will also be affected by the degree to which the firm is risk averse. The more risk averse a company, the more likely it is to prefer a safe (even if lower) return. For this reason, it may try to compete with the dominant design for a share of its market.

An Alternative Approach

We come to the same conclusion if we analyze the expected return on assets for the two alternatives shown in Figure 11.6a. Note that return on assets (ROA) is defined as[30]

$$\text{ROA} = \frac{\text{Net profit}}{\text{Assets}} = \frac{\text{Net profit}}{\text{Sales}} \times \frac{\text{Sales}}{\text{Assets}}$$

We can compare the returns of emulators to those of niche players as follows: Let us denote the various quantities by the subscripts "np" for niche player and "em" for emulator. Then we have

$$(ROA)_{np} = (Net\ profit/Assets)_{np}; (ROA)_{em} = (Net\ Profit/Assets)_{em}$$

The ratio of these two returns is $(ROA)_{np}/(ROA)_{em}$ which can be expressed as

$$m/n \times \frac{(Net\ Sales)_{np}}{(Net\ Sales)_{em}}$$

where m = ratio of margins and n = ratio of net assets.

If the returns for niche players (the unshaded area in Figure 11.6a) are higher than those for emulators, then $(ROA)_{np}/(ROA)_{em} > 1$ or

$$(NS)_{np} > (n/m) \times (NS)_{em}; n > 0\ and\ m > 0.$$

We can formally write this ratio in terms of the expected sales as

$$E(NS)_{np} > E(n/m) \times E(NS)_{em}$$

The ratio (n/m) compares the ratio of assets required by the alternatives to the relative margins. Very often, the net asset requirements for niche products are lower than for emulators and, as we discussed earlier, the margins of niche products are higher than those of emulators. Under these conditions, *niche players will have higher returns than emulators,* unless the expected sales of the niche product are very low (because the niche was too small) or the expected sales of the emulator are very high (because the firm is exceptionally well positioned).

Maturity to Decline

Similar arguments hold as the innovation evolution moves from maturity into decline. As shown in Figure 11.7, the choice is either to compete with existing suppliers of the dominant design or firms producing flankers, niche products, and so on, or to focus on emerging market needs, in this case for a lower-priced product. The market sizes of the new segments are smaller, however, the intensity of competition is likely to be lower, at least initially. While prices of second brands/private labels will be lower than those of main-line products, their relative production and marketing costs are also likely to be lower. With the innovation mature and technological change virtually nonexistent, there will be little difference in basic product costs, while manufacturers of private-label or "clone" brands typically have much lower manufacturing overheads and R&D costs. Marketing costs will also be lower because these products will be sold through low value-added channels, with corresponding savings in distribution and related sales costs. (We discuss these changes in channel roles in greater detail in Chapter 13.)

Implications for Individual Players

Thus far, we have analyzed overall product tactics without considering how they might differ for different players within an industry. We will now examine how strategy choices—differentiation, cost leadership, or focus—and competitive position—leader, follower, or new entrant—affect new product choices.

Leaders

During the growth phase of an innovation, the objectives for differentiated leaders must be to (1) maintain differentiation, and (2) achieve market control. For these reasons, such firms must concentrate on *flankers* and *key complements*. Flankers are essential to provide a broad product line. Key complements such as spare parts, critical accessories (in the case of PCs, systems and utility software), and important application programs such as word processing are also crucial to maintaining differentiation. Niches should receive lower priority, even if they are likely to be highly profitable, in order to concentrate resources on achieving the overall strategic goal of differentiation. The only exceptions to this are niches that could emerge as major segments in the future, for example, laptops in the PC industry.

The differentiated leader's new product choices become particularly difficult as the innovation matures and enters the decline phase. At this point, a firm must choose between either introducing second brands or concentrating its resources on identifying and participating in the new innovation.[31] Either choice is risky. Second brands take revenues and profits away from the main brand; however, the alternative (not introducing them) is to watch the revenues accrue to competitors. Second brands divert resources from efforts to discover the next innovation. What is more, timing is crucial. If a firm focuses its resources on creating the next innovation too early, it could lose valuable revenues and share during the long gestation period. Further, it is taking the risk that it will be successful (again) in creating the dominant design.[32] However, if the leader tries to extend the life of the innovation beyond a certain point, it risks losing its dominant position to a new innovation created by a new entrant (or occasionally a competitor).

During the growth phase, firms following the cost leadership strategy must choose between new product investments to establish/maintain market control and process investments to lower product costs. The implications are (1) fewer flankers and (2) the bare minimum of complements. Niches should be avoided; note that a cost leadership strategy requires ". . . aggressive construction of efficient-scale facilities (and) . . . avoidance of marginal customer accounts."[33] Niches requiring special products and/or specific marketing efforts are counter to this entire philosophy. As the innovation enters the decline phase, the cost leader's choices are similar to the differentiated firm's—introduce second (that is, lower-priced) brands or invest resources in creating the new innovation.

Followers and Entrants

Followers should concentrate on identifying emerging opportunities during the growth and maturity phases. Especially during the innovation growth phase, followers should use new product tactics to (1) create defensible niches (for example, through specialized complements and adaptations to suit specific segment needs) or (2) enhance their value to would-be purchasers such as the dominant design manufacturer.[34]

During the growth phase, entrants can (1) attack the dominant design with an alternative standard, (2) produce products that are compatible with the dominant design, or (3) introduce flankers, niche products, or complements. Opportunistic entrants (see Chapter 7) have few or no restrictions on their choices, other than likely returns and risks. Firms entering the market for competitive reasons, such as the need to protect their positions in related markets, must endeavor to replace the dominant design with their own designs. If that is too difficult—if the dominant design is too well-established—then they should introduce compatible products that compete either on price or features. Price competition may be less effective during the growth phase of the innovation as buyers are less aware of, and sensitive to, price differentials. Consequently, we believe that competitive entrants should concentrate on feature-based competition, changing the price/performance ratio in their favor. As the innovation matures and starts to decline, entrants should be introducing "clones"—products compatible with the main design but significantly cheaper.[35]

Summary

Our framework shows the vital role played by leverage in new product tactics. Leverage is particularly important in "high-tech" industries. In such cases, rapid technological change coupled with typical product development cycles virtually ensure that "emulators" will always lag far behind. Only by understanding the factors affecting leverage and how they will change as the technology and market needs evolve can a company anticipate and exploit new product opportunities.

12

How Strategic Leverage Influences Product Tactics

AREA POSITIONING
TARGET MARKET

Product tactics such as the timing of a new product entry, brand extension, creation of a second brand, bundling a product (or service) and its accessories/complements, and so on, play a major role in achieving a company's objectives and strategies. Which tactic will be most effective depends heavily on the nature of industry payoffs and the company's strategic leverage. Being "second but better" in introducing new product or service innovations might be the best tactic for the leader in a mature, concentrated industry. But the same tactic could be disastrous for a follower. Further, a "second but better" approach would be doomed to failure, regardless of the position of the firm, in a rapidly growing market where technological leadership changes daily.

We will begin our analysis of the relationships between these tactical issues, industry payoffs and strategic leverage, by considering a specific situation in the U.S. large appliance market. This example provides considerable insight into the decision, "Should we move first or should we wait in entering a new market segment?" In addition, it provides a "model" for discussing other product tactics such as brand extensions versus second brands, the role of complementary products, and the bundling of products and services.

The "Aging" Market in the United States:
GE versus Whirlpool[1]

In the mid-1980s, product planners at each of the leading U.S. large appliance manufacturers were asking, "Should we be the first to introduce a product line specifically tailored for the emerging "aging" market, that is, the segment composed of buyers 55 years of age and older? Or would it be preferable to wait and see if there really *is* such a market before making sizable investments in product development and tooling?" Proponents of early entry argued that the elderly would be a major segment in the late 1980s and 1990s, with considerable purchasing power and special needs such as easier-to-use controls, smaller capacities, and more features. Thus, their contention was that the first firm to make a product line designed specifically to meet these needs would be well set to capture a commanding share of the aging market.

Opponents of early entry pointed out that the information regarding the purchasing power of this segment was, at best, mixed[2] and that even if the elderly had money, there was no guarantee that they would spend it on special appliances. Further, it was not clear whether their needs were unique; different market research results contradicted one another. Viewed in this light, the "aging" segment offered uncertain returns while requiring substantial investments in product design and manufacturing equipment.

Background

U.S. suppliers of large appliances—clothes washers and dryers, dishwashers, cooking ranges/ovens, and refrigerators—included four full-line manufacturers, namely, General Electric (GE), Whirlpool Corporation (Whirlpool), White Consolidated Industries (WCI), and Maytag Company (Maytag), together with specialty makers such as Speed Queen, KitchenAid, Revco, and Fedders.[3] Total U.S. sales of large appliances in 1982 were $8.2 billion. The market was mature and sales were cyclical; industry shipments had declined steadily in the mid-1970s and had recovered only recently.

There were two main segments in the market, served by very different channels. Appliances installed in new homes accounted for 25 percent of total industry sales. This segment was highly cyclical, with sales rising and falling in concert with new home starts. Manufacturers sold their products directly to approximately 80,000 to 100,000 builders. These sales were typically on a contract basis, and buyers tended to be price sensitive with little brand loyalty.

The other major segment was replacement sales. The typical U.S. household purchased 2.5 sets of large appliances—washers, dryers, refrigerators, and cooking ranges—over its lifetime. These replacement sales accounted for 75 percent of the total market. The main channels of distribution were mass merchandisers such as Sears, J.C. Penney, and Wards, department stores, discount outlets such as Kmart, Caldors, Korvette's, and appliance dealers of all sizes. There was considerable brand loyalty among buyers, who did not appear to be overly price sensitive within a particular price range.

GE and Whirlpool were the industry leaders in both share and pricing, with revenues in 1982 of $2.2 billion and $1.8 billion, respectively. WCI was third, with annual revenues of $1.3 billion, while Maytag had revenues of $600 million (see Figure 12.1). GE, Whirlpool, and Maytag followed differentiation strategies, whereas WCI's approach was overall cost leadership. Other, smaller manufacturers followed a variety of focus strategies, for example, KitchenAid concentrated on high-end appliances, Speed Queen on laundromats, and so forth. The industry had undergone several phases of consolidation, most recently with WCI's purchase of appliance divisions of all the automobile manufacturers and of Westinghouse's appliance operations.[4] After a period of steady growth in the late 1970s, sales had declined by 17 percent in 1981 and 1982 leaving few opportunities for increasing share except through acquisitions. Partly as a result, price competition was intensifying, especially in the builder market.

Analysis of Company Market Share by Product Category							
Companies	Product	1982	1981	1980	1979	1978	1977
				Percent			
Whirlpool	Washers	41	40	40	40	40	45
	Dryers (E)	40	40	40	40	40	40
	Dryers (G)	40	40	40	40	40	40
GE/Hotpoint	Washers	20	20	20	20	20	20
	Dryers (E)	20	20	20	20	20	20
	Dryers (G)	15	15	15	15	15	15
Maytag	Washers	15	15	15	15	15	15
	Dryers (E)	15	15	15	15	15	15
	Dryers (G)	15	15	15	15	15	15

Joseph L. Bower and Nass Dossabhoy, "Note on the Major Home Appliance Industry." Boston: Harvard Business School, case 385-044. Copyright © 1984 by the President and Fellows of Harvard College. Reprinted by permission.

Figure 12.1 Summary of company revenue and industry statistics.

The Aging Market

The combination of low overall industry growth, increasing price competition, and the high degree of brand loyalty in the replacement market had led to increased industry interest in exploring potential product/ market niches. One niche of particular interest was the aging market, consisting of purchasers over 55 years of age.

The combination of continually decreasing family sizes, the end of the postwar baby boom, and increased longevity due to improved medical care meant that the median age of the U.S. population was increasing and that the aging market would soon become the fastest-growing consumer segment.[5] By most estimates, this segment contained 45.5 million consumers and would grow at the rate of 21 percent per year (see Figure 12.2). Furthermore, the median incomes of the aging would be substantially higher than in the past, thanks in large part to inflation-indexed social security payments and rising real estate prices. Disposable income, in particular, was projected to grow rapidly, due to increasing incomes and lower expenses. These changes were accompanied by significant changes in lifestyles. Better health meant that they would be more active, and increased income enabled them to spend more on such things as travel, clothing, accessories, and appliances.

The last possibility had naturally stimulated the interest of the major appliance makers. GE and Whirlpool had both conducted various surveys to study the aging to determine any unique needs regarding product features, capacities, or performance. The results of these studied appeared, at best, to be mixed. For example, initially market researchers and designers believed that this market would require appliances with easy-to-read controls, oversized knobs, and other features to help better cope with the infirmities of age. But by and large, this market rejected such designs in favor of "high tech" features and appearance.

While neither firm had committed itself to producing a line of appliances specially geared for the aging, both companies had carried out engineering studies to estimate the likely investments in product redesign and tooling. Preliminary figures indicated that producing a complete line of appliances for this segment would require an investment of the order of $25 million by each firm. This figure covered only additional tooling and product R&D; the products would use the same plants and distribution channels.

Key Issues

There was considerable controversy within the industry and within the major firms about product strategies for this potential market segment.

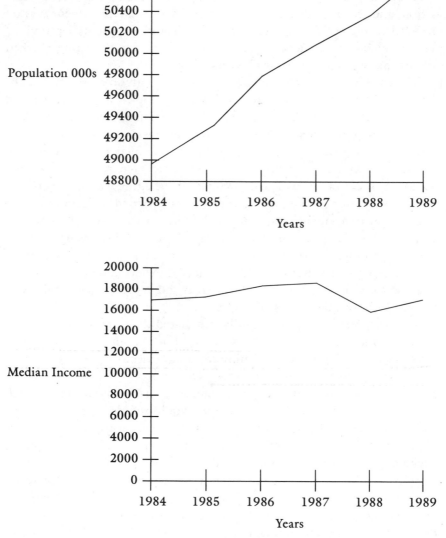

Figure 12.2 The aging segment (55+)—population and income growth.

The different arguments—and their underlying concerns—could be summarized as follows:

- Did the aging have unique needs and would consumers in this segment replace their existing appliances with new products meeting these needs?

- What types of appliances would they purchase, that is, specially designed, easy-to-use or high-tech, high-touch appliances, or up-scale models with some features to assist the aging?
- What were the costs and risks in entering or passing up this segment, both the financial costs as well as likely opportunity costs?

The question of costs and risks was obviously of great concern to all participants. The costs incurred in introducing a product line with special features for the aging were relatively easy to determine; estimates ranged between $20 million and $30 million, depending on what assumptions were made regarding the likely annual volume, selling prices, and initial investments in design and tooling.

The opportunity costs of *not* producing such a line were considerably harder to define. Briefly, they depended on whether the aging market indeed materialized and, if so, which of the other participants was producing a line of products tailored to this segment's needs. For many reasons, this came down to a contest between GE and Whirlpool. The general feeling was that Maytag and WCI would probably opt out of this segment, although for different reasons, while the smaller players did not pose a significant threat—GE and/or Whirlpool could easily acquire them or use their own superior marketing resources and market position to push them aside. For either GE or Whirlpool, the opportunity costs could potentially be high, especially if failure to introduce such a line of products led to reductions in their respective market shares. Some analysts placed the potential long-term share losses as high as five percentage points; given total company sales of $2 billion, this represented a revenue loss of over $100 million. This was considered rather high; more conservative estimates indicated that the price of late entry could be between two and three share points, or between $40 million and $60 million in 1982 revenues.

Analyzing the Choices

We summarized the choices faced by GE and Whirlpool in Figure 12.3. For simplicity, each firm is assumed to have two choices—to produce a line of products for the aging or not to produce such a line. The outcomes then depend on whether there is, or is not, a market among the aging for such special products.

Let us consider the alternatives from GE's perspective.[6] If GE enters the market while Whirlpool does not, GE could gain as much as $100 million in additional revenue and five points in share, *provided the aging market exists* (indicated by Y in the diagram). If there is no real market for

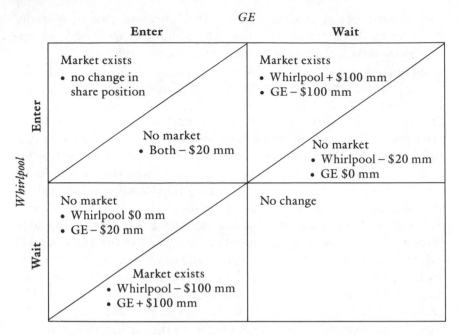

Figure 12.3   GE versus Whirlpool—the payoff matrix.

these special products and they have to be abandoned, GE loses $20 million out of pocket (pretax). Conversely, if GE elects not to produce these products while Whirlpool does produce them, the situation is reversed; if the market exists, GE stands to lose three to five points of market share and corresponding revenues, whereas if the market does not exist, Whirlpool loses $20 million out-of-pocket (pretax), but GE has no tangible monetary benefits.

Let us see what happens if GE and Whirlpool both decide to produce special products for the aging. Assuming for simplicity's sake that they both produce similar types of products, then they both share the revenues of the aging market if it exists, and they have similar losses if there is no real market for these products. Conversely, if they both elect *not* to produce such products, there are no gains or losses. In either case, the net share position stays the same; neither firm gains on the other.

Given these payoffs, GE has every incentive to cater to the aging market if it has the slightest inkling that Whirlpool may do so as well. In other words, GE stands to lose more by *not* producing such a special product line, *even if it believes that there is no real market,*, than it stands to gain by abstaining.[7] The reasoning is as follows: If there is even a moderate chance that there is a market for such appliances, the expected losses in market share and revenues due to not participating outweigh the likely losses if the market fails to materialize. The same also holds for Whirlpool; it, too, is better off developing special products for the aging than risking the possibility that GE might gain share by outflanking it.[8, 9]

Thus, in this industry, the major players' product tactics were restricted by the competitive situation and the fact that industry conflict was stalemated. Consequently, product-related decisions cannot be examined in isolation; managers must analyze the impact of industry structure and likely competitive reactions before choosing specific tactics. Given the investments and risks involved, they may also want to use market signals, as discussed in Chapter 9, to minimize preemptive moves by either party. However, market signals may not be effective in such a situation especially if the projected share gains are large, in which case the incentives to cheat on any tacit or implied agreement would be irresistible.

Finally, note that we could use the same rationale and come to similar conclusions regarding other tactical issues such as product-line extension and bundling. In other words, given the degree of concentration in the U.S. large appliance industry, its cost structure, and the low overall growth rate, any moves by one of the major players regarding bundling or product-line extension must be immediately matched by the others.

Implications for Product Tactics

The appliance industry situation described above also provides a useful framework for analyzing, more generally, how different industry forces affect product tactics. Specifically, we can use this example to determine how the nature of the payoffs, industry structure, cost characteristics, and overall industry growth affect maneuver and returns and how these two factors, in turn, affect product tactics.

To understand how these different forces affect product tactics, we must recognize that GE's (and Whirlpool's) choices were limited because of the asymmetrical nature of the payoffs; the expected returns (or losses), adjusted for risks, were overwhelmingly in favor of one alternative, making tactical choices obvious. These asymmetrical returns were the result of

- The nature of industry payoffs
- Industry concentration
- Industry cost characteristics
- Overall industry growth rate.

In this example, all four factors combined to create extremely lopsided payoffs. In more typical situations, one or two factors are of primary importance, with the remainder having little or no influence.

The Nature of the Payoffs.   If industry conflict is win/lose or lose/lose, then payoffs may be skewed; the risks of not being first to enter a new product/market segment tend to outweigh the likely costs, other things being equal. If there is very little conflict within the industry—a win/win case—then managers have much more freedom when deciding tactics. Finally, in industries where conflict is limited, it is hard to determine the exact impact on the payoffs.

Industry Concentration.   The greater the concentration within an industry, the more likely that it will skew the returns. In terms of the travel agency examples discussed in Chapter 2, the large corporate travel agency does not have much flexibility regarding first entry, product-line width, or bundling of products and services. It must match the moves of key competitors or risk a possibly irretrievable loss of share. The small, local travel agency can do what it pleases, within general industry norms.

Industry Cost Structure.   As we might expect, industry costs and margins have a significant influence. Firms in industries with high (in relation to total costs) fixed costs or storage are often forced to emulate competitors' moves as the alternative (abstaining) is often too expensive. The large appliance industry described above is one example; another is the airline industry's response to changes such as new fares, seating arrangements, or other service offerings introduced by a major player.

Overall Industry Growth Rate.   When the industry is growing rapidly, there is usually considerable uncertainty about the likely technological feasibility and market success of different product tactics. Consequently, the expected payoffs, adjusted for these uncertainties, are usually comparable, and industry participants have more freedom of maneuver. This explains, in part, why personal computer software and hardware producers do not have uniform policies regarding warranties and support services. This is in contrast to the automotive industry where any changes to warranty policies, coverage tend to be copied rapidly, especially if the initiator of the changes is one of the major producers.[10]

These factors are very often correlated, as shown in Figure 12.4. Consequently, asymmetrical payoffs are much more likely when industry growth matures or starts declining. For the same reasons, tactical questions such as the advantages of moving first, product-line extension,

Nature of Industry Conflict	Industry Concentration	Industry Cost Characteristics	Overall Growth Rate
Win/Win	Low	?	High
Win/Lose or Limited Warfare	Medium to high	Some economies of scale	Medium to low
Lose/Lose	High	Some economies of scale	Low or negative

Figure 12.4   Typical interrelationships between the forces.

creation of second brands, and bundling of products have more relevance during the growth and early maturity stages of an industry when there is more room for maneuver.

We will now proceed to examine these tactical choices individually. First, we will consider the question, "Under what conditions do firms who move first gain tactical or strategic advantages?" Next we will review the several issues connected with product-line extension and creation of a second brand. We will then examine decisions related to complementary products and services, including, as a special case, product support. Finally, we will briefly discuss product/service bundling and unbundling, deferring a detailed analysis to Chapter 14.

First Entry—Pros and Cons

Should a firm be first to market with a particular product? Or should it be "second but better," that is, should it wait until the technology or customer needs have stabilized and then enter the market, thereby avoiding some of the costs of pioneering?[11]

First movers have several advantages, such as clear differentiation and positioning in customers' minds as the innovators or technological leaders, creation of switching costs, the ability to set standards and, occasionally, pre-emptive positioning (see Table 12.1). Leica in 35mm cameras and Apple in personal computers are just two examples of first-mover advantages with regard to differentiation. By being first, Wang was able to create significant switching costs for users of its minicomputer-based word-processing systems. By being the first to market color televisions, RCA was able to set video standards for the U.S. television industry.

Being the first to market also has disadvantages. The costs of pioneering can be prohibitively high, particularly if the technology ultimately fails to work. Demand is often uncertain, with the result that early

Table 12.1   Advantages and disadvantages of first to market.

Advantages	Disadvantages

Reputation
    Leica, Apple
	Pioneering Costs
	    Rolls Royce in carbon filaments
	    Univac in computers

Pre-Emptive Positioning
    Sears, Merrill Lynch, CMA
	Demand Uncertainty
	    Color TVs, LANs
	    Fiber optic long distance cable

Switching Costs
    DEC minis
    Wang word-processors
	"Wrong" Technology
	    Philco in transistors
	    Sony in VCRs
	    Sylvania in tubes

Standards Definition
    RCA in color TVs
    CP/M	

entrants have to produce at uneconomic volumes. Finally, there is always the danger that the firm may have invested heavily in technology that will be superseded by fresh advances. In 1971, Rolls Royce went bankrupt, nearly taking Lockheed with it, when its gamble on carbon filament technology for jet engine blades failed; this was a case both of pioneering costs being too high and of choosing the "wrong" technology or more precisely, the wrong application for the technology. Carbon filament composites were not suited for jet engine blades but are now being used elsewhere. The demand for color television in the U.S. grew far more slowly than corresponding penetration levels for black-and-white television, with the result that pioneers' costs were quite high. More recently, demand for fiber optic long-distance transmission has grown far more slowly than anticipated, creating large amounts of excess capacity.[12] Another example of the "wrong" technology is germanium versus silicon transistors; early entrants such as Hughes, Sylvania (part of GT&E), and Transitron, who based their designs on germanium, lost out to Texas Instruments and Motorola, who used silicon.[13]

Which approach is best? There are no general rules[14] and, to some extent, the choice appears to depend on a firm's predisposition; some firms are more aggressive while others are more conservative in entering new product/market areas. In order to determine which approach is best suited to any given situation, we must analyze factors such as

- The initial investment requirements
- The impact of learning curve effects
- The degree to which first entry can create switching costs

- The rate of technological change
- The speed with which the innovation is likely to penetrate the market
- The importance of "network effects," that is, benefits that depend on the existence of an installed base of users of the innovation.

Other things being equal, large initial investments argue for caution in entering the market. It may be preferable to let smaller, less well-capitalized players test the market and the technology and then enter via acquisition. If significant learning curve effects or switching costs are likely, then first entrants have major competitive advantages that may be difficult to overcome. If technological change is occurring very rapidly, "second but better" is not likely to be a feasible approach; the later entrant will always be lagging technologically and, therefore, its overall strategic leverage will be lower. Similarly, if the rate at which the innovation penetrates the market is high, then "second but better" may not succeed, especially if the second entrant's approach/design is incompatible with the pioneer's; early buyers will be reluctant to switch and later buyers, lacking the infrastructure provided by the first design, will have little incentive to select it in preference to the established pioneer. The implications of network effects are difficult to predict; the need for a large installed base of users could deter *any* entrants; on the other hand, the first firm to create the minimum installed base necessary would possibly have a commanding lead over later entrants.

Second Brands versus Brand Extension

Second brands are products aimed at different (often more price sensitive) segments of the market. They are usually introduced to help preserve the positioning of the primary brand or product line while capturing sales from other segments. Examples of second brands are numerous: Sears with its Craftsman™ and Companion™ line of hand tools; the Companion™ line is lower priced and offers significant differences in quality and has little or no warranty protection. In men's clothing, Brooks Brothers offers 346 and Brooksgate lines of clothes; the former is more expensive and is, presumably, for the older male, while the Brooksgate line is less expensive and aimed at young men. Not all second brands need be aimed at lower-priced segments. Outboard Marine Corporation, for example, sells its products under both the Johnson and Evinrude labels, while Whirlpool sells its products through Sears under the Kenmore label and through other distribution channels under the Whirlpool name.

Second brands may be created for a number of reasons, including the following:

- To capture incremental revenues from the lower price end of the market without affecting the positioning and image of the primary brand (to capitalize on available returns)
- To combat price-based competitors and prevent them from taking share from the flagship brand (to maintain freedom of maneuver in pricing)
- To pre-empt channels that might otherwise be inclined to seek out an alternative or "house brand"—a second brand relieves some of this pressure and protects the flagship brand (again, maintaining freedom of maneuver in pricing)
- To assist during an unbundling strategy by creating different brands, thereby making direct comparisons difficult.

Key Trade-Off

Managers considering second brands must choose between extending an established brand, one with clear name recognition, and launching a new brand, without name recognition. The advantages of extending an existing brand are obvious: immediate name recognition, credibility, economies of scale in advertising and promotion, access to established distribution channels, and the use of a common salesforce. Given these conditions, the incremental revenue from such an extension often appears very attractive.

By contrast, creating a second brand from the beginning is a much riskier and more expensive proposition. It often requires substantial investments in advertising and promotion, start-up costs to establish separate distribution channels, potential apathy on the part of the existing salesforce necessitating the need for special incentives or a dedicated salesforce, and added overhead expenditures for product management. Thus it is no surprise that firms tend to opt for brand extension rather than taking on the uncertain task of creating a new brand.[15]

However, product-line extension is also risky and may result in lowering the total sales of *both* the flagship and the second brand. Ries and Trout put it aptly, "Line extension is like a teeter totter. One name can't stand for two different products. When one goes up, the other goes down . . . [i]n the long term, line extension is usually a loser's strategy."[16] The reasons become evident when we recognize that the objective of either line extension or a second brand is *price discrimination,* tapping a different segment of buyers who previously were nonbuyers. A different (second) brand, with its own identity, distribution, and pricing has little impact on purchases of the flagship brand; neither set of customers is particularly interested in the other brand. Product-line extension, on the other hand, stimulates the interest of buyers in both segments; in this sense, common advertising works against the long-term interests of the firm by making flagship brand buyers aware that (1) a different product with the same name exists, and, if the extension is at the low-priced end, (2) that it has most of the features of the flagship brand but a lower price.

Figure 12.5 illustrates this situation using the perceived quality/ perceived price matrix described earlier. Assuming that the flagship brand is positioned in the best-value (high perceived quality, low perceived price) box, brand extension into the "cheap goods" segment risks a firm's position in the majority of the market while offering incremental sales in a small (10 to 15 percent of the total market) segment. In other words, brand extension is actually a "high risk, low return" investment. By contrast, a second brand allows the firm to insulate its main offering while contesting for a share of the "cheap goods" segment.[17]

Who Can Introduce a Second Brand

Generally speaking, differentiated players can offer second brands. A second-brand strategy is inconsistent with cost leadership, as it would divert resources from cost reduction and would increase marketing costs. Low-end focus players usually find it difficult to go upscale, while firms

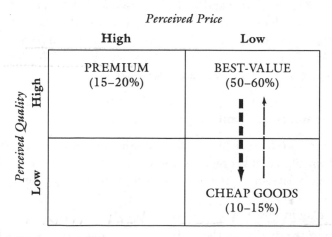

Figure 12.5   Brand extension versus second brands. Many more high-end customers migrate to lower end (or to other brands), very few low-end customers migrate up.

offering premium-priced niche products (for example, Rolls Royce in automobiles) risk losing their distinctive identity if they offer a second brand. Rolls Royce is, in fact, a case in point; in the early 1960s, Rolls offered a "second brand," namely, the Austin Princess, an upscale Austin (a mass market nameplate in the U.K.) with a Rolls Royce engine. The project was abandoned as it was difficult to sell these cars and, moreover, threatened to affect Rolls' reputation for exclusivity and quality.[18]

When to Introduce Second Brands

Assuming that a second brand is lower in price, it should logically be introduced as the market starts to mature, provided there is spare production capacity. The rationale should be to counter price-based competition; as such, the second brand may need to be judged on the basis of its incremental contribution, that is, its profitability in terms of variable (out-of-pocket) production and marketing costs only. Burdening it with allocated overheads, divisional and/or corporate, tends to divert attention from its real purpose, namely, to attack low-end competition.

Complementary Products

Complements are products that are used in conjunction with the main product and support its function in some way. The classic example is the original safety blade introduced by King Gillette in 1895. In this design, the blade was sold separately and was to be used and then discarded; the razor was the complement to the blade, which was the main product. Other examples are the special filters sold with coffeemakers such as Melitta and Mr. Coffee, the creme rinse and conditioners sold along with shampoos, and computer software and peripherals.

Why Complements Are Important

Complementary products help increase a company's leverage by increasing its freedom of maneuver and/or increasing the returns from changing its product positioning. Specifically, complements are crucial for

- Promoting innovation diffusion
- Ensuring the quality of the main product
- Providing a basis for differentiation
- Generating additional sales of the main product.

Complements are often essential for rapid innovation diffusion, as demonstrated by the case of the microwave oven. Household microwave ovens did not really penetrate the market until frozen food manufacturers introduced packages designed for such ovens. Similarly, a key to Matsushita's success with the VHS format was the (relatively) rapid creation of a large library of movies and other entertainment using this format. Matsushita recognized, correctly, that the real appeal of the videocassette recorder was in watching feature-length movies at home, not necessarily in taking (and viewing) home movies.

Early in the life of an innovation, complements are essential for ensuring that the main product delivers the expected quality. For example, Xerox insisted on using its own toners and powder. Given its proprietary technology, other manufacturers' products might have created problems, affecting the perceived quality of Xerox's copying machines. Complements such as repair parts and field service are often essential if a new technology is to successfully penetrate the market.[19]

Complementary products also create an important dimension of additional differentiation by providing features/services that may not be available elsewhere. Apple's LaserWriter, in conjunction with the Macintosh, made desktop publishing possible and provided Apple an entry into the corporate market, traditionally dominated by IBM. Superior after-sales support has helped differentiate Caterpillar and John Deere equipment in their respective markets. After-sales support is also a good example of how complementary products and services can generate additional sales of equipment, by increasing market share.

The Need to Control Complements

Managers need to control the design, introduction, and positioning of complementary products if they are perceived as complements by customers, or if they are important to overall competitive position, or both.

Products such as spare parts, consumables, application software, and supplies are usually perceived by customers to be closely connected with the main product. Often they will purchase these complements from the supplier of the main product without considering alternative sources, as is generally the case with service contracts for office equipment. Even when products are not perceived as complements, controlling them may be important to maintain freedom of maneuver in pricing. An example is financing for new equipment to permit "one-stop" shopping and retain pricing flexibility.

We can classify the alternatives as shown in Figure 12.6. The cases of interest are (1) when complements are perceived as complements and as

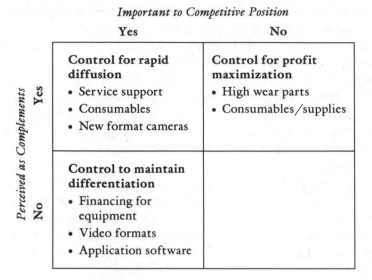

Important to Competitive Position

	Yes	No
Perceived as Complements — Yes	**Control for rapid diffusion** • Service support • Consumables • New format cameras	**Control for profit maximization** • High wear parts • Consumables/supplies
Perceived as Complements — No	**Control to maintain differentiation** • Financing for equipment • Video formats • Application software	

Figure 12.6   Controlling complementary products.

being important for competitive position, (2) when they are important for competitive position even though they may not be perceived as complements, and (3) when they are perceived as complements even though they are not important for competitive position. (If none of these conditions is true, then we need not concern ourselves with complements.) We can now define specific objectives for product tactics with the help of this framework as follows:

- If they are perceived as complements and as being important to competitive position, then managers must control these complements to achieve rapid diffusion. The tactical focus must be on supporting the sales growth of the main product, with profitability of complements a secondary concern. Ideally, a firm should retain the design and generation of these complementary products and services; failing that, it should use exclusive arrangements to retain operational control.

- If they are important to competitive position, but are not necessarily perceived as complements by customers, then the objective must be control to maintain differentiation. The current argument in the personal computer industry over page description languages is a clear example of the importance of such complements in maintaining differentiation. Such software is used to control the appearance of type on screens and of text output to laser printers. The vast majority of PC users are only vaguely aware of these languages' functions; they certainly do not perceive page description languages in the same light as system software or service support. The de facto standard was Postscript, a language developed by an independent supplier, Aldus Corporation. With the importance of such software increasing, two major players—Apple Computer and Microsoft—have announced plans to create their own standards. The fact that Apple was an initial investor in Aldus merely highlights the importance of these complements; Apple sold its Aldus stock prior to the agreement with Microsoft to ensure its freedom of maneuver.

- If they are perceived as complements, but are not important to competitive position, then the objective should be profit maximization. High wear parts and accessories carrying the brand of the main product are two examples. However, while seeking to maximize profits, it is important to avoid pricing these complementary products so high as to invite other firms to offer competing products, particularly if the main product is "bundled" with these complements. In such cases, there is considerable danger of "cream skimming" by competitors providing only the high volume/high profit items while leaving the manufacturer of the main product with the responsibilities (and costs) of supplying the remaining items.[20]

Control Mechanisms

Companies must control various elements relating to complements. If the objective is to ensure rapid diffusion, then every one of the 4Ps may be important. If the complement is being controlled for profit maximization, then control over pricing is important to avoid "cream skimming"; in turn, this may require careful control of channels. Firms can control complements by

- Bundling the main and complementary products together
- Subsidizing the complementary product
- Developing and selling both main and complementary products
- Licensing third-party providers to create and market suitable complements.

Bundling Main and Complementary Products.   This is appropriate when rapid innovation diffusion is desired and tight control of complements is essential for maintaining quality and/or maximizing profits. The computer industry is replete with examples of such bundling, starting with IBM's bundling of hardware and software in the mid-1960s, to the more recent bundling of word-processing and graphic software in the early stages of the Apple Macintosh. As we discuss in Chapter 14, bundling creates economies of scale in production, distribution, and marketing. More importantly, it speeds innovation diffusion by enabling the buyer to realize the benefits of the innovation quicker. This, for example, was a major element in IBM's success in mainframe computers; by bundling the hardware and software, IBM offered complete solutions to payroll, accounting, and other operating problems.

Subsidizing the Complementary Product.   If the product is not perceived as a complement but control is essential to maintain differentiation, firms often subsidize the complementary product. Often termed the "razor-and-razor-blade" approach, after King Gillette, such cross-subsidization is used in financing for equipment as well as in pricing of important/essential accessories.

Selling Both Products.   This approach can be used to achieve any of the three objectives described earlier, namely, rapid innovation diffusion, maintaining differentiation, or profit maximization. It avoids the dangers inherent in bundling and cross-subsidy; however, on occasion it may inhibit the development of necessary complements by third-party providers.[21]

Licensing Third-Party Providers.   If "network economies" and/or the presence of an installed base of users or devices are essential to the success of an innovation, then firms may license their technologies to third-party providers of complementary products. Such third-party licensing was a major reason for the success of Matsushita's VHS standard versus Sony's Betamax, as it created a large library of movies for viewing at home.[22] It is also the rationale behind AT&T's licensing of its UNIX V operating system on very generous terms. Largely as a result, UNIX has emerged as an important standard in a number of areas such as government procurements of computers and engineering and scientific applications.

Product Support[23]

Spare parts, repair services, warranties, training, and other elements of support are an important special case of complementary products. These products (and services) fit in all of the three categories just discussed—they may be necessary for rapid diffusion, for maintaining differentiation, or for profit maximization. Support requirements also have definite implications for product tactics and for pricing decisions.

Product support is a key concern in situations where the interruption of benefits provided by the product—dishwasher, tractor, mainframe, or personal computer—imposes costs on the user. These costs can be categorized in terms of the various costs of equipment malfunction or failure and are broadly grouped into two categories: costs that are independent of the duration of failure or fixed costs, and those that vary with the length of the failure or variable costs:

- Fixed costs on failure are those related to the actual repair of the equipment together with any transactions and information costs. Repair costs are usually out-of-pocket costs, unless the item is still under warranty. Transactions and information costs are harder to determine explicitly and often have to be inferred from other costs.

- Variable costs on failure consist of those costs that increase with increasing duration of failure. These can be subdivided into out-of-pocket costs and opportunity costs.

Generic Support Strategies

The various approaches used to meet customers' support requirements can be grouped according to whether they are related to (1) product or design, (2) support system, and (3) reduction of purchasers' or users' uncertainties.

Design-related strategies can be further subdivided into three generic types: strategies focusing on increasing product reliability, those focusing on repair time by making the product more modular, and those building in redundancy. Reliability improvements reduce customers' total costs by reducing the frequency of failure. Modular design lowers the variable costs on failure, while redundancy reduces both fixed and variable costs of failure by limiting both the frequency and the duration of failures.

Support system-related strategies are designed to reduce repair time, improve system response to failure, or both. Repair times can be reduced through investments in the training of technicians, on-site diagnostic equipment, and built-in diagnostics. System response to failure can be improved by having additional technicians, positioning them closer to the customers' sites, and providing overnight delivery of repair parts.

Strategies that reduce customers' risks include warranties and service contracts. Warranties minimize customers' out-of-pocket costs immediately after purchase and ease fears about product reliability, an important consideration for new entrants and for followers. Service contracts limit the buyers' uncertainties regarding repair and maintenance costs.

We can classify these generic strategies in terms of the framework discussed previously (see Figure 12.7). Strategies to reduce customers' uncertainties are important for rapid diffusion. Occasionally, other strategies such as higher reliability or a superior support system may also assist in speeding product acceptance. Design- and support system-related strategies are important for maintaining differentiation. Any of these strategies may also be used for profit maximization; however, this presupposes that support is not important to competitive position, which is rarely the case.

Conceptual Framework

In practice, manufacturers must balance the conflicting demands of customer requirements, their willingness to pay for superior support performance, technological feasibility, manufacturing and support costs, and so on, when choosing a specific approach. However, if we plot different products in terms of their relative fixed and variable costs on failure, we can get a general framework for analysis that provides a picture of commonly used support strategies (see Figure 12.8). In terms of this framework, small household appliances such as toasters fall into the low fixed

| | *Important to Competitive Position* | |
	Yes	No
Perceived as Complements — Yes	**Rapid Diffusion** Risk reduction • warranties • service contracts	**Profit Maximization**
Perceived as Complements — No	**Differentiation** Design-related • reliability • modularity etc. System-related • system response • repair time	

Figure 12.7   Tactical roles of support strategies.

cost, low variable cost (low, low) end, large appliances such as washers and automobiles fall in the high fixed cost, low variable cost (high, low) segment, tractors, minicomputers, large copiers, and so on, fall in the low (relative) fixed cost, high variable cost (low, high) end, and airplanes, large mainframe computers, life support equipment, and so on, fall in the high fixed cost, high variable cost (high, high) segment.

The analytical significance of this framework lies in the fact that, for each segment, *one particular support strategy dominates all others.* We have labeled the four segments disposables, high reliability, rapid response, and never fails; in each of these segments the optimal strategy is different, with corresponding changes in the implications for product and pricing tactics.

Disposables. If the buyer's fixed and variable costs on failure are very low, a disposable strategy dominates, provided replacement costs

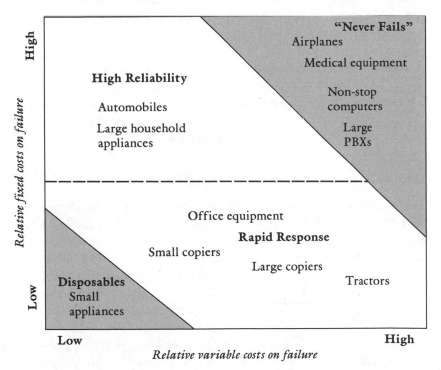

Figure 12.8 Conceptual framework for support strategies.

as well as the likelihood of a failure occurring in a short time period are both low. The classic example is Timex, which virtually eliminated watch repair in the late 1940s by introducing a low-cost, reliable watch that was not even intended to be repaired and was backed by a one-year warranty.

High Reliability.   When the buyer's fixed costs on failure are high relative to the variable costs, then the dominant support strategy is high reliability. In other words, products have a relatively high level of reliability (although not as high as disposables) and are designed to keep out-of-pocket repair costs low. However, ease of repair is secondary to design reliability and manufacturing costs.

Rapid Response.   In the first two cases, design-related strategies were dominant. In this segment, variable costs of failure are of prime importance with the result that the best approach is to use product design and support systems to minimize *total* downtime. In general, this requires a balanced approach, for example, a modular design *and* rapid logistic support.[24]

Never Fails.   Finally, when both the fixed and the variable costs of failure are high, a "never-fail" design or support strategy is dominant. This means either component-or system-level redundancy, stringent maintenance programs, continuous monitoring, and/or on-site repair personnel to minimize service interruption.

Implications for Product and Pricing Tactics

The significance of this classification is emphasized when we recognize that the shapes of the segments are determined by customers' expectations, their costs, and technological feasibility. Consequently, the dimensions of these segments are fluid and will change over time, with changes in technology and in customers' relative fixed and variable costs.

The implications for product tactics are twofold: First, managers must correctly identify which segment their products currently occupy and choose the dominant strategies. A corollary is that managers must recognize that the keys for success in different segments will be very different. For example, with "disposables," the key is the ability to bring the total price below the threshold at which customers will no longer pay for a repair, while in the "rapid response" segment success requires the ability to improve total system performance, from design through manufacturing to in-field support.

Second, managers must recognize that changes in technology and customers' relative costs change the leverage of various product and pricing tactics. Word processors are a case in point; in the early 1980s they were part of the rapid response segment, but increasing reliability and changes in technology have reduced their unit costs threefold and shifted word processors to the high reliability segment. Today, most firms can afford a second word processor (usually a personal computer), eliminating the need for on-site support. This reduces the manufacturers' freedom of maneuver in product design and in pricing support services.

Changes in technology and customers' relative costs also mean that bundling of products—and any associated cross-subsidies—will be more difficult to maintain for any length of time, and pricing of complements will be crucial to deter entry by would-be competitors or entrants. Rapid changes in technology will lead to customers having greater choices with regard to support. This will make bundled approaches to support, such as service contracts, less attractive to many customers; they will soon discover other, more economical alternatives. This will also make pricing of support-related complements crucial, as competitors will rapidly detect any monopoly profits, for example, overpriced spare parts and warranties/service contracts, high-volume supplies, and so forth and enter those areas selectively.

Bundling the Product Offering

The concept of bundling is combining several products into a single package that is sold at a given (bundled) price. The individual components of the bundle may or may not be available separately to customers. If they are sold separately, then the bundled price is generally lower than the sum of the items purchased individually.

There are numerous examples of bundling. In the United States, the former Bell System bundled local telephone services under the concept of "universal service."[25] The result was that local calls were not metered separately; the monthly charge was a flat rate, regardless of actual usage. "Full service" brokers and gasoline stations are other examples of bundling, as are the various "option packages" put forth by automobile manufacturers.

Bundling can create leverage by increasing the returns on product changes and raising the barriers to market entry, thereby increasing freedom of maneuver in pricing and product/service design. Especially in the early stages of industry evolution, bundling can speed innovation diffusion by reducing customers' search costs and uncertainties; this is particularly attractive in an emerging industry where suppliers for necessary complements may not yet be established. Bundling creates entry barriers by forcing would-be entrants to make additional investments in support and manufacture of accessories, complements, or other components of the bundle customers have come to expect as part of the standard product offering. Bundling may also increase differentiation by providing unique product or service offerings. Finally, bundling can increase profitability through economies of scale in production, distribution, and marketing, combined with barriers to entry that, other things being equal, allow a firm to charge higher prices.

However, continuing to bundle as an industry matures and leverage becomes restricted makes a company vulnerable to cream skimming. It also invites entry by creating unfilled needs. Cream skimming occurs when competitors concentrate on the more lucrative services, ignoring other, less profitable areas. In automotive after-market, for instance, third-party firms focus their efforts on profitable areas such as brakes and mufflers, leaving other maintenance tasks requiring greater investments in facilities and training to the dealer. The other drawback of bundling is that it overservices some segments and underservices others. This creates openings for potential competitors.

We can summarize the major questions relating to bundling as follows:

- Should we bundle the product at all?
- What should be the composition of the bundle, that is, which products, complements, and accessories should be included in the bundle?
- How should the bundle be priced?
- Should we offer individual elements of the bundle separately?
- When and how should we unbundle?

The basic decision to bundle a product is affected by the stage of the product life cycle and a firm's long-term objectives. Bundling is attractive primarily in the emerging and growth phases of a product or a new technology, where it could assist innovation diffusion. Further, bundling is likely to be more attractive to players pursuing differentiation, either across the board or in a particular market niche. Choosing the components of the bundle requires balancing customer requirements and costs. If there are more items than necessary, overall costs will be too high, either creating a loss or making the product unaffordable to most potential buyers. Conversely, if the bundle does not meet most requirements of the majority of customers, it becomes unattractive.

Unbundling, that is, making customers purchase—and pay—separately for items that they have always received as a package, is the reverse of bundling. The issues are similar: When should the firm unbundle? Which components should be unbundled? What should be the prices of the individual components? In addition, in unbundling the firm must consider competitors' likely reactions, whether they will unbundle in their turn or instead lower the prices of their (bundled) packages to gain share.

Broadly speaking, bundling is most prevalent during the emerging and growth stages of industry/technology evolution. As the industry matures, there is a tendency towards unbundling. Larger customers are usually the first to want an unbundled offering, reflecting their greater capabilities to assemble the package internally, as well as their greater buyer power. Followers or new entrants are often the first to provide unbundled offerings, either partially or completely disassembled. Unlike the leaders, they enjoy few or no benefits from bundling; in fact, new entrants may see bundling as an entry barrier that should avoided or circumvented.

Summary

Industry payoffs and strategic leverage affect product tactics, while tactics can be used to change leverage by changing maneuver or creating returns. In this chapter we saw how asymmetrical (lopsided) payoffs affected GE's and Whirlpool's decisions about entering a new market segment. We also examined how second brands increase leverage by maintaining a company's freedom of maneuver, while brand extensions exploit the potentially higher returns; and how complementary products, product/service bundling increased freedom of maneuver and/or returns by neutralizing buyer power, creating barriers for potential entrants.

13

Why Channels Can Become Industry "Fault Lines"

Channels represent a major, often underutilized area for strategic innovation, especially if the channel choices have not changed despite changes in the underlying costs, roles, and responsibilities. In such cases there is usually considerable—if untapped—strategic leverage to be gained by making major changes to channel roles. The new entrant or, occasionally, an incumbent who successfully taps this source of leverage can virtually re-make the industry landscape. For this reason, we term channels an industry's potential "fault lines"; apply the right pressure, and you may create a landslide or even an earthquake!

Our primary focus in this chapter will be on how firms can identify and exploit such strategic opportunities. First, we will describe how the patterns of distribution change over time. Next, we will introduce a framework that relates changes in channel requirements to changes in the product/industry life cycle and corresponding shifts in buyers' needs. Using this framework, we can identify when companies must either force existing channels to change or switch to entirely different channels in order to remain competitive. We will then illustrate how overly rigid channel choices can induce strategic myopia with disastrous effects for a firm's competitive position. Finally, we will analyze the implications for suppliers and for channels.

How Distribution Patterns Evolve

Over time, the mix of channels used by an industry varies considerably. Channels that once played a central role are sidelined, while others become dominant. This pattern is repeated in industry after industry:

- Large household appliances like television sets and washing machines, once sold exclusively through franchised outlets, are now available from discount stores, mass merchandisers, and in some cases, by direct mail!

- Small office copiers were first sold exclusively through the manufacturer's direct salesforce. Then some firms started to market them through office equipment dealers. Today these machines are distributed through a variety of channels—manufacturers' sales organizations, dealers/distributors, and mail order.

- Office supplies such as copier paper, paper clips, staples, file folders, and so forth, long sold primarily through high-service local dealers are being increasingly sold through discounters and mail order.[1]

- Financial services such as investment advice, estate planning, and so forth, once marketed only through a bank's trust department are now available from "financial mass merchandisers" such as Sears and Merrill Lynch.

Furniture Retailing.   From 1970 to 1980, furniture sales grew at rates of 10 to 20 percent annually. But in the early 1980s, the industry suffered a severe slump, and one-third of the traditional furniture dealers closed their doors. During the same period, the furniture mail order business grew fivefold. Where traditionally 80 percent of all furniture in the United States was sold through furniture stores, that figure has dropped to between 55 and 60 percent. Department store sales have similarly fallen to 10 to 12 percent from their 15 percent share in the early 1980s.[2]

Auto Parts.   The U.S. automotive after-market parts industry's history over the past 30 years provides an excellent illustration of how distribution patterns change over time. The retail auto parts industry grew steadily through the 1950s and 1960s and into the early 1970s, reaching its peak volume around about 1972. Since that time, the market has declined in absolute volume (see Table 13.1). Throughout this period, a variety of channels were in use—automotive dealers, parts jobbers, farm stores, gas stations, mail order, hardware stores, general merchandise stores and "white goods" chains such as Sears and Montgomery Wards. However, historically four channels have accounted for the vast majority of after-market parts sales—automotive dealers, gas stations, parts distributors (jobbers), and general merchandise stores.

In the early 1960s, when industry sales were growing, auto dealers had the lion's share of the market with approximately 33 percent of total sales, while gas stations were virtually tied for second place with parts jobbers with 22 percent of the market to the latter's 27 percent. During the next 15 years, however, dealers and gas stations saw their market shares dwindle to 22 percent and 9 percent respectively. Their combined share plummeted from 55 percent in 1962 to 30 percent 20 years later. On the other hand, the volume of parts sold through parts jobbers and general merchandisers doubled, with the result that nearly two-thirds of the market was controlled by these two channels.

Industrial Products. We find similar patterns in the distribution of industrial items such as electrical apparatus, electronics, machinery, supplies, and chemicals (see Table 13.2).[3] From 1963 to 1982, industrial distributors grew steadily in importance in nearly every category and accounted for half or more of all sales for industrial items other than chemicals. Factory branches, such as, direct salesforces, generally declined, with the only exception being electronic parts where the factory salesforce actually increased its share. Finally, agents have declined in influence, gaining in one industry (electrical equipment) while losing their share in the others.

Apparel Retailing. In 1958, Malcolm McNair introduced the concept of a "wheel of retailing" to describe the changes experienced by channels in the apparel industry (see Figure 13.1). The cycles of the wheel begin with specialty shops, followed by department stores, discount stores, and lastly, off-price outlets.[4] The channel members within each cycle begin with an innovative idea, expand on it, trade up with

Table 13.1   Changes in automotive parts distribution.

	1962	1967	1972	1977	1982
Total sales in billions	6.2	9.4	16.5	21.2	31.0
Automobile dealers (%)	33	34	33	22	22
Auto parts dealers (%)	27	28	31	44	52
Gas stations (%)	22	21	19	13	9
General merchandise (%)	8	11	13	16	16

Table 13.2 Industrial distribution pattern.

Groups	1963	1982
Electrical apparatus and equipment (SIC 5063)		
Total sales ($000,000)	$ 8,478	$ 53,956
Total sales accounted for by		
distributors	34%	45%
factory branches	58%	41%
agents	7%	14%
Electronic parts and equipment (SIC 5065)		
Total sales ($000,000)	$ 4,296	$ 40,365
Total sales accounted for by		
distributors	36%	40%
factory branches	28%	32%
agents	36%	28%
Industrial machinery and equipment (SIC 5084)		
Total sales ($000,000)	$ 8,695	$ 68,630
Total sales accounted for by		
distributors	45%	57%
factory branches	37%	29%
agents	18%	13%
Industrial supplies (SIC 5085)		
Total sales ($000,000)	$ 7,424	$ 39,800
Total sales accounted for by		
distributors	49%	49%
factory branches	42%	43%
agents	9%	8%
Chemicals and allied products (SIC 5161)		
Total sales ($000,000)	$12,562	$ 76,103
Total sales accounted for by		
distributors	16%	26%
factory branches	80%	71%
agents	4%	4%
All categories		
Total sales ($000,000)	$41,455	$278,854
Total sales accounted for by		
distributors	34%	43%
factory branches	54%	45%
agents	12%	12%

Source: U.S. Census of Wholesale Trade, *Geographic Area Statistics, 1982,* Table 1, "Summary Statistics for the United States: 1982," and *Summary Statistics, 1963,* Table 2: "United States by Kind of Business: 1963."

From E.R. Corey, F.V. Cespedes, and V.K. Rangan, *Going to Market: Distribution Systems for Industrial Products.* Boston: Harvard Business School Press, 1989. Reprinted by permission.

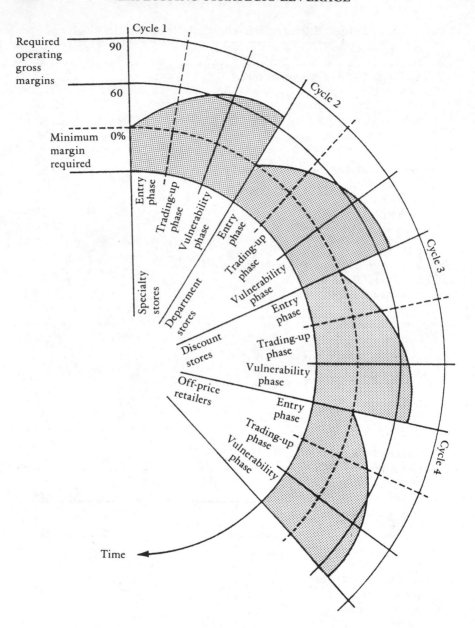

Figure 13.1   Wheel of retailing.

additional innovations to embellish the original, and then become vulnerable as competition intensifies and consumers become more price conscious.

Relationship to Industry Life Cycle

A common feature of these shifts in distribution patterns is the progressive displacement of higher value-added channels (with higher margins) by channels that add less value and, therefore, have lower margins.[5] This is not accidental but is related to the changing role played by channels as industries evolve and the freedom and returns to using different channels change. Specifically:

- *Channel changes follow a predictable pattern.* Channels with high value-added and high margins mark the emerging/growth phases of an industry (or product).[6] Medium to high value-added channels, with lower margins, emerge in the late growth/early maturity stages. As the market matures, outlets with low value added and low margins satisfy customers' requirements for fewer services at a lower cost. And when low cost becomes customers' primary focus as the market declines, channels with little or no added value and very low margins predominate.

- *Two factors explain these changes.* One is the value added by the channel, *as perceived by the purchaser.* The other is the growth rate of the market/industry.

- *Different channels are most effective at different stages of industry evolution.* In the early stages of industry/product evolution, channels that aggressively "push" the product are needed; these channels provide services such as market research, promotion, matching of buyers and sellers, and so on, that volume-driven, "pull" channels cannot cost-effectively supply. As the product matures, however, the latter become competitive and eventually dominate the market.

The Value Added versus Market Growth Matrix. We can better understand these changes and the underlying relationships when we consider the 2 by 2 matrix shown in Figure 13.2, which maps the value added by the channel against the market growth rate. The first variable, value added by the channel, measures the economic value to the purchaser of the various services provided by the channel before, during, and after the

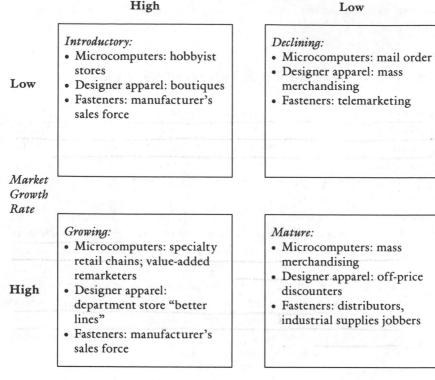

Value Added by the Channel

	High	**Low**
Low	*Introductory:* • Microcomputers: hobbyist stores • Designer apparel: boutiques • Fasteners: manufacturer's sales force	*Declining:* • Microcomputers: mail order • Designer apparel: mass merchandising • Fasteners: telemarketing
High	*Growing:* • Microcomputers: specialty retail chains; value-added remarketers • Designer apparel: department store "better lines" • Fasteners: manufacturer's sales force	*Mature:* • Microcomputers: mass merchandising • Designer apparel: off-price discounters • Fasteners: distributors, industrial supplies jobbers

Market Growth Rate (row label, at left)

Figure 13.2   Value added versus market growth matrix.

transaction. Services provided by the channel include needs analysis, product selection, time and place utility (that is, the right goods or services available where the buyer needs them and when he needs them), after-sales support, warranties, and guarantees. The second variable, market growth rate, measures the speed with which the demand for that type of product is growing.

In terms of this framework, the pattern of channel evolution is from high/low (high value added/low market growth) through high/high, low/high and finally to low/low. Specifically:

- *Emerging/early growth.* Products/markets that are still in their nascent stages use specialist channels that add considerable value by spotting trends, screening or selecting new introductions, developing both sources and customers, and enabling two-way communication between manufacturers and leading-edge customers. Hobbyist stores played this role in the development of the PC, while boutiques provide a similar function in the evolution of clothing fashions.

- *Growth/early maturity.* Once the market takes off, it typically moves into channels that can handle the higher volumes but do not provide all the services offered by the specialists. For personal computers, this meant a shift to specialized retailers such as Computerland and BusinessLand. For designer clothes, the shift is from boutiques to major department stores.

- *Maturity.* Once the market nears maturity, the emphasis shifts to lower cost channels, offering lower prices with fewer services. At this point, the channel adds little value beyond time and place utility. For personal computers, this meant a shift to mass merchandisers and discounters. For designer clothing, this means a change from department stores toward mass market outlets such as Penncys.

- *Decline.* As the market moves into the decline stage, channels that add even less value become dominant, for example, mail order in the case of PCs, off-price discounters such as Marshalls for designer clothes.

The intensity of distribution also varies. During the emerging/early growth stages, firms have exclusive relationships with a very limited number of noncompeting channels, sometimes with only one member of one type of outlet. Once market growth takes off, wider coverage is essential, with the result that exclusive channels are replaced by selected, high quality ones. However, channel conflict is still minimal. The situation changes dramatically when market growth slows. Now firms must abandon selective distribution in favor of intensive market coverage. As a result, channels overlap extensively, and there is incessant channel conflict. Lower-cost, lower-service channels aggressively undercut established outlets, eroding the latter's market share or even forcing them to drop the product. Price competition is intense and maintaining price differentials between segments becomes extremely difficult.

Finally, there is a consolidation of channels in the decline stage. Manufacturers discard high-cost, high-service intermediaries in favor of the most cost-effective ones. Alternatives such as direct mail, catalogs, and telemarketing become dominant, while direct sales, agents, distributors, and dealers are downgraded or eliminated entirely.

Innovation Diffusion: The Driver. These changes occur due to changes in the level of support/assistance required by buyers and

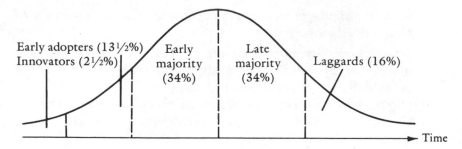

Figure 13.3   Innovation diffusion cycle.

changes in the relative efficiency of suppliers and channels as a new innovation spreads through the target market. Working in tandem, these two factors change the returns provided by different types of channels. They may also change a company's freedom of maneuver, especially if they raise buyer power.

In the beginning, purchasers' needs for support are high. Potential buyers need services such as information regarding likely sources, assistance in assembling the various offerings into viable systems, training in operation, customization, location of sources for supplies and accessories, and so forth. At the same time, the market is small—composed primarily of the innovators and early adopters[7] (see Figure 13.3)—and suppliers are fragmented and numerous. Consequently, the channel is more efficient than suppliers/manufacturers at meeting purchasers' needs, with the result that value added by the channel, as perceived by the customer, is high (see Table 13.3).

At the other extreme, when the market has started to decline and the late majority and the laggards are purchasing the product, customers' support and information needs are few or are met more efficiently by manufacturers, specialist suppliers, or third parties. At the same time,

Table 13.3   Value added changes with innovator category.

Target Market	Innovators Early Adopters	Early Majority	Late Majority	Laggards
Market Growth	Low	High	Medium/ low	Low to zero
Support Requirements	Very high	High to medium	Medium to low	Low
Value Added by Channel	Very high	High	Medium	Low

many of the functions initially performed by the channel—awareness creation, needs identification, matching of buyers and suppliers, and so on—can be performed more efficiently by the manufacturer. For these reasons, the value added by the channel (in the customers' eyes) is low.

The transition between these two extremes occurs when market growth takes off, that is, when the early majority start to purchase the product. At the start of this phase, buyer needs are still high, and the channel is still more efficient than the manufacturer at performing various functions. Thus, the value added by the channel is high. But as the market expands, the value added by the channel continues to drop as buyer needs decline or are met more efficiently by the manufacturer or by third parties. As this occurs, the manufacturer becomes more efficient at creating awareness and identifying customer needs.

Another way of looking at the situation is that in the early stages of an innovation, channels, or intermediaries, play a major role in creating the market and acting as facilitators and catalysts for change. Once the market takes off, however, economies of scale in demand creation shift to the supplier. Further, the very growth of the market fosters "network economies" that can be exploited by third parties; for example, once a critical mass of users is reached, third-party providers of repair services can enter the market. Inevitably, the value added by the channel starts to shrink, from its original role as the market creator to, ultimately, merely providing time and place utility.

Air-Powered Fasteners.   The manner in which distribution patterns have changed in the U.S. air-powered fastener industry during the past 40 years provides a good example of these forces at work. It also illustrates the strategic opportunities created when manufacturers are reluctant to change traditional channels. (For a more detailed discussion of this industry with regards to price bundling, see Chapter 14.)

Air-powered fasteners such as nails and staples were introduced into the automotive industry in the late 1940s and gradually spread to other industries, in particular, housing, mobile homes, furniture, and packaging.

In the early years of the industry (late 1940s to mid-1950s), there were few established intermediaries; at the same time, potential purchasers required considerable attention before they would change their production methods to take advantage of these new techniques. For these reasons, manufacturers used their own salesforces to educate would-be customers. To facilitate sales, manufacturers also provided users with tools and support services essentially free of cost. Companies also designed special tools and fasteners for particular applications, such as fine-wire tools for the furniture industry.

The industry's growth stage ended in the early 1970s, yet manufacturers hesitated to change channels. They continued to market through their direct salesforces and still provided tools and repair services essentially free of charge. By continuing to use this high-service, high-margin channel, manufacturers forced the prices of fasteners to remain high at a time when users were looking for a product with fewer services at a lower cost.

In the early 1980s, European and Taiwanese imports seized this opportunity provided by the domestic manufacturers' reluctance to change. Imports offered the most popular fastener sizes at prices 30 to 50 percent less than those charged by the major U.S. manufacturers. But the imports did not provide free tools, repair services, or training; instead, they designed their fasteners to work in the majors' tools.[8] Not surprisingly, imports soon accounted for nearly 15 percent of total industry sales and began to dominate in some segments. As a result, domestic manufacturers' profits dropped significantly, forcing them to make major changes in their channels of distribution in order to stay competitive. Most firms have abandoned or drastically reduced their direct sales efforts, with one company's total sales force shrinking in size from 800 in 1982, to under 250 in 1988. Instead, they now rely on distributors and dealers to sell their fasteners. Manufacturers have also "unbundled" fastener prices, separating their nails and staples from their tools and spare parts. Finally, telemarketing is increasingly used to supplement dealers' efforts, especially in marketing spare parts and accessories.

Strategic Myopia: Amana in Microwave Ovens

Amana's experience in the microwave oven industry is another example of changes in channels changing strategic leverage. It also illustrates the reluctance of manufacturers to change distribution patterns and the disastrous consequences of such strategic rigidity on a firm's long-term competitive position within the industry.[9]

Background

The microwave oven was originally developed and patented by Raytheon in the mid-1940s. Until the mid-1960s, its applications were restricted to the institutional market. In 1967, Amana (which was acquired by Raytheon in 1965) introduced the first consumer microwave oven in the United States. Amana was followed rapidly by Litton Industries, which had licensed the technology earlier from Raytheon, and by other appliance makers such as GE, Tappan, and Sharp (an importer), and by mass merchandisers such as Sears and Montgomery Wards.

The market grew rapidly, from virtually no penetration in 1971 to nearly 10 percent of U.S. households by 1978. In 1978, annual sales passed the $1 billion mark and almost $2^{1}/_{2}$ million units were sold nationwide (see Table 13.4). Microwave oven sales were now important to retailers, surpassed only by refrigerators and washing machines in total volume. Further, microwaves were the fastest-growing and also the most profitable segment of the appliance market, an increasingly competitive retail environment.

Rapid growth attracts entrants and the microwave oven industry was no exception. Numerous firms, both U.S. and foreign—primarily Japanese—entered the market, with the result that by 1975, 30 producers were offering 27 brands in more than 150 styles/models. This increased by 1978 to 35 brands and about 200 different styles/models. Litton and Amana, the pioneers, lost their commanding two-thirds share of the market; by 1977 their sales represented about 30 percent of the total market. There was a second tier of three firms—GE, Sharp, and Tappan—which captured a quarter of the market, while the remainder was accounted for by approximately 15 other firms. By late 1977, the rate of entry slowed down, and several firms dropped out of the market. A potentially ominous development was the increasing importance of Japanese suppliers. They were ahead of U.S. makers on the learning curve, owing in part to the faster development of their domestic market;

Table 13.4 Market size and household penetration.

	Units Shipped[a]			Percent Household Penetration[b] (%)
	Total (thousands)	Imports (%)	Retail Value ($million)	
1970	50	—	25	0.1
1971	100	—	45	0.2
1972	325	44	130	0.6
1973	440	41	167	1.2
1974	715	30	286	2.2
1975	1,000	26	400	3.7
1976	1,660	32	654	5.9
1977	2,100	26	850	8.3
1978 (est.)	2,400	33	984	11.4

[a] Total U.S. shipments plus imports.
[b] In 1977, 1% represented about 759,000 homes.

Robert D. Buzzell and Fred D. Wiersema, "Note on the Microwave Oven Industry." Boston: Harvard Business School, case 579-185. Copyright © 1979 by President and Fellows of Harvard College. Reprinted by permission.

almost 20 percent of Japanese households owned a microwave oven in 1976.

However in mid-1978 the industry was in turmoil. Growth slowed down, placing considerable pressure on marginal producers and companies with excess capacity. Price competition was increasing, and some observers were predicting a shakeout. There were indications that the affluent/convenience-seeking customer segment was becoming saturated. At the same time, mass market consumers, who formed the vast majority of the market, seemed more interested in replacing their existing major appliances than in purchasing new ones such as microwave ovens. While some observers viewed the slowdown as merely temporary, caused by severe winter weather that reduced consumer shopping, others were concerned about the long-term future of the industry. The sense was that there would be a pause in sales before the true mass market evolved. As one person put it, ". . . [the microwave oven] has reached the first 8 percent of households . . . The next 8 percent are going to have to be highly educated, motivated, and that's going to take time."[10] Another analyst believed the market would develop more like the dishwasher market, which took more than 20 years to achieve a 30 percent penetration of households.

Balancing these pessimistic assessments were the decidedly more optimistic views of many participants. Several industry spokesmen predicted continued growth, with estimates of between 5 and 5½ million units in sales by 1981 to 1982 and household penetration approaching a fifth of all U.S. homes. This was consistent with the low levels of penetration then prevalent and the continuing changes in demographic patterns and buyers' needs. The proportion of women in the work force was increasing, placing greater emphasis on convenience. In addition, lifestyles were changing, involving new cooking and eating habits such as snacks and single meals; these changes tended to place increased emphasis on speed and convenience, thereby enhancing the appeal of the microwave oven.

Products and Pricing. There were two basic types of ovens—countertops and combinations. Originally all ovens were countertops of relatively modest size, 0.7 cubic feet. Over time, they increased in capacity to their present levels of 1 to 1.3 cubic feet. Countertops were further divided into three broad classes: high feature, top-of-the-line models, medium-priced models, and low-priced models. Combination ovens were conventional rangetops with a microwave oven in the bottom or with both a conventional and a microwave oven built in. These were introduced later and gradually increased in importance until, in 1978, they accounted for approximately 10 percent of all units sold.

Prices of countertops ranged between $150 and $600 with the high-feature models costing between $450 to $600, and the low-priced models costing anywhere between $150 to $350. Combinations were more expensive, starting at $850 and going higher. Average retail prices decreased substantially in the period 1970 to 1973, after which they stabilized. However, prices of the two popular capacity countertops—the 600-watt and the 400-watt models—fell by approximately 50 percent in the period 1973 to 1978. In addition, price promotions were used frequently by manufacturers and retailers alike. Retailers' gross margins on these items were in the 20 to 23 percent range, with department stores aiming at 30 percent, appliance retailers, 25 percent, and discount retailers, 18 percent.

Distribution.   Microwave ovens were distributed through appliance stores, national department store chains, and other mass merchandisers (see Table 13.5). Sears was the largest chain retailer of microwave ovens, under its Kenmore brand name. In 1977, Sears' major suppliers were Litton, Sharp, and Sanyo. National chains were supplied directly by the manufacturers, while appliance stores and other mass merchandisers were typically serviced by wholesale distribution channels. The latter consisted of both independent distributors and manufacturer-owned branches. The top two brands, Amana and Litton, relied exclusively on independent wholesalers, while all of GE's output was distributed through its own branches. Factory-owned distribution required a broad line of appliances and sizable share especially in major metropolitan markets; consequently, manufacturers with limited lines were almost always forced to use independent distributors with their attendant higher costs.

Table 13.5   Market shares of various retail channels in microwave oven industry—1977.

		Market Share (%)
Appliance Store		49
Department Store		32
National chain	21%	
Local store	7	
Discount store	4	
Housewares/Hardware		8
Other		10

Robert D. Buzzell and Fred D. Wiersema, "Note on the Microwave Oven Industry." Boston: Harvard Business School, case 579-185. Copyright © 1979 by President and Fellows of Harvard College. Reprinted by permission.

Microwave oven manufacturers used a combination of "push" and "pull" strategies. By 1977, manufacturers were spending more than $35 million to advertise microwave ovens, far more than any other category of major appliances. In addition, the major producers offered extensive user education programs to familiarize potential buyers with the benefits of microwave cooking. These programs included single-session "cooking schools," in-store demonstrations, informational brochures, support for specialized cookbooks, and feature articles in national and local media. Both Amana and Litton, the market leaders, believed that user education was essential before the real mass market—middle income and middle class—would start buying the product. At the beginning of 1977, Litton planned to support more than 1,000 cooking schools and field 2,000 Litton home economists. While Amana's plans were not as specific, the firm had always been a strong supporter of consumer education and would continue to aggressively support its schools and in-store demonstration programs.

Amana's Strategy. Amana was the pioneer producer, along with Litton, and was considered the industry's quality and reliability leader. It competed almost exclusively in the top-of-the-line segment retailing for between $450 and $600. Amana had introduced the first consumer countertop in 1967 and, in 1970, had more than 60 percent of the unit share. However, by 1976 its unit share had fallen to about 18 percent, somewhat below that of Litton, the industry leader (see Table 13.6).

Table 13.6 Market shares of major players microwave oven industry—1978.

Maker	1975	1976	1977	1978
Litton	21	19	18	17
Amana	15	18	11	12
GE	10	11	12	11
Sharp	7	8	10	10
Tappan	5	5	5	4
Sears	14	14	15	16
Wards	12	8	7	7
All others	16	17	22	23
Total	100%	100%	100%	100%
Total Imports	26%	32%	26%	33%

Robert D. Buzzell and Fred D. Wiersema, "Note on the Microwave Oven Industry." Boston: Harvard Business School, case 579-185. Copyright © 1979 by President and Fellows of Harvard College. Reprinted by permission.

While a subsidiary of Raytheon, Amana was relatively autonomous and, within the appliance industry, had a reputation for being both innovative and different from other competitors. In developing the market for microwave ovens, Amana had stressed quality and reliability and built a strong network of distributors and dealers, consistent with its overall approach to business. Customer service and consumer education were central features of this approach; Amana focused considerable attention on training dealer sales personnel, displaying and demonstrating its products, and providing cooking schools. The firm did not believe in price competition, as evidenced by its total absence from the home builders' market and its lack of interest in private-label sales.

The company's distributor and dealer network was perceived as being particularly strong. Amana worked through a network of 49 independent distributors and nine Amana-owned branches. These in turn supplied approximately 5,000 appliance dealers across the country. Amana paid considerable attention to this network; as the (then) president put it, "I don't understand how a high-end appliance can be sold by a tire salesman, or . . . a temporary clerk at Kmart. A strong, independent retailer is a true professional who has some stability." Amana took considerable care when selecting its distributors and expected them to be equally careful in choosing retail outlets. It had formal policies regarding the services it expected distributors and dealers to provide; these went far beyond merely stocking and selling the product and included extensive requirements regarding product demonstration, consumer education, and post-sales support.

Despite Amana's strong emphasis on product quality and its strong distribution, competitors gained in strength through the 1970s. Amana had been displaced by Litton as the share leader and was now being threatened by Sears' private-label brand. Yet the internal perception was that Amana "had been number one from the beginning; we started off and we're still number one—(we) can't be bothered by what our competitors say."

By the fall of 1977, it was evident that Amana's position was slipping badly, with the result that its market share might drop to 11 percent from 18 percent in 1976. While a number of factors were at work, Amana's management was particularly concerned about the actions of unauthorized dealers, especially Service Merchandise, a major nationwide chain of discount stores. Management's sense was that ". . . in areas that were relatively free of this kind of activity, [Amana's] results were still good."

A major factor was transshipping, whereby (authorized) Amana distributors (sometimes dealers) who had overstock would unload this oversupply on unauthorized dealers outside their own market areas, at prices below those charged by Amana's distributors. In many cases, unauthorized dealers purchasing these transshipments retailed the items at prices close to the authorized dealers' costs. The net result was channel conflict and a lowering of the value of the Amana franchise, especially at the distributor level. This last was particularly important to Amana; as one executive put it, "It is really important that [the distributor] has some assurance that, if he invests all this money and does all this work, he will reap the rewards."

What Happened

Over the next four years, Amana devoted considerable resources to eliminate transshipping. In the process, it conducted a lengthy court battle against Service Merchandise to affirm Amana's right to require dealers to meet its service standards and, implicitly, respect its suggested territorial restrictions.[11] In 1982, Amana won the lawsuit and its right to insist upon service and support requirements was upheld.[12]

However, it proved to be a hollow victory. The sales slowdown experienced by the industry in 1978 was merely a pause in its headlong growth. Between 1979 and 1982, microwave oven shipments exploded and household penetration of microwave ovens increased rapidly (see Table 13.7). In 1982, unit shipments exceeded 4.2 million.

Table 13.7 Microwave ovens—post–1977 summary statistics regarding revenues, shipments, and penetration.

Analysis of Company Market Share					
Companies	1982	1981	1980	1979	1978
Whirlpool	5%	4%	—	—	—
GE/Hotpoint	16	19	21%	13%	13%
White (incl. Frigidaire)	18	18	18	18	18
Magic Chef (Admiral)	4	4	—	—	—
Maytag (JennAir & Hardwick)	1	1	—	—	—
Raytheon (Amana & Caloric)	10	14	13	20	20
Electrolux (Tappan)	12	8	8	13	13
Litton	11	14	14	23	20
Sharp	10	11	8	13	13
Sanyo	15	9	—	—	—
Matsushita	5	4	—	—	—
Others	10	10	36	18	21

Joseph L. Bower and Nass Dossabhoy, "Note on the Major Home Appliance Industry." Boston: Harvard Business School, case 385-044. Copyright © 1984 by the President and Fellows of Harvard College. Reprinted by permission.

AMANA Held its share of the High End Market But the Middle and Low End Gpleaded. Amana Became Uncompetitive (Spending Fixed Costs! Invest)

This rapid growth in demand was accompanied by a radical change in patterns of distribution. Appliance dealers, which had been dominant in the years leading up to 1978, were displaced by mass merchandisers as the primary channel of distribution. Further, within mass merchandisers, it appeared that discounters had captured a major share (see Table 13.8).

The implication was obvious; customers were either not requiring the education, training, and other support services, or (what was more likely) they were going to the dealers for the information while making their purchases at the discount outlets (at significantly lower prices). In economic terms, customers were "free riders": they took advantage of training and other services offered in the expectation that they would purchase the product from the dealer providing these services; yet they made their purchases elsewhere. Essentially the dealers were training the customers for the mass merchandisers. As a result, dealers' net profits were severely squeezed. Their costs were higher, yet competition from discounters placed a limit on their prices. The result was inevitable; a steady loss of share to the mass merchandisers.

Amana's fortunes paralleled those of its dealers. Preoccupied with its struggle to maintain what it perceived to be very necessary service standards, reluctant to engage in price competition, and at a cost disadvantage relative to Japanese producers due to their head start on the learning curve, Amana relentlessly lost market share. From being the industry leader, Amana had less than 6 percent of the market in 1983. It was now perceived as a specialty premium brand, with good name recognition but a very low share of the market.

Table 13.8 Microwave ovens—post-1977 patterns of distribution, the market shares of different channels.

Percent of Sales by Type of Outlet—Microwave Ovens					
Type of Outlet	1982	1981	1980	1979	1978
Appliance stores	36	37	37	38	40
Catalog/chain stores	27	24	23	24	23
Department stores	8	10	11	11	11
Discount stores	11	11	11	10	11
Furniture stores	4	4	5	6	7
Catalog showroom	4	4	4	3	2
Builder/contractor	2	3	3	3	2
Kitchen remodeler	4	4	3	3	3
Other	4	2	3	2	—

Joseph L. Bower and Nass Dossabhoy, "Note on the Major Home Appliance Industry." Boston: Harvard Business School, case 385-044. Copyright © 1984 by the President and Fellows of Harvard College. Reprinted by permission.

Tactical Obsession . . . and Strategic Myopia

While numerous other factors contributed to Amana's loss of market position—the over-valued dollar in 1980 to 1984 made imports cheap, market growth was hastened by rapid demographic changes that were difficult to forecast accurately, the shift to mass merchandisers and discounters occurred faster than anyone anticipated—they are not sufficient to explain how a firm that had more than 60 percent of the market a decade earlier could be virtually driven out of the market it had created. We believe the real explanation lies in an unfortunate combination of *tactical obsession* and *strategic myopia*.

It appears that, at a critical period in the evolution of the microwave oven market, Amana's management was preoccupied with just one element of the marketing mix—channels. It did not understand how strategic leverage in the microwave oven industry had shifted, from product and promotion to place and price. Thus, Amana's management virtually ignored other tactical considerations, especially in regards to confronting an increasingly price-sensitive market. Specifically:

- *Amana was overly committed to high-service, high-cost channels.* The firm had built its market position by providing superior service and, on particular, by offering consumer education through product demonstrations and cooking schools. As management's various comments indicated, Amana fervently believed that high-service dealers were essential to its continued growth and success. Consequently, management could not even imagine that the situation might change and, when that occurred, these service requirements would become major handicaps. The final proof, if proof is necessary, is its decision to invest resources in a long and expensive legal fight against discounters, as represented by Service Merchandise, at a time when discounters were becoming an increasingly important channel of distribution.

- *It was blind to changing marketplace needs.* Management failed to recognize that the major factor inhibiting sales was price; that once prices came down, the mass market would start to buy in earnest. This was particularly sad because in the early 1970s, Amana had stimulated the market by pricing ovens at 85 percent of its manufacturing costs, using the volume this generated to create learning curve effects that eventually reduced costs.

- *It failed to recognize the growing power of intermediaries.* The large retail chains, for whom appliance sales represented a sizable portion of revenues and profits, were intensely interested in increasing their share of what they saw as a lucrative and growing market. This interest, combined with their ability to purchase in volume, large advertising budgets, and a huge customer base, made them formidable competitors and dramatically changed Amana's strategic leverage. Refusing to provide private-label ovens for these chains, as Amana did, merely provided an entry for other, mostly foreign, competitors who used the volume to further lower their production costs.

- *It was unwilling to compete on price.* The firm appeared to have consistently overestimated the price premium it could command in the marketplace, that is, it did not understand how its freedom of maneuver was limited. This rigidity on prices carried through to its distributor margins and to its unwillingness to enter price-sensitive segments such as private-label sales and the home builders' market.

These tactical miscues resulted from Amana's shortsighted approach to its overall business strategy. Some of the symptoms of this strategic myopia were evident: Amana's managers failed to recognize that Litton had surpassed them and that Sears' private-label brands were gaining on them. They added capacity too slowly, in relation to the rate of market growth. While they understood the importance of revenue growth, they did not appear to have had specific market share goals.

In terms of the strategic framework we have developed, Amana made the following basic mistakes:

- *Amana did not realize that industry payoffs had changed.* First and foremost, Amana's management appeared not to have understood that the payoffs had changed—from limited warfare to win/lose. In the period 1970 to 1978, the nature of conflict was first win/win and, later on, limited warfare. As the market reached a critical size, however, some players, notably the Japanese and the mass merchandisers, were playing for keeps.

- *Amana failed to recognize that its competitive position had weakened.* In the early 1970s, Amana could set the rules. However, by 1978, it had lost its ability to determine the terms of competition, in part because it had ceded the middle price range to other players. Amana no longer set the standards for product innovation (Litton was the perceived leader here), for pricing (the mass merchandisers were taking over in this area), or for quality and durability (the Japanese suppliers had the edge in these attributes).

- *Amana had no clear long-term positioning.* In terms of our basic paradigm, managers never asked the fundamental questions, "Can we realistically remain/regain number one? Can we even remain number two? Or is it preferable to identify a defensible niche now and create mobility barriers? If so, which niche?" Consequently, the firm had no context in which to make tactical decisions such as, "Should we supply the private-label market? What is our price positioning and how important is price in relation to market share? What should be the focus of our investments in product innovation? What is the relative importance of investments in features versus manufacturing costs?" Such questions appear to have been addressed on an ad hoc basis, without an explicit, unifying theme.

- *Amana failed to realize that the role of channels had changed.* Last but not least, the company did not appreciate that the asset it had created—its high-service, high-margin dealer network—was becoming a liability. As the market grew and started to mature, intensive distribution was the key to success, *even at the price of lower channel margins and increased channel conflict.* Viewed in this perspective, Amana should have been working with discounters such as Service Merchandise instead of suing them; these discounters would be key to increasing volume and helping it maintain some share. However, such an approach was antithetical to Amana; its entire strategy to date had stressed the value of the Amana franchise and the importance of service in maintaining that value. The firm simply didn't understand that customers were no longer interested enough in these services to pay for them.

Unfortunately, Amana's experiences are not unique. All too often, both manufacturers and channels fail to adapt to changing market needs. This typically creates opportunities for entrants as well as the (few) incumbents who are willing to make necessary changes.

Strategic Implications

Changes in the value added by the channel parallel the shifts in strategic focus that occur as the product proceeds through its life cycle. In the beginning, the emphasis is on market creation. As growth takes off, the strategic emphasis shifts to market expansion. As the product/market matures, market share is the key concern. And in decline, the major strategic goal is moving the customer to new technologies or products. Thus, by comparing the strategic focus at each stage with the value added by the channel, we can decide which channels to choose, how many different types of channels should be used, and how to set channel incentives and measure their performance.

Table 13.9 summarizes our conclusions regarding these various issues. In addition, firms should avoid the following common mistakes in channel tactics:

- *They should not assume that one channel will suffice.* AT&T learned this lesson the hard way, when it chose to market its telephone handsets exclusively through its Phone Center stores. Caught between lower-cost outlets and its own expensive overhead, AT&T found itself losing share. Only after the firm abandoned its exclusive marketing strategy in favor of broad-based mass merchandising did it regain some of the share it had lost.

  Firms with large, salaried direct sales forces are especially vulnerable to this "one channel fits all" mentality. Reluctant to add new channels or to consider alternatives, they reason that legal restrictions, alienation of existing channel members, and the perceived difficulties of controlling unfamiliar channels make change unfeasible. Such reluctance can slow down a firm's growth or even prove fatal to long-term competitive position. IBM's reluctance to use "discount" and mail order channels for its personal computers is a prime example; Dell Computer and others have become major players by exploiting IBM's disdain.

Table 13.9   How channel strategies change with the product life cycle.

	Introduction	Growth	Maturity	Decline
Strategic Focus	Market creation	Market expansion	Company share	Migration of customers
Value Added by Channel	Very high	High/medium	Low	Very low
Channel Characteristics				
Number	Few; exclusive	Several; selective	Many; intensive	Few; exclusive
Margins	High	High to medium	Low	Very low
Examples	Boutiques Manufacturer's representatives Value-added remarketers	Franchisees Exclusive dealers Value-added distributors Integrated systems vendors Direct sales force	Discount stores Off-price retailers Commission sales force	Direct mail Mass marketers

- *They should not assume that they can control the evolution of channels.* A particularly seductive trap is to convince oneself that customers *prefer* being served by a particular channel because of the added services it offers. Over time, this is usually a false, if not self-serving, assumption; customers may like the added services but often are not willing to pay a noticeable premium for them. This is particularly the case as the product becomes mature and buyers have more experience with them. When this occurs, the price premium they are willing to pay for additional services usually vanishes.

- *They should not be slow to change channels as the market evolves.* The common mistake is to stay with a channel much too long, even when all the evidence indicates that the channel is not cost effective. This prevents a firm from entrenching itself in new segments of the market, or else it creates new competitors—firms that are not hampered by the same emotional ties. Amana's devotion to its dealers is merely an extreme example; the U.S. color television manufacturers were too slow to recognize the emerging power of the mass merchandisers when they refused to create private-label sets for sale through these outlets. The Japanese quickly filled the void, thereby gaining access to the U.S. market.

- *They should not use the wrong incentives or measurements to control the channel.* It is essential that firms know what their channels can and cannot use. Offering volume-oriented channels larger margins to fund market research or market development activities is fruitless; they are simply not oriented to act as "push" channels, regardless of the monetary incentives. Conversely, discounts to exclusive channels, in the hope that they will use those discounts to lower buyer prices, are usually futile. Almost always, such channels will pocket these discounts instead of launching price promotions. Typically, exclusive channels are quite ineffective at price competition.

If any of these tactical errors becomes an industry practice, it creates a potential industry "fault line." New entrants often exploit these fault lines, thereby changing industry structure to their benefit. Entrants are free agents and have no investment, financial or emotional, in existing practices. Further, they may have products or services that can eliminate the need for the services traditionally provided by existing channels. As a result they can compete profitably at significantly lower prices—as in the case of the importers of "generic" air-powered fasteners—and gain share rapidly while incumbents are struggling to adapt their strategies to the new realities.

Implications for Channels

Just as companies risk losing their competitive position if they do not change channels at different stages of market evolution, so channels also risk becoming isolated and irrelevant if they fail to adapt to changes in customer requirements or technological evolution. In particular, they must recognize the following:

- Change is inevitable.
- It is difficult, if not impossible, to reverse the cycle.
- Anticipation is essential.

Regardless of intentions, almost every supplier who promises to remain exclusive will be forced to change—or risk becoming irrelevant. Intermediaries, therefore, should be careful when making significant investments in facilities, training, or inventories, particularly in a market that is changing rapidly. Otherwise, they run the risk of being stranded with unproductive assets.

Under competitive pressure, channels often convince themselves that the solution is to offer even more services and increase the value added as perceived by the customer. The idea is that, "Once customers *really* understand all the services we provide, they will happily pay more and buy from us." Unfortunately, if the changes have occurred due to external forces—increased buyer awareness, education by early adopters or early majority, greater familiarity with the product or services offered, and so on—then such efforts only increase overhead costs without materially improving revenues or profits. Microcomputer dealers such as Businessland have tried to become "value-added remarketers" without notable success. Similarly, automotive dealers have tried to sell the value of the dealership's service department without slowing the exodus to mass marketers such as Midas, Sears, Goodyear, and AAMCO.

Just as suppliers must make positioning decisions, channels too must anticipate and choose their positioning in a market that is evolving. There are only two basic choices—keep services and change products, or cut services and keep products. The first alternative recognizes that the channel cannot (or does not wish to) reduce the services it offers its customers. In which case, the channel must seek out new products or customers where its services genuinely add value, in terms of the buyer's willingness to pay for these services. Bloomingdale's department store, for example, has taken this approach in meeting the competitive threat from off-price retailers; it has added/changed labels and merchandise and refocused its efforts on customers who want a pleasant shopping experience (and are willing to pay for it). Alternatively, the channel may decide to cut the services it offers and continue selling the same products to the same customers at lower prices. This is analogous to a department store opting to become an off-price retailer itself.

Summary

Channels affect leverage by influencing both freedom of maneuver and return. Strong channels such as mass merchandisers in appliances, discounters in apparel and furnishings, and discounters and mail order firms in personal computers can change and may even dictate the terms of competition in an industry. There may also be considerable returns in switching to new types of channels, particularly as an industry matures and buyers are familiar with the new innovation. By carefully analyzing the leverage available and anticipating how it changes, companies can make major strategic gains even in (or especially in) mature industries.

14

Using Pricing
to Create Maneuver
and Maintain Leverage

Payoffs and leverage, in conjunction with a company's objectives, define the overall importance and the role of pricing tactics. They determine how and to what extent prices are constrained, the returns for different tactics, and how pricing must change as the industry evolves.

These relationships also work in reverse. Pricing tactics can change a company's strategic leverage, and they may even radically alter industry payoffs. Successful price discrimination, for example, increases a company's freedom of maneuver and its leverage in the target market dimension. Using this tactic, a company may compete as a mainstream player in one segment and an up-market or premium-priced player in another. Mercedes Benz is a mass-market competitor in Europe, especially Germany, and a luxury carmaker overseas.

Earlier we described how industry structure and company position affected a company's leverage in pricing. We also considered the crucial role of pricing (and price-based promotions) in market signaling. In this chapter we will discuss specific pricing tactics that can be used to exploit or change strategic leverage. First, we review how tactical pricing decisions are influenced by a company's freedom of maneuver. Next we discuss price bundling, namely selling a number of products or services for one price. We show how price bundling in the early stages of an industry can create attractive returns. However, trying to maintain bundled

269

prices as the industry matures limits freedom of maneuver. It may prevent a firm from competing in certain rapidly growing segments. It makes the company vulnerable by offering opportunities for competitors or potential entrants to "skim the cream." Price discrimination allows the company to (legally) sell the same product or service at different prices to different groups of customers. Successful price discrimination increases freedom of maneuver and leverage. But it can also create opportunities for competitors, and especially for third-party suppliers (gray markets).

A related issue is how to price complements, especially after-market complements such as spare parts, repair services, etc., so as to exploit a company's leverage. Complements provide ample opportunities for bundling and price discrimination; not surprisingly, these same tactics can leave the firm vulnerable when industry structure and strategic leverage shift.

Tactical Pricing

Tactical pricing issues, such as whether to match or exceed competitors' price changes, how to determine the timing of price changes, how to react to customers' price pressures, and when to make changes in discount schedules, occupy a great deal of management's time. In part, this is because the actual implementation of such changes throughout a large sales organization and widespread customer base is time-consuming. However, much time is also wasted on needless activity and, worse, pricing changes that accomplish little and may even prove counterproductive. This occurs because managers either have not defined their long-term pricing objectives and approaches or because they have failed to analyze their freedom of maneuver and their leverage. As a result, they usually have no idea which, if any, pricing moves will have the desired effect.

We can categorize these short-term, tactical pricing issues according to whether they are concerned with one of the following questions:

- How should a firm respond to competitive changes in prices, i.e., the *nature* of the response?
- How fast should a firm respond to these changes, i.e., the *speed* of the response?

We can analyze how a firm should respond to competitive moves in terms of its freedom of maneuver by considering how its ability to change prices is affected by buyer power and the ease with which competitors can learn about price changes.[1] If buyer power is high (customers are price sensitive) and price changes are transparent to other players, then there is relatively little freedom of maneuver and, therefore, little leverage in pricing. In this case, participants must match any changes in price (see Figure 14.1). If buyer power is low and price changes are "opaque" to other competitors, then there is considerably more freedom of maneuver and pricing offers some leverage. The first situation—high buyer power and considerable price visibility—corresponds to a commodity sold to large purchasers, for example, basic chemicals, aluminum, and long-distance transmission services.

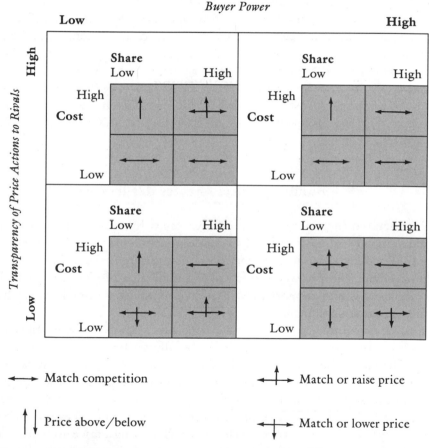

Figure 14.1 Tactical pricing and a firm's freedom of maneuver. Reprinted by permission of *Harvard Business Review*. An exhibit from "Making Money with Proactive Pricing" by Eliot B. Ross (November–December 1984). Copyright © 1984 by the President and Fellows of Harvard College; all rights reserved.

The second is typical of catalog items sold to retail customers. In the case of commodities, other participants must match any price changes; on the other hand, they should not lower prices to avoid a downward spiral. In the case of catalog items, by contrast, companies have much more flexibility as the average catalog shopper has relatively limited information about price levels and changes, and is not very price sensitive within his or her particular category.

The speed of responses to pricing changes is also important. If a firm is too slow to respond to price changes it could lose valuable share and, in the case of the leader, create an impression that it is vulnerable to attacks by competitors. If industry conflict is limited, it is the leader's duty to police prices, initiate changes instead of passively reacting to them, and vigorously attack any destabilizing price tactics by competitors. A firm's competitive position also affects the timing of the response. A well-placed firm whose share is high and costs are low relative to its competitors should speedily match any price *decreases;* it has more latitude in responding to price increases.[2] By contrast, a weak follower—a firm with low share and high costs relative to its competitors—has to be slower in following price decreases but quick to profit from any general price *increases.*

Bundling Prices Creates Returns

As discussed in Chapter 12, bundling speeds innovation diffusion by reducing buyers' costs and risks when purchasing a new product or service. Bundling also raises the barriers to entry; potential entrants cannot just provide the primary product; they must also provide the various complements and support services. Thus bundling creates leverage by raising returns and increasing freedom of maneuver.

How the bundle is priced directly determines how well a company can exploit the leverage available from bundling. Improperly executed, bundling may fail to generate the level of sales anticipated, or it may cannibalize other, successful product lines. Further, the price of the bundle cannot be static. As the industry evolves, managers must continually review and, when necessary, adjust the price of the bundle. They must also be ready to unbundle in time, or else they risk creating a price umbrella for competitors and entrants. As we shall discuss, such price umbrellas can be extremely costly, even downright fatal to a company's market revenues and market share.

In this section we will address the question, "How should we price the bundle so as to fully exploit our strategic leverage?" We will then examine how changes in leverage make continued bundling an untenable tactic and highlight the tradeoffs that must be considered when unbundling prices.

Pricing the Bundle

As we indicated briefly in Chapter 12, pricing problems in bundling fall into one of two cases. The first is when prospective purchasers have no information regarding the prices of the different components of the bundle. The second category is when the prices of some or all elements of the bundle are widely known. New innovations, such as Xerography or Polaroid color film, fall into the first category, while the bundling of options such as radios and stereo systems by automobile manufacturers and dealers is an example of the second.

When Purchasers Have No Information.   In this case, pricing the bundled offering is no different from pricing other, unbundled new products. The only considerations are the overall positioning of the product in the marketplace and how the perceived value of the bundle compares with the proposed price.

This approach to pricing the bundle works as long as the manufacturer can suppress or control the prices of the various components. However, sooner or later, customers learn the prices of some items. Once this occurs, a company's freedom of maneuver and its leverage shrink drastically, and the pricing problem changes to the second category.

When Purchasers Know Prices of Some or All Components.   In many cases, customers have access to information regarding some or all of the components of the bundle. For example, the prospective car buyer has (or can obtain) the prices of the car radio or stereo system when purchased separately. In this case, for the bundled offering to be attractive it must be either (1) cheaper than purchasing the car and radio or stereo systems separately, or (2) more convenient or reliable, or (3) both.

The requirement that the price of the bundle be less than the total price of its components, plus search, aggregation, and transaction costs, also offers insight into why bundling is most effective early in the life cycle of an innovation and why there is a tendency towards unbundling as a product or technology enters maturity. In the early stages of innovation, customers have little or no information regarding the components of the bundle. Consequently, finding alternative sources of components, obtaining necessary items, assembling them, that is, recreating the bundled offering, is both expensive and risky. By comparison, the bundled offering appears quite attractive; in other words, there is considerable freedom and leverage in bundling. As the product technology matures, the situation changes. Third parties start offering key components or services and the widespread diffusion of technology means less uncertainty about how to assemble the various elements together, for example, how to install the third-party radio or stereo in the automobile. These developments lower customers' costs, thereby decreasing the perceived value of the bundle.

These relationships also show that, for bundling to be successful, managers must either (1) lower their costs of producing the bundle to the levels required for customer acceptance, (2) control or raise the prices of components sold separately (increase maneuver), or (3) concentrate on the more risk-averse segments of the market or those segments where the perceived opportunity costs are high, that is, go where the return is high. In practice, firms use all of these approaches when creating and pricing bundled products. Japanese automotive manufacturers apparently lowered their costs by including traditional extras such as air conditioning and radios in the base price of the car. Equipment manufacturers often make their service contracts more attractive by raising their prices for noncontract service calls and parts. Appliance manufacturers sell extended warranties to risk-averse householders.

Service Contracts: An Example*

Service contracts are used extensively in providing after-sales support—parts, on- or off-site repair, documentation, training—for a variety of industrial, office computer, and telecommunications equipment.[3] Such contracts are usually priced as bundles, that is, they provide some or all of these products and services for a single annual fee.

Service contracts illustrate vividly the several issues involved in pricing product or service bundles. First, they show how the availability of "reference prices" and other information that allows prospective purchasers to estimate the costs of various elements reduces a company's freedom of maneuver and/or its leverage. This, in turn, places limits on the pricing of the total package. Service contracts also demonstrate the key factors for the success of a bundling strategy, namely, keeping the costs of the bundle low, raising or controlling the prices of reference items, and marketing bundles to risk-averse segments. Last but not least, service contracts illustrate how the pressures for unbundling increase as

---

*This subsection is somewhat technical and can be skipped without any loss of continuity.

the technology matures and highlight the problems often encountered in unbundling prices.

Consider a piece of equipment, such as a personal computer, that is subject to failure. When it fails, a customer has two alternatives: he can repair it and pay for the repair on a "time-and-materials" basis, that is, parts, labor, and any transportation charges, as incurred. Or else he may purchase a service contract that covers all these costs. Thus, a buyer's choice is between a predictable cost, namely, the price of the service contract, P_{sc}, and the risk that annual repair cost will exceed P_{sc}.

Figure 14.2 represents a buyer's choices as being between a certain cost P_{sc}, and a lottery with the expected outcome being the average repair cost[4] but with a small, nonzero probability that the repair costs could be very high. If a buyer is rational (that is, not risk averse), then the service contract must cost less than the expected repair cost, ERC. Otherwise a buyer would have no incentive for choosing the service contract.

However, if the buyer is risk averse, then a known, fixed price (P_{sc}) will be preferable to the possibility of a large loss. In this case, P_{sc}, the service contract, can be priced as

Average annual repair cost $\leq P_{sc} \leq p_m * M *$ degree of risk aversion

where p_m represents the probability of a major failure and M is the cost of repairing the major failure.

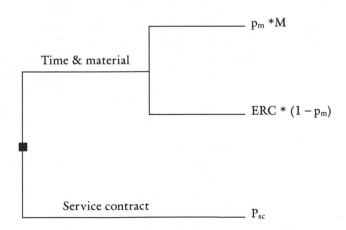

p_m = Probability of a major failure
M = Maximum repair cost, time & material basis
P = Price of service contract
ERC = Expected or average repair cost

Figure 14.2   Evaluating service contracts.

This inequality helps us understand how reference prices and other information can influence the price of the bundled offering. First, note that M, the cost of repairing a major failure, places a definite upper bound on P_{sc}. Further, the more risk averse the buyer, the greater the latitude on the service contract price. Next, note the following:

- Buyers often estimate M using perceived reliability (average number of failures per year) and their estimates of average repair costs, using the information on time-and-material prices. The average annual cost of repairs therefore becomes a reference price.

- For items whose prices are low in relation to a buyer's asset base or income stream, the replacement cost of the item becomes a reference price for M, provided there are few or no opportunity costs. Thus, M is equal to the replacement price for "disposables" such as Timex watches and some small household appliances such as toasters.

- If the perceived reliability of the item is high, then the ERC drops. In turn, this often lowers customers expectations regarding the *likely* cost of a major failure,[5] thereby placing downward pressure on service contract prices.

Thus, the prices quoted for time-and-material repairs, together with customer perceptions about the frequency of failure, have a definite impact on the price of the service contract, the bundled offering.

A concrete example will make this clearer. Assume that the personal computer cost $3,000, the average number of failures is 0.5 per year, the ERC (labor and materials) is $100, the cost of repairing (or replacing) the most expensive component is $800, and the probability of this component failing is 5 percent. Then the service contract should be priced between $50 (the average annual cost of repairs) and $800 per year. In reality, customers will use some multiple of the average annual cost of repairs to judge the value of the service contract. A corollary is that a service contract priced too high, say at $500 per year, will be taken as an indication that the equipment itself is not very reliable; customers will perceive that the manufacturer expects it to fail often. Thus, service contracts also send signals to potential buyers regarding the inherent reliability of the product.

The relationship between ERC, P_{sc}, and the maximum repair cost also confirms our statements regarding the keys for the success of a bundling strategy. First, the lower the bundled price, P_{sc}, the greater its attraction to potential buyers. Second, raising prices for time-and-material work raises the reference prices, permitting greater latitude in pricing the service contract. Similarly controlling information about the frequency of failure adds to a buyer's uncertainty regarding likely repair costs, once again increasing the attractiveness of service contracts. Finally, the more risk averse the customer, the higher the upper limits on P_{sc} and the greater the freedom in pricing service contracts.

Shrinking Leverage Forces Unbundling

As the industry goes from growth into maturity, a company's leverage declines, making bundling progressively less tenable or profitable. Maintaining bundled prices under these conditions makes a company increasingly vulnerable to competitors and entrants. Where bundling is an industry-wide practice, it may even create potential "fault lines." Down the road, such fault lines can lead to cataclysmic changes and an extremely painful industry restructuring, as demonstrated by the experiences of the air-powered fastener industry in the mid-1980s.

Two factors cause leverage to shrink and make bundling an endangered tactic. Changes in industry structure such as increased buyer power or greater rivalry reduce freedom of maneuver, thereby lowering a company's flexibility in setting prices. At the same time, increased buyer familiarity with the product or service, the availability of some or all of the components of the bundle from third parties, and the rise of substitutes lower the attractiveness of the bundled offering to customers. As a result, the returns from bundling decline.

We begin by categorizing the pressures forcing unbundling. Next we highlight the strategic implications of unbundling and discuss the various tradeoffs. Last, we examine when and how to unbundle prices.

Pressures Forcing Unbundling

Before discussing the detailed tactical questions involved in unbundling, we must recognize that unbundling becomes an issue of if and only if,

- The bundled price, P_B, is greater than the sum of the perceived or actual prices of individual components, ΣP_i, i.e., $P_B \geq \Sigma P_i$, and
- Perceived or actual search, aggregation, and transaction costs exist.

When these conditions hold, the seller is charging a premium over the "free market" price of the bundle.[6] This premium makes bundling an attractive strategy by offering above-market returns. In turn, these above-market returns create pressures for unbundling by attracting new entrants and by providing an incentive to buyers for exerting buyer power.

New entrants use this premium as an umbrella, offering key components of the bundle at substantially lower prices, thereby increasing their share. This is a signal to the incumbent that leverage is changing. At this point, the original seller can either ignore the threat, lower the price of the bundle, or unbundle and compete directly with the new entrants. Ignoring the threat merely postpones the decision; worse, by allowing new entrants to gain share without retaliation, it makes subsequent adjustments even more painful. Lowering the bundled price is usually not economically feasible; the new entrant has substantially lower costs because it has not incurred the initial R&D expenditures, and it is not providing services required by only a few customers or segments. This leaves unbundling the package and meeting entrants head-on as the only viable alternative. However, as we shall discuss later in this section, unbundling also imposes costs and risks.

As the technology starts to mature, buyers have more information and wider choices. As a result, they revise their estimates of the likely search, aggregation, and transaction costs, thereby lowering the returns for bundling. These changes in buyers' perceived or actual costs make the premium appear "excessive" or monopolistic. If buyers have power, they increase price pressures on the firm, causing it either to lower the price of the bundled package or, alternatively, unbundling partially or completely.

Strategic Implications

This premium also explains why firms are reluctant to unbundle: Any firm disaggregating a bundled offering incurs substantial costs. Nearly always, unbundling leads to lower total revenues, at least in the short term. At the same time, the firm's costs fail to adjust to the reduction in revenues. Consequently, unbundling causes a drastic fall in the firm's short-term profitability.

Why Revenues Fall.   In general, all the components of a given bundle are not equally attractive. Bundling exaggerates the true demand for the various components of the bundle. The corollary is that unbundling lowers demand and, therefore, total revenues.

We can intuitively understand how this occurs by considering a bundle consisting of a car and a stereo system. Given a choice, not all car buyers will elect to purchase a stereo system. Bundling thus raises unit demand for stereos without significantly lowering the demand for the car. Conversely, unbundling will lower demand for the stereo, again without affecting the demand for the automobile. Provided that demand for stereos is price elastic, total revenues will drop.

Revenues fall precipitously if there is significant, unbundled competition for the high volume components and demand is price inelastic. In such cases, unbundling forces the prices of key components to the levels set by competition. However, with demand inelastic, such price changes merely affect market share; they do not raise overall revenues. We shall discuss this point in more depth when we analyze price unbundling in the air-powered fastener industry.

Why Costs Fail to Adjust Rapidly. Inefficiencies in sales or operations, implicit or explicit cross-subsidies, and a reluctance to eliminate services no longer valued by customers explain why costs fail to adjust rapidly to changes in revenue caused by unbundling. Often, these factors are interrelated. For example, bundled selling generally requires high service channels, with corresponding high costs, such as high margins or expense-to-revenue ratios. When a firm unbundles, such channels are inefficient; they provide more services than customers want, and they are not cost-effective at providing the basic services buyers require. Lowering these costs takes time due to a firm's slowness in recognizing that traditionally provided services are no longer wanted (in the sense that customers are willing to pay for them), and difficulties in terminating existing channel arrangements and finding lower cost alternatives.

Similarly, the high volume items of the bundle cross-subsidize other components by distorting operating overhead allocations that are volume-based. This encourages investments in less profitable product and services that might not be justified if the lines were judged on their own merits. Unbundling highlights these cross-subsidies, but eliminating unnecessary costs takes time.

The combination of a sharp drop in revenues and continuing high costs reduces profits drastically. Not surprisingly, unbundling is therefore viewed as a last resort by most companies. However, postponing the decision to unbundle is dangerous; in the interim, a firm stands to lose market share and, more important, customer loyalty, once buyers perceive the firm's prices as excessively high in comparison with unbundled competitors.

Whether to Unbundle

When unbundled competitors enter a market that was previously bundled, a firm selling bundled packages has three choices: it can stay bundled; it can be the first to unbundle; or it can create pressure for across-the-board unbundling by all players in the industry.

If the firm remains bundled, it risks a continuing loss of market share as rivals attack the high-volume, high-margin components of its offerings. If the firm initiates unbundling, it takes the risk that other firms may stay bundled and merely match its (unbundled) prices, in an effort to gain share. Now the firm can either cut its prices further in an effort to force industry-wide unbundling, or it can retreat and become bundled again. Neither option is attractive. Further cuts risk widespread price warfare; on the other hand, rebundling means a general lowering of prices without the fundamental changes necessary to counter unbundled entrants. Finally, the firm can create pressures for industry-wide unbundling by lowering the prices of its packages, selling key components separately, or unbundling its prices in key, price-sensitive segments (see Figure 14.3).

In choosing among these three alternatives, a firm must consider the implications for its revenues and profits, its ability to influence or control prices in the industry, its market share and overall competitive position, and likely reactions of both bundled competitors and unbundled entrants.

Implications for Revenues and Profits. As discussed earlier, unbundling reduces revenues and profits, at least in the short term. Thus, a firm must decide between a sharp, "one-time" drop or a slow, steady erosion of revenues over a longer period of time (see Figure 14.4). Viewed in this light, the choice depends upon whether the short-term revenue (or profit) losses are outweighed by the long-term revenue (or profit) gains provided by unbundling.

As we can see from Figure 14.4, a key issue is, "How fast will bundled revenues drop to the level of unbundled revenues, that is, what is the time

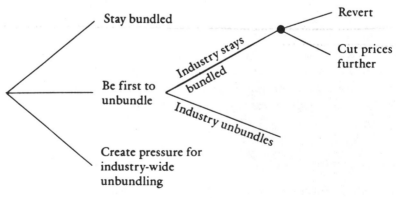

Figure 14.3 Whether to unbundle.

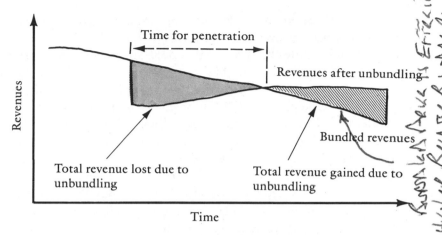

Figure 14.4   Revenue tradeoffs.

for penetration?" At one extreme, if the interval is extremely long, then the firm gains by staying bundled. Conversely, if the interval is likely to be extremely short, then unbundling is preferred. How long bundled revenues will stay above the level of unbundled revenues depends on

- The perceived or actual differences in prices
- How rapidly buyers will discover unbundled alternatives
- Buyers' aversion to risk.

If the difference in prices is large, information spreads quickly, and buyers are not particularly risk averse, then bundled revenues will drop rapidly. Conversely, small perceived or actual price differentials, slow diffusion of information, and highly risk-averse buyers will slow the erosion of bundled revenues for a long time.

Buyer power is a major influence on the speed with which unbundled offerings will penetrate the market. Large corporate buyers will tend to discover unbundled offerings more rapidly and, being larger, they are less risk averse. Consequently, unbundling is preferable in markets or segments where buyers are powerful. In markets where buyers are weak (as is the case for many consumer goods and services), a firm should stay bundled as penetration by unbundled competitors will be relatively much slower.

Price Control and Market Share.   These generally go hand-in-hand; market share is essential if a firm wishes to maintain price control, and price control is vital to retaining market share. The entry of unbundled competitors threatens both. By offering unbundled products and services at significantly lower prices, they affect the price positioning of the (bundled) industry leader. If the leader does not respond immediately or aggressively, it risks losing its ability to set the terms of competition and control industry conflict. Further, unless the leader can regain control, over time its market share will be "nibbled" away by unbundled entrants.

Therefore, in industries where controlling price and market share is important, the leader must attack unbundled entrants vigorously, unbundling early and forcing the rest of the industry to follow suit. Followers, especially niche players, have little to gain by initiating price unbundling; they should be among the last to unbundle. They need not unbundle at all, if their customers face switching costs or are particularly risk averse. In industries where price or share leadership are difficult due to structural instabilities or high fixed costs, the choice is less clear. Unbundling in such industries may result in prolonged price wars, a general lowering of prices without bundling, or both.

Competitors' Reactions.   Before unbundling a firm must also assess the likely reactions of the other players. These can be divided into two groups, existing (bundled) competitors and new (unbundled) entrants. Existing competitors can either unbundle at the same time, wait without lowering their prices, or stay bundled but lower prices in an effort to gain share. If they unbundle simultaneously, there is no change in the status quo. If they do not unbundle and maintain previous price levels, the firm unbundling has the opportunity of increasing market share. However, if other competitors lower prices without unbundling, the firm is in a difficult position, as discussed earlier.

New (unbundled) entrants tend to lower their prices as existing players unbundle; they want to maintain their price positioning and market share. This means that the revenue drop will be larger than estimated. These reductions could also lead to a price war, with each side progressively cutting prices in a vain attempt to close or maintain the gap between their relative prices.

When to Unbundle

Basically the rule is unbundle early if you are the industry leader and later if you are a follower. Leaders should err on the side of unbundling earlier rather than later, particularly in industries where

- Share is important for economies of scale in manufacturing or marketing

- Regaining customers who have switched is difficult
- A firm's market share makes it vulnerable to "cream skimming" by unbundled entrants.

Unfortunately, leaders frequently ignore such threats and postpone unbundling until far too late, choosing to maximize near-term revenues.[7]

Followers should unbundle much more slowly, particularly if they are niche players in well-established, defensible niches. Followers are much less vulnerable to attack by unbundled entrants because their markets are smaller, and the needs of their customers are unique or different. An unbundled entrant therefore faces higher costs and lower returns, making any attacks on niches much less attractive.

How to Unbundle

As we have seen, a variety of approaches ranging from gradual to immediate ("flashcut") unbundling are feasible. For example, a firm offering service contracts for hardware or software support can

- Price routine maintenance services separately
- Provide training as a separate, unbundled option
- Offer multiple bundles, for example, routine support with emergency requirements on a time-and-materials basis, standard support, and 24-hour support at additional cost
- Create a second, unbundled brand of products or services, sold through separate channels
- Negotiate unbundled contracts with large users, charging separately for parts, on-site service or technical support, and training.

Gradual unbundling minimizes revenue losses due to unbundling. It also enables a firm to "price discriminate," that is, keep on marketing bundled packages to certain segments.

Sometimes, such a gradual approach risks price attrition rather than true unbundling, depending on how rapidly leverage is changing and on the underlying industry payoffs. In this case, a company should unbundle its prices virtually overnight by

- Announcing separate, unbundled prices for all components of the bundle
- Lowering prices of high volume items to make them competitive with unbundled entrants

- Discontinuing low-demand/high-cost products and services
- Making deep cuts in marketing costs by either reducing sales personnel, changing channel margins, or if necessary, dropping existing channels in favor of lower-cost alternatives.

Such rapid unbundling is traumatic for the entire organization, not to mention to the channels affected. It also carries high risks—new channels may be slow to take hold, the firm may not be able to trim its expenses fast enough, or customers may leave if certain long-standing products are discontinued. However, sometimes it is the only option.

The U.S. Air-Powered Fastener Industry

Air-powered fasteners such as nails and staples are used in a number of different industries including automotive upholstery, furniture, residential construction, manufactured housing and packaging. (For a discussion of changes in distribution patterns in this industry, see Chapter 13.) U.S. firms traditionally bundled tools, spare parts, training, and support into fastener prices. In the 1980s, the industry came under attack from "generics"—suppliers that sold only fasteners not tools or accessories. In five years, generics captured nearly 15 percent of the market, using fastener prices that were between 20 and 40 percent lower than those of their bundled competitors. The presence of generics also created customer dissatisfaction with what they perceived as the excessively high prices of bundled or "full-line" suppliers. These pressures were compounded by slow overall demand, which further reduced industry profitability. Full-line suppliers therefore had to decide whether they should unbundle fastener prices and, if so, how they should unbundle.

The full-line manufacturers' difficulties in responding to unbundled competition illustrate the very real problems in unbundling prices. This case also illustrates

- How changes in structure cause leverage to shrink, making bundled pricing untenable
- How persisting with bundling for far too long creates industry "fault lines"
- How unbundling is difficult and risky when the terms of competition are unstable and/or there is no clear industry leader
- Why market signals are essential in unbundling prices
- How traumatic unbundling can be if left until too late.

Background

The air-powered fastener and nail industry started in the late 1940s in response to the automotive industry's need to speed up production to meet to postwar demand. Two or three manufacturers developed air-powered staplers to replace manual stapling. These air-powered staplers used stacks of staples, similar in shape (but not in size) to office staples. These stacks were loaded into a pneumatically driven tool that "fired" each staple individually with great speed and uniformity, thereby improving productivity and quality. Initial applications were in attaching cloth to the interior of automotive fixtures, which was subsequently extended into automotive upholstery. The natural extension was into furniture, which occurred in the mid-1950s. Subsequently, as appropriate tools became readily available, air-powered fasteners spread into mobile and manufactured housing and, in the late 1960s, into on-site construction. In 1984, total industry sales amounted to approximately $500 million.

Staples and nails are manufactured from steel wire in a variety of sizes to suit different applications. They may be left uncoated or covered with plastic or other finishes. Tools typically consist of a housing that contains the air-driven firing system, and a feeding system for the nails or staples. The housing is generally made of metal, and must successfully withstand pressures of 60 to 120 pounds per square inch. Tool manufacture involves close tolerances to insure smooth, safe operation of the nailer or stapler (the terms are used interchangeably). In general, tool manufacturing is a low volume operation, with annual production runs averaging under 300 pieces.[8]

Fastener manufacturing is automated to a considerable degree and is thus relatively more capital intensive than tool production. However, capital is not a particular barrier to entry; several small firms have produced fasteners. In 1985, a typical manufacturing plant represented an investment of $15 to $18 million, net of land acquisition costs. Economies of scale were significant only in wire purchasing and in castings for tools.

Industry Organization

The players in this industry can be organized into two categories, full-line or *major manufacturers* and *generics*. In 1985, major manufacturers accounted for 80 percent of total industry volume, divided approximately equally among five participants: NailTite, Signode, AeroNail, Bea, and Senco Products. However, there were wide differences in ownership, motivations, and market focus. NailTite and Signode were subsidiaries of larger, diversified organizations, while Senco and AeroNail were privately held, and Bea was based in Italy. Signode concentrated almost exclusively on the packaging segment, while Bea had the lion's share of the upholstered furniture market. Only NailTite, AeroNail, and Senco competed across the board. Industry profitability was hard to estimate, as all participants were either privately held or subsidiaries of larger organizations. In the period 1982 to 1985, profits were virtually nonexistent, with all participants experiencing losses in one segment or another.

These firms marketed the common fasteners (staples and nails) that were used in tools supplied by the majors. Historically, generics were small, low-overhead operations, concentrating in a limited geographic area. Consequently, the majors tended to ignore generics. From 1981 to 1985, generic competition intensified due to imports, primarily from Germany and Italy. A strong dollar, depressed demand for steel wire in Europe, and government subsidies allowed importers to undercut the majors' prices by 20 to 40 percent and still be profitable.

The market had four distinct segments, namely, on-site construction, mobile and manufactured housing, furniture, and industrial packaging. On-site construction and packaging were the two largest, followed by furniture and mobile and manufactured housing. (Figure 14.5 summarizes the characteristics of each of these segments and the market shares of the major players.)

Marketing Strategies

Historically, the major manufacturers adopted a razor/razor blade approach in order to speed market development. Typically, they supplied tools and support services such as training, parts, and repairs free to customers purchasing fasteners. Generally, only medium-sized and large customers received tools free; smaller accounts had to purchase their tools. However, even small accounts received support services directly from manufacturers, usually free of charge.

Channels. The industry used three primary channels—direct sales, distributors and dealers, and specialty dealers—but their roles varied by segment. Direct sales was the only channel in mobile and manufactured housing, while all three channels were used in on-site construction. Due to its highly fragmented nature, industrial packaging was served almost exclusively by distributors/dealers. Finally, in the furniture segment, large and some medium-sized accounts were handled by the direct sales force, while the others were funneled to distributors/dealers. Generic

On-site construction
  Segment volume: $140 million
  Customer characteristics   Market shares
  Small accounts: 80–85% of total customers   Senco   24%
                  40% of sales   NailTite   18%
  Large accounts: 10–15% of total customers   Signode   17%
                  60% of sales   AeroNail   13%

Industrial packaging
  Segment volume: $70 million
  Customer characteristics   Market shares
  Highly fragmented customer base   NailTite   30%
                                                  Signode   23%
                                                  Senco   10%

Furniture
  Segment volume: $85 million
  Customer characteristics   Market shares
  Similar to on-site construction, i.e., 15% of   Bea   27%
  customers purchase 60% of total segment volume Senco   24%
                                                  AeroNail   21%
                                                  NailTite   10–12%

Mobile and manufactured housing
  Segment volume: $70 million
  Customer characteristics   Market shares
  Primarily large accounts, relatively concentrated Senco   45%
                                                  AeroNail   26%
                                                  Signode   10%

As of 1985; estimates only.

Figure 14.5 Characteristics of major segments—air-powered fasteners.

manufacturers had no direct sales of their own and used dealers and master distributors exclusively.

Pricing. Nominally the industry had four levels of pricing: list price, dealer price, a master distributor price, and a large account price. Small accounts nominally paid list prices. Dealer and master distributor prices were between 20 and 30 percent below list, with large accounts paying somewhat more than master distributors. In reality, the industry lacked price (and channel) discipline, and the distinctions between these price levels were hopelessly blurred. Dealers purchasing large volumes or medium-sized accounts purchasing comparable volumes of fasteners and tools could often negotiate individual discount schedules. Large accounts had considerable buyer power and used it to extract periodic price concessions by playing one supplier against another. Direct sales personnel occasionally undercut their own dealers to keep vital accounts in-house. Finally, the majors competed intensely on prices, with the result that price concessions offered to induce key accounts to switch suppliers often resulted in across-the-board price reductions.

The Threat from Generics

Generic suppliers added to the price pressures by offering discounts as high as 40 percent on key, high-volume fastener sizes. This created the impression of a substantial price disparity between the generics and the majors, disregarding the fact that the majors offered a complete line as well as tools and support services, while generics carried only a narrow line of the most popular, high volume sizes.

By mid-1985, generics had captured almost 20 percent of the on-site construction market, placing them on a par with the majors. They were also making considerable inroads into the furniture market and, to a lesser extent, the packaging market. As yet, generics had not entered the mobile and manufactured housing; however, it was only a matter of time before players in this segment also faced generic competition.

The full-line manufacturers were even more alarmed by the breathtaking speed with which the generics penetrated the market. While there were always a few regional generic suppliers, they never accounted for more than 5 percent of the total market. The current surge in generics was led by overseas—primarily German and Italian—manufacturers of fasteners. Possessing far greater marketing and financial resources than the previous group of generic suppliers, these new players were much more aggressive in both their pricing and their sales efforts. As a result, generics' sales grew more than 30 percent annually in the period 1981 to 1985, while overall industry growth in the same time period averaged less than 4 percent per year.

Choices . . . and Tradeoffs

Faced with the growing power of generics in the on-site construction, packaging, and furniture segments and knowing that it was only a matter of time before generic competitors attacked mobile and manufactured housing, full-line manufacturers realized they had to rethink their traditional, bundled pricing strategies. Unfortunately, changes would be both expensive and risky, as shown in Figure 14.6, which illustrates the several choices and their likely outcomes.

One possibility was to maintain current bundled pricing, making tactical adjustments to retain accounts. The reasoning was ". . . generics have grown because the dollar was overpriced. Once the dollar drops to a

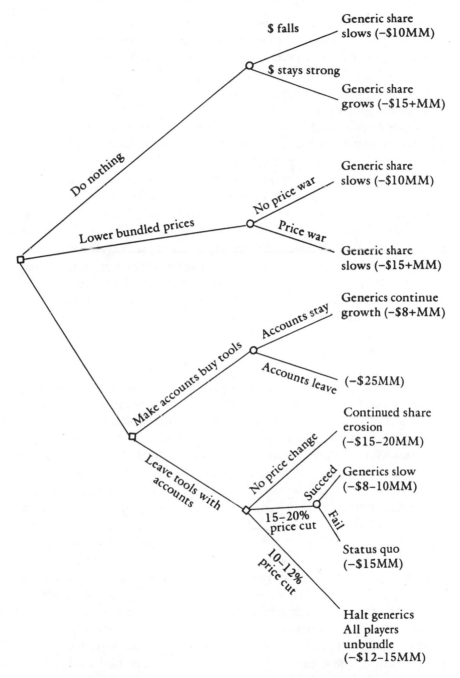

Figure 14.6 Full-line manufacturer's choices and trade-offs.

more realistic level, generics will lose their price advantages and their growth will slow down." This dealt with European imports; however, it still left open the possibility that generics would merely source their fasteners from other countries such as Taiwan and South Korea, as subsequently occurred. This approach also entailed continuing share erosion, revenue and profit losses, or both.

A second option was to stay bundled but lower prices of high-volume fasteners to halt the inroads of generics. This would be extremely expensive and could potentially ignite an industry-wide price war. To halt generic competition, a major manufacturer would have to cut the prices of high-volume lines at least 15 to 20 percent. Given that these items accounted for more than 80 percent of their sales volume, such a cut would lower revenues approximately 12 to 15 percent, or about $10 million per year.[9] However, this assumed that other players would not perceive such a cut as an attempt to gain share at their expense. If they did, a major price war was a distinct possibility, in which case the likely revenue losses might be much higher, perhaps as high as $20 million.

The third choice was to unbundle fasteners, tools, and spare parts and sell them all separately. This raised two questions, namely, "Do we make customers buy tools they are currently using or only those tools they may need in the future?" and "How should we price the high volume fasteners?" Charging customers for tools in place turned out to be a nonstarter; the risk that customers would switch if asked to purchase their tools was simply unacceptable. Deciding the prices of high volume fasteners was more difficult. Not cutting prices at all was not feasible; it provided no incentive to the other manufacturers to unbundle, and it merely ensured that customers would switch, either to other, unbundled major suppliers or, more likely, to generic suppliers for the bulk of their high volume requirements. On the other hand, a small price cut might not be enough; given the intense rivalry in the industry, the other major players might be tempted to lower their prices a matching amount without unbundling, in order to capture market share. If this occurred, the net result would be merely a general price reduction, without changing the practice of bundling and its associated costs. Yet too deep a price cut would be expensive and ran the risk of inciting a general price war.

The lack of price discipline and an acknowledged price leader complicated the situation further. Given the historically chaotic nature of price competition in the industry, firms wishing to unbundle could not predict accurately how other full-line suppliers might react to any changes. In addition, the differences in ownership—two firms were privately held, two were subsidiaries of much larger corporations, while the fifth was foreign owned—made it difficult to judge the likely motivations and staying power in any prolonged price war. One of the private firms (Senco) had a profitable subsidiary making surgical staples and could be expected to stay in the game a long time. Similarly, the corporate parents of both Signode and NailTite were profitable and could probably afford the costs of a long price war. An added complication was the lack of clear share leadership in any segment, implying that firms would find it difficult to abandon a particular market area. In short, price changes perceived as threatening could create a downward spiral, a successive series of price reductions as each player fought desperately to maintain share in the face of competitors' actions.

This example also shows the importance of signaling when unbundling prices. As Figure 14.6 shows, the preferred outcome is that all firms unbundle, with the prices of high volume fasteners being cut between 10 and 12 percent, that is, large enough to slow generics but small enough to minimize revenue losses. For this to occur, however, the other bundled players must cooperate by unbundling instead of lowering their (bundled) prices to gain share at the expense of the player to unbundle first. Market signals could help achieve this result, particularly if a clear share leader in a segment (such as Bea in furniture) unbundled while signaling that it was not a predatory move. The danger is that, lacking a clear market leader, other players may ignore the signals and cut prices without unbundling, forcing the initiator to either cut prices further in order to force unbundling or abandon the idea of unbundling and revert to bundled pricing.

Price Discrimination . . . and Gray Markets

Price discrimination occurs when a firm sells the same product or service to different groups of customers at different prices.[10] For example, in certain ethnic restaurants the price of an item may vary depending on whether it is ordered from the English or the ethnic-language menu, with the ethnic-language price being lower. Similarly, a department store and a specialty retailer often sell the same branded garment, perfume, or appliance at very different prices.

Firms use price discrimination to increase or exploit their leverage. Specifically:

- *To maximize profits.* Firms want to capitalize on differences in price sensitivity among different groups of customers. As mentioned earlier, Mercedes Benz's prices in the United States are consistently higher than in Europe, reflecting the willingness of U.S. purchasers to pay more for a Mercedes.

- *To create a second brand.* The same or similar item may be sold at different prices reflecting differences in perception or positioning, as for example Bentley versus Rolls Royce in automobiles.

- *To unbundle prices.* When unbundling a product or service, the same components may be sold at different prices either to encourage migration of customers to different (for example, lower service) channels, to differentiate on the basis of service, or both.

- *To maintain channel and segment separation.* Firms may deliberately market the same item to different segments through very different channels at markedly different prices. This is particularly the case in services; banks offer similar services at very different prices to encourage some customers (for example, well-to-do, ATM users) and discourage others.

- *To compensate for differences in costs.* Firms often charge different prices for the same item because the costs of serving different groups of customers vary. Examples are volume discounts, prices that vary with distance due to transportation costs, and "factory outlet" versus retail prices.

When Is Price Discrimination Feasible?

Consider the situation shown in Figure 14.7, in which a marketer is selling the same product to two different, distinct segments, A and B, at prices P_a and P_b, respectively. For the firm to successfully maintain a higher price in segment A than in segment B, there must be

- *Limited or no information exchange* between the two segments, that is, buyers in one segment must be ignorant of prices in the other segment

- *Perceived differences in usage or application* between the two segments, for example, antistatic spray sold to household users, and the same spray sold to computer users to minimize the effects of static on their equipment

- *Search, aggregation, or transaction costs* incurred in remarketing goods from segment B (the lower-price segment) to segment A, for example, buying an European automobile in the United States versus buying it for a lower price in Europe, shipping it over, getting it certified for U.S. safety and emission requirements and so forth

- *Perceived or actual risks* in remarketing goods between the two segments, for example, the manufacturer may not honor the warranty if purchased from an unauthorized dealer/distributor.

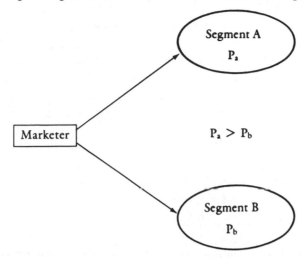

Figure 14.7   Price discrimination.

Furthermore, these differences must be high in relation to the price differential $(P_a - P_b)$. In other words, if price discrimination is to work, the perceived or actual costs (adjusted for the risks) of remarketing goods from segment B to segment A must be significantly higher than the potential profit.

Volume discounts to end users provide one illustration of how these conditions apply in practice. In most cases, the perceived or actual costs of remarketing exceed likely profits; consequently, even high-volume end users rarely compete with their suppliers. However, in long-distance telephone services, many large end users are also resellers. The reason? Price differentials are substantial and marketing costs low, especially when marketing to certain segments, for example, a firm's employees, dealers, and vendors.[11]

Gray Markets

These conditions also explain why it is difficult to price discriminate over the long term. Changes in awareness, wider information availability that reduces search or transactions costs, improvements in technology reducing the perceived risks of failure and, by extension, the value of warranties—these and other factors reduce the costs of remarketing, making it more attractive. This reduces the company's freedom of maneuver in pricing, making price discrimination more difficult to maintain. Increasing buyer awareness of price differences creates customer dissatisfaction. Buyer awareness also provides the incentive and the means for arbitrage, that is, for intermediaries who remarket goods from the lower-priced segment to the higher-priced one. In many cases, these intermediaries are the firm's own dealers and distributors, creating channel conflict.

Sustained price discrimination leads to "gray markets"—the cross-selling of goods from one segment to the other by resellers. These resellers may be "unauthorized" in that they have no formal connection to or support from the manufacturer, or they may be authorized to sell goods to one segment but are reselling outside their assigned market without the manufacturer's permission. The classic examples of gray markets occur in international marketing, where differences in exchange rates create opportunities for price arbitrage. In the early 1980s, a strong dollar coupled with Mercedes Benz's U.S. pricing policies enabled buyers to purchase automobiles in Germany, ship them to the United States, convert them to meet local emission and safety requirements, and still save thousands of dollars. In 1985, the gray market accounted for almost 40 percent of total Mercedes sales in the United States.[12]

Gray markets can also be created by inadvertent price discrimination, that is, unplanned or unanticipated differences in prices for the same product or service. Such inadvertent price discrimination can occur due to

- *Pricing policies,* for example, steeply graduated discount schedules that encourage overordering, prices that vary by type of transaction or channel[13]
- *Differences in channel costs,* which create price discrimination giving rise to a gray market
- *Channel strategies/policies,* such as selective distribution, that provide price umbrellas for unauthorized resellers when demand is strong, as IBM discovered when marketing its PC.[14]

Strategic Implications

When confronted with a gray market, a firm has three choices: It can try and eliminate the gray market; it can tolerate the gray market; or, on occasion, it may actually encourage the gray market.

To eliminate a gray market, a firm must increase its freedom of maneuver and/or maintain its leverage by making arbitrage unprofitable. That is, the company must ensure that (see Figure 14.7).

The price differential $(P_a - P_b)$ < Expected search, aggregation, or transaction costs, adjusted for risks

The company's choices are change the prices, reducing the differential, $(P_a - P_b)$, making reselling from segment B (the lower priced segment) to segment A unattractive, or confuse competitors regarding likely returns by such tactics as

- Changes in product packaging or identification, making it more difficult to compare products across segments
- Product registration to detect the flow of goods to unauthorized resellers, or
- Product warranties that are not valid outside designated sales areas.

Naturally, each of these approaches has costs and risks. Reducing the price differential $(P_a - P_b)$ by lowering P_a means foregoing lucrative profits. On the other hand, raising P_b risks losing customers in segment B to lower-priced competitors. Changes to product packaging or identification are often expensive and usually do not deter resellers for long. Tracking products is time-consuming and expensive, and punishing offenders carries legal risks. Finally, limited warranties are difficult to enforce and create customer dissatisfaction.

Given the high costs of eliminating gray markets, firms sometimes prefer to tolerate them, either as a temporary condition or because they believe that a gray market helps them reach different, more price-sensitive customers. Toleration may be the only remedy for temporary gray markets such as those caused by short-term currency fluctuations. However, tolerating gray markets as alternative means of reaching price-sensitive customers is both fallacious and dangerous. While it is true that gray market customers may include those who have not previously purchased the product, more typically they are buyers migrating from other, higher-priced channels. Tolerating gray markets in such cases creates channel conflict without corresponding benefits for the firm. Such tolerance is useful only if the firm has decided to change its channel strategy from selective to intensive distribution, as discussed in Chapter 13. In this case, a firm may actively encourage price discrimination (and any associated gray markets) in order to force changes in the structure of its channels.

Pricing Complements to Maintain Leverage

Complements such as peripherals, accessories, spare parts, and ancillary goods and services represent major sources of revenue and profit. Controlling the prices of complements is important to ensure rapid innovation diffusion or to maintain product positioning. However, companies often overlook the importance of pricing complements in maintaining their overall leverage. Instead, they price them as stand-alone items. As a result, firms often become attractive targets for "cream skimming" by competitors or third-party suppliers. Such cream skimming is sometimes exacerbated by cost-based pricing procedures that provide a price umbrella under which competitors flourish. Companies may also fail to control prices that channels charge for complements, thereby inviting competitors to enter. Finally, poorly priced complements distort the demand for the main product if channels find it more profitable to order basic models and package them with complements purchased from other sources.[15]

In Chapter 12, we categorized the roles of complementary products depending on whether they were perceived as complements by customers or were important to overall competitive position, or both. We then defined a firm's objectives in marketing complements as being either to promote innovation diffusion, maintain differentiation, or maximize profitability (see Figure 14.8).

We can use the same framework to determine pricing tactics for complementary products. We can draw the following conclusions:

- If complements help promote innovation diffusion, then pricing is crucial to maintaining and exploiting leverage. Prices of complements should be judged in terms of the overall rate of market growth, a firm's share of the market for complementary products, and its overall market share. Using margins alone is likely to result in prices that are too high, especially during the early stages of the innovation. Firms should use bundled pricing as and where appropriate.

Important to Competitive Position

	Yes	No
Perceived as Complements — Yes	**Control for rapid diffusion** • Bundle prices • Set price levels to maximize penetration	**Control for profit maximization** • Price independently to maximize profit
Perceived as Complements — No	**Control to maintain differentiation** • Use defensive pricing • Set price levels to maintain penetration, share	

Figure 14.8 Pricing complementary products.

- If complements are important to differentiation, then complements should be priced defensively, that is, so as to maintain a firm's quality (or feature)/price position relative to its competitors yet low enough to prevent cream skimming by competitors. Prices should be compared with those of third-party providers, and any premiums scrutinized with great care. Firms should not expect substantial price premiums over and above the price levels of independent suppliers of complementary products such as peripherals, accessories, supplies, and commonly available repair parts.

- If complements are used to maximize profitability, only then can they be priced without reference to the pricing and positioning of the main product.

The Attraction of a Large Installed Base of Customers

Firms encounter a number of problems when marketing complements, especially if they did not understand how their leverage may by limited. Common problems are (1) cream skimming by independent suppliers, (2) difficulties in controlling or maintaining a firm's market share in complements, (3) failure to control the prices charged by channels, and (4) substitution by channel members.

These problems occur because managers either fail to realize the attractiveness of their installed base of customers, or they assume that it can be protected from competition indefinitely. This leads to pricing policies that, over time, deviate from a firm's overall objectives of innovation diffusion or maintaining differentiation. Instead, blinded by the high profit potential of complements, managers increasingly price monopolistically, that is, they ignore how structure and payoffs restrict maneuver. Such high prices coupled with few or no barriers to entry virtually invite competition.

For example, consider the market for repair parts used in agricultural or industrial machinery. Vendors supply parts to equipment makers, who install them in production machinery and also distribute them to their authorized dealers for after-market sales (see Figure 14.9). We can now ask ourselves the question, "Under what conditions will third parties market spare parts or other complements?" The answer is, "When the potential profits exceed the costs of entry, adjusted for risks," that is, when

Margin × Volume > > Production, distribution, and marketing costs

If production, distribution, or marketing costs are high, for example, third parties have to create a logistics and sales network from scratch,

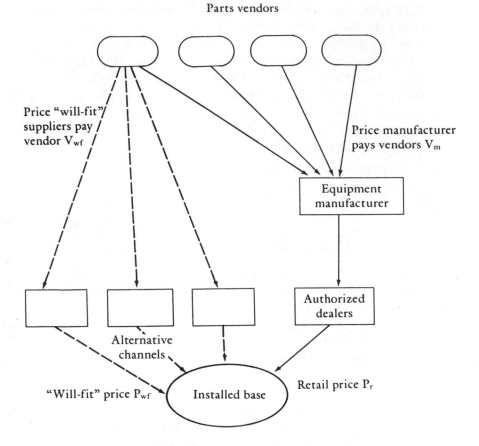

Figure 14.9   The attraction of the installed base.

then they act as entry barriers—increasing equipment makers' freedom of maneuver—and third-party competitors are not a threat.

But if third parties are already marketing other products to the same customers, then marketing and distribution costs are no longer effective entry barriers. Third parties then have an incentive to sell spare parts in competition with the manufacturer whenever (1) the potential volume is large in relation to the fixed costs, (2) the margins are inviting (that is, much higher than those available in their existing product lines), and (3) no proprietary technology is necessary for manufacturing the parts.

The potential volume depends on the size of the installed base, that is, the total number of machines in operation at any point in time. It is also affected by the usage of the item; other things being equal, frequently used items such as supplies and parts replaced regularly during routine maintenance will offer higher potential sales. Margins will be inviting if either the manufacturer's wholesale prices are much higher than the costs of sourcing, purchasing, and distribution, or dealer prices are higher than "free market" prices, that is, if either the manufacturers or the dealers or both are pricing monopolistically. Finally, the requirement that no proprietary technology be used implies that externally sourced items or attachments will be the primary focus of competition.[16]

Viewed in this light, we can predict that third-party competitors will concentrate their efforts on high volume models that have been in production for some time and on maintenance or wear parts that are either source from outside vendors or can be "reverse engineered" without significant investment. Further, the speed with which such competitors enter will depend on the price premium that manufacturers charge for such items.

In fact, if retail prices (P_r in Figure 14.9) are high enough, vendors will have an incentive to create or encourage third-party competitors in order to capture more of these profits for themselves—supplier power in action. Essentially parts vendors will compare V_m—the prices they receive from manufacturers—with V_{wf}, the prices they would receive from third-party distributors (or "will-fit" suppliers as they are often termed in the industry). If will-fit suppliers are prepared to pay substantially more than V_m, parts vendors have every incentive to sell to them. Especially when equipment makers have low or no buyer power relative to parts vendors, sales to will-fit suppliers are inevitable as there is no downside risk; manufacturers will still keep buying their present and future needs from these vendors. Thus we can expect will-fit competition in items where there are only a few suppliers or where purchases from the manufacturer are either guaranteed or likely to decline, for example, parts for machines that have been in production for some time.

Strategic Implications

Firms with an installed base of customers must recognize that any attempts to charge higher prices, that is, $P_r > P_{wf}$, and maintain share in the market for complements is price discrimination. In other words, they must not destroy their own leverage in pricing. It will work only if will-fit suppliers concentrate on other segments and current customers are unaware of the price differential or have significant search, transactions, or opportunity costs. Usually neither of these is true; will-fit suppliers naturally want to sell to the largest segment and it is difficult if not impossible to keep current customers ignorant about price differentials. Thus, a firm has two choices: It can keep complement prices high and try to maintain share through other means. Or it can keep the difference between its prices and those of will-fit suppliers to a minimum, thereby reducing the threat from such competitors.

- If a firm chooses to keep complement prices high, it must reduce customers' and competitors' expected returns in order to maintain its market share. Proprietary packaging or unique features increase search costs and risks, reducing returns; buyers who cannot directly compare part numbers or are uncertain whether the part will work properly in their equipment are less likely to switch. Voiding warranties if unauthorized (or will-fit) parts and complements are used also accomplishes the same purpose.

- If a firm wants to keep its prices competitive, it must control the prices it charges its channel members, as well as the prices channels charge customers. It must also establish targets for its prices in relation to will-fit prices to ensure that, over time, prices do not drift higher.

Each of these approaches entails costs and risks. Changes in packaging, unique features, or other product alterations increase a firm's costs and may not be feasible. Voiding warranties is difficult to enforce and creates customer dissatisfaction. Overhead allocations that are volume-based can make it difficult to keep prices to the channel competitive without raising prices of low volume captive items substantially, something that firms are often loathe to do. Finally, controlling retail prices creates tension with the channel and may lower sales of the primary product if channels raise prices to compensate for lower profits on complements.

Summary

Pricing tactics can dramatically alter a company's returns and therefore its leverage. On the long-term, poor or inadequately designed pricing tactics can significantly reduce a company's freedom to maneuver, so to speak, backing it into a corner.

Notes

CHAPTER 1

1. This is assuming no discontinuous changes in their resources or capabilities.
2. Hamel and Prahalad call this "searching for loose bricks." See Gary Hamel, and C. K. Prahalad, "Strategic Intent," *Harvard Business Review,* May–June 1989.
3. Hamel and Prahalad, *ibid.*
4. The detailed references are presented in Chapter 7, together with some caveats and critiques of the industry/product life cycle concept.
5. The game metaphor for business strategy has a long tradition; an excellent exposition of the game-theoretic approach of business strategy is contained in *The Game of Business* by John MacDonald.
6. C. K. Prahalad, and Gary Hamel, "The Core Competence of the Corporation," *Harvard Business Review,* May–June 1990, pp. 79–91.

CHAPTER 2

1. Technically, the structure of the industry influences/decides the nature of the payoff matrix, using the game-theory definition of the term.
2. Strictly speaking, we should add the caveat "other things being equal." As we shall see later, even here a "cooperative solution" is possible and likely.
3. For example, in the U.S. beer industry, Schlitz and Budweiser were alternately number one and number two over the period 1951 to 1956. As Ries and Trout point out, "These were the crucial years when half efforts were not good enough. The truth is, the victory could have gone to either brand. A few million extra dollars for advertising might have tipped the scale." Al Ries and Jack Trout, *Marketing Warfare* (New York: McGraw-Hill, 1986) p. 138.
4. Thomas C. Schelling, *The Strategy of Conflict* (Cambridge, MA: Harvard University Press, 1980) Chapter 3, especially the section on limited wars.

See also Carl von Clausewitz, *On War,* Michael Howard and Peter Paret, (ed. and trans.), (Princeton, NJ: Princeton University Press, 1976).

5. Michael Porter, *Competitive Strategy,* (New York: The Free Press, 1980) Chapter 3. Schelling, *ibid.,* also discusses the likely reactions of participants/opponents in a game or bargaining situation.

6. For example, F. M. Scherer, *Industrial Market Structure and Economic Performance* (Boston, MA: Houghton Mifflin, 1980) p. 191, indicates that, ". . . Most consumer goods manufacturers are well aware that adherence to accepted pricing points facilitates coordination and discourages price warfare. They go to considerable pains to preserve the system . . . Tampering with accepted pricing point structures threatens industry discipline and may induce price warfare."

7. Porter, *op. cit.,* p. 266.

8. The cyclical nature of the airline, farm equipment, and telecommunications equipment industries are classic examples of such lose/lose situations.

9. Kathryn Rudie Harrigan, "Strategies for Declining Businesses," doctoral dissertation, Graduate School of Business Administration, Harvard University, 1979.

10. Porter, *op. cit.,* pp. 22–23.

11. The statistics and some of the economic analysis in this section were obtained from F. M. Schrerer, "The Breakfast Cereal Industry" in *The Structure of the American Industry,* Walter Adams (ed.) (New York: Macmillan, 1982) pp. 191–217.

12. Scherer, *op. cit.,* p. 194.

13. Porter, *op. cit.,* pp. 17–20.

14. Scherer, *op. cit.,* p. 203.

15. "Can John Sculley Clean Up the Mess at Apple," *BusinessWeek,* July 29, 1985.

16. "Case Study in Determination," *Forbes,* October 30, 1989, pp.126–127; "Navistar Starts on the Road Back," *Sales and Marketing Management,* July 1986, pp. 49–51.

17. These are three generic strategies defined by Porter.

18. "Why Word-Processor Companies Are the Talk of Wall Street," *Fortune,* December 31, 1979, pp.76–77; Roderick Edward White, "Structural Context, Strategy and Performance," doctoral dissertation, Graduate School of Business Administration, Harvard University, 1981. White found that ". . . the more surprising observation is the lack of any significant relationships between environmental and competitive conditions, and strategic intentions." He goes on to add that ". . . interactions between environmental and competitive position variables were also examined for associations with strategic intentions. None of significance were found."

CHAPTER 3

1. *Standard and Poor's Industry Surveys,* Standard and Poor's Corp., December 22, 1988, p.28.

2. "International Capacity Glut to Shrink Prices," *Network World,* June 6, 1988, pp. 9–10.

3. Often the threat of bypass was enough to force the local carriers' to lower their access charges to a level comparable to that offered by the alternative technologies. The net result was the same; access was no longer a significant source of supplier power.

4. "Big Three of Long Distance Slug It Out," *New York Times,* October 9, 1990. Sec. C, p. 1.

5. David G. Hamer, "Users Response to Evolving International Competition," speech presented to the Intelevent 1985 Conference, Cannes, France.

6. "Is the FCC Putting Humpty Dumpty Back Together?" *BusinessWeek,* July 16, 1984, p. 35.

7. *New York Times, op. cit.*

8. "McGowan: The Man Who Cracked AT&T," *BusinessWeek,* January 21, 1985, p. 69.

9. "Anderson Clayton Foods," by the President and Fellows of Harvard College, Harvard Business School, Boston, MA, 1980.

CHAPTER 4

1. *Barrons,* July 28, 1986, p. 11; *BusinessWeek,* April 28, 1986, p. 39; and *The Economist,* August 10, 1985, p. 66.

2. Michael Porter, *Competitive Strategy* (New York: The Free Press, 1980) p. 24. We have organized these slightly differently from Porter's treatment. In particular, we have defined the general conditions under which buyers will have power in the introduction to this section more along the lines of Williamson. Oliver E. Williamson, *Markets and Hierarchies* (New York: The Free Press, 1975).

3. Survey of Fortune 500 CFOs conducted by Milind M. Lele, 1983.

4. Theodore Levitt, "Marketing Intangible Products and Product Intangibles," *Harvard Business Review,* May–June 1981, pp. 95–102.

5. Porter, *op. cit.,* p. 27.

6. Martin Mayer, *The Bankers* (New York: Weybright and Talley, 1974) p. 410.

7. The relationship isn't entirely one-sided. The Fed needs the dealers as much as they need the Fed, especially when the Treasury decides to finance its deficits by borrowing, as it has done in the 1980s.

8. Porter, *op. cit.*

9. Again, *ceteris paribus.* If exit barriers are also high, then competitive intensity will be very high.

10. F.M. Scherer, "The Breakfast Cereal Industry," *The Structure of American Industry,* Walter Adams (ed.) (New York: Macmillan, 1982) pp. 191–217.

11. This is consistent with Caves and Porter who suggest that ". . . entry is likely to occur along a circuitous path into groups whose capital requirements for entry are large. . . ." R. E. Caves and M.E. Porter, "From Entry

Barriers to Mobility Barriers," *Quarterly Journal of Economics, 91,* 1977, pp. 241–262.

12. "The PC Wars," *BusinessWeek,* July 28, 1986, pp. 62–68.

13. David S. Landes, *Revolution in Time* (Cambridge, MA: Belknap Press, 1983) pp. 339–340.

14. Porter, *op. cit.*

15. "A Market of the Future Gets Ahead of Itself," *BusinessWeek,* August 12, 1985, p. 29.

16. John Newhouse, "A Sporty Game," *The New Yorker,* June 14, 1982.

17. "Five Big Firms Gird for Air-Fare Battle," *Crain's Chicago Business,* March 30, 1987, p. 1. A good PIMS-based reference is Craig S. Galbraith and Curt H. Stiles, "Firm Profitability and Relative Firm Power," *Strategic Management Journal, 1,* 14, 1983, pp. 237–249. Their discussions of the impact of buyer and supplier power on ROS is particularly interesting.

CHAPTER 5

1. "An Upstart Airline Goes Upscale," *BusinessWeek,* May 30, 1983, pp. 37–38.

2. "Clipping Its Wings to Make It Fly," *Venture,* January 1986, pp. 86–88.

3. Strictly speaking, their expected losses adjusted for risks.

4. "Infighting Intensifies Over UNIX Standard," *Electronic News,* March 6, 1989, p. 1.

5. "The PC Wars: IBM vs. the Clones," *BusinessWeek,* July 28, 1986, pp. 62–68.

6. F.M. Scherer, *Industrial Market Structure and Economic Performance* (Boston, MA: Houghton Mifflin, 1980) pp. 180–181, for a discussion of price coordination in the U.S. automotive industry. See, for example, Ruth S. Raubitschek, "A Model of Product Proliferation with Multiproduct Firms," *The Journal of Industrial Economics,* V. XXXV, No. 3, March 1987, pp. 269–279.

7. "Why Bigger *IS* Better in the Airline Wars," *Fortune,* March 31, 1986, pp. 52–55.

8. "Can American Cars Come Back," *Fortune,* February 26, 1990, pp. 62–63; "Here Comes GM's Saturn," *BusinessWeek,* April 9, 1990, pp. 56–61.

9. Michael Porter, *Competitive Strategy* (New York: The Free Press, 1980) p. 85.

10. "Who's Afraid of IBM?" *BusinessWeek,* June 29, 1987, pp. 68–74; "The Verdict on IBM's System/2," *BusinessWeek,* May 4, 1987, pp. 118–121.

11. U.S. auto industry vs. Japanese imports in the small car market, e.g., David Halberstam, *The Reckoning* (New York: Morrow, 1986).

12. "Will the Auto Glut Choke Detroit," *BusinessWeek,* March 7, 1988, pp. 54–62; "Have Cheap Incentive Rates Worked Too Well?" *Advertising Age,* February 23, 1987, p. 56.

13. Michael Porter, "How to Attack the Industry Leader," *Fortune,* April 29, 1985, pp. 153–166.

14. Michael Porter, *Competitive Strategy, op. cit.,* p. 35–37.

15. Scherer, *op. cit.,* pp. 176–184.

16. Victor J. Cook, Jr., "Marketing Strategy and Differential Advantage," *Journal of Marketing,* V. 47, Spring 1983, pp. 68–75.

17. Victor J. Cook, Jr., *ibid.*

18. Victor J. Cook, Jr., *op. cit.*

19. "Can American Cars Come Back?" *Fortune,* February 26, 1990, pp. 62–63.

CHAPTER 6

1. Michael Porter, *Competitive Strategy* (New York: The Free Press, 1980) Chapter 2.

2. Milind M. Lele, *The Customer Is Key* (New York: John Wiley, 1987) p. 20; "The World's Best Airlines," *Institutional Investor,* June 1989, pp. 195–198.

3. "Lorenzo Braves the Airwaves," *New York Times Magazine,* November 29, 1987, p. 17.

4. "Tandy Adds to High-End of Desktop PC Line," *Electronic News,* August 10, 1987, p. 17.

5. Al Ries and Jack Trout, *Marketing Warfare* (New York: McGraw-Hill, 1986) p. 142.

6. Robert D. Buzzell and Bradley Gale, *The PIMS Principles: Linking Strategy to Performance* (New York: The Free Press, 1987) p. 112.

7. "The Northwest Fares Clipping JAL's Wings," *BusinessWeek,* August 16, 1982, p. 36.

8. "A Slimmer IBM May Still Be Overwieght," *BusinessWeek,* December 18, 1989, pp. 107–108; "Why Nothing Runs Like a Deere," *Production,* December 1989, pp. 70–74.

9. Lele, *op. cit.,* p. 15.

10. Naeim H. Abougomaah et al., "Elimination and Choice Phases in Evoked Set Formation," *Journal of Consumer Marketing,* Fall 1987, p. 67–73.

11. Anthropologists have found that social groups without a formal counting system could not "clearly perceive or precisely express numbers greater than four." George Ifrah, *From One to Zero: A Universal History of Numbers* (New York: Viking, 1985) pp. 6–7.

12. Carl R. Anderson and Carl R. Zeithaml, "Stage of the Product Life Cycle: Business Strategy and Business Performance," *Academy of Management Journal,* 1984, V. 27, N. 1, pp. 5–24.

13. Ries and Trout, *op. cit.,* p. 32.

14. "Apple's Comeback," *BusinessWeek,* January 19, 1985, pp. 84–89; "Apple Part Two," *BusinessWeek,* January 27, 1986, pp. 96–98.

15. "Big Changes at Big Blue," *BusinessWeek,* February 15, 1988, p. 92–98; Marquise Cvar, "Competitive Strategy in Global Industries," doctoral dissertation, Graduate School of Business, Harvard University, 1984; Michael

Porter, Ed., *Competition in Global Industries* (Boston, MA: Harvard Business School Press, 1986) pp. 485–492.

16. The analogy is not exact; one could argue that Volkswagen was a differentiated player. However, its focus on the single Beetle design and its emphasis on economy and production costs suggest that it followed a cost leadership strategy whereas the Japanese came in with a broader line of economy cars and lower production costs only partly due to lower labor rates.

17. *Planning Review,* January–February 1989, V. 17, pp. 40–45.

18. Richard Foster, *Innovation: The Attacker's Advantage* (New York: Summit Books, 1986) pp. 125–126.

19. F.M. Scherer, "The Breakfast Cereal Industry," *The Structure of American Industry,* Walter Adams (ed.) (New York: Macmillan, 1982), pp. 92–94.

20. "Can't Get Off the Ground," *Barrons,* May 7, 1984, pp. 36–43; "Welcome Aboard," *BusinessWeek,* January 19, 1987, pp. 61–62.

21. Apple faced a similar problem with its "educational consortium" discounting policies for the original Macintosh. However, Apple (unlike IBM) did not have a significant base of corporate customers who could exert buyer power and force prices down. The situation has changed in the case of the Macintosh II.

CHAPTER 7

1. Robert Buzzell and Bradley Gale, *The PIMS Principles: Linking Strategy to Performance* (New York: The Free Press, 1987) p. 136.

2. Buzzell and Gale, *ibid.*

3. Carl R. Anderson and Carl P. Zeithaml, "Stage of the Product Life Cycle, Business Strategy and Business Performance,"*Academy of Management Journal,* 1984, V. 27, No.1, pp. 5–24.

4. Philip Kotler, *Marketing Management: Analysis Planning and Control,* (5th ed.) (Englewood Cliffs, NJ: Prentice-Hall, 1984) pp. 369–370; Chester R. Wasson, *Product Management,* Challenge Books, St. Charles, IL, 1971; David J. Luck, *Product Policy and Strategy* (Englewood Cliffs, NJ: Prentice-Hall, 1972).

5. Buzzell and Gale, *op. cit.;* Michael Porter, *Competitive Strategy* (New York: The Free Press, 1980) pp. 158–162.

6. Nariman K. Dhalla and Sonia Yuspeh, "Forget the Product Life Cycle Concept," *Harvard Business Review,* January–February 1976; Rolando Polli and Victor J. Cook, "Validity of the Product Life Cycle," *The Journal of Business,* October 1969, p. 385; Theodore Levitt, "Marketing Intangible Products and Product Intangibles," *Harvard Business Review,* May–June 1981, pp. 95–102.

7. William J. Abernathy and James M. Utterback, "Patterns of Industrial Innovation," *Technology Review,* MIT Alumni Association, Cambridge, MA, 1978.

8. Abernathy and Utterback, *ibid.;* Michael E. Porter, "The Technological Dimension of Competitive Strategy," *Research on Technological Innovation Management and Policy,* 1 (Greenwich, CT: JAI Press, Inc., 1983).

9. Porter cited earlier in note 5 regarding the role of economies of scale.

10. David A. Hounshell, *From the American System to Mass Production: The Development of Manufacturing Technology in the United States* (Baltimore, MD: The Johns Hopkins University Press, 1984) pp. 217–219.

11. Richard Foster, *Innovation: The Attacker's Advantage* (New York: Summit Books, 1986) p. 103.

12. See for example, R. Schmalensee, "Product Differentiation Advantages of Pioneering Brands," *American Economic Review,* V. 72, No.3, June 1982, pp. 349–365.

13. Buzzell and Gale, *op cit.,* pp. 30–51.

14. "The PC Revolution: IBM Sets the Industry Standard," *USA Today,* August 12, 1986, p. 6B; "AT&T—Still King of the Hill," *Standard and Poor's Industry Surveys,* Standard and Poor's Corp., December 22, 1988, pp. 28–37.

15. "Technological Edge Will Let Firms Survive Computer-Design Shakeout," *Marketing News,* October 11, 1985, p. 14.

16. We can speculate which of these conditions are necessary and/or sufficient. While a gradual transition to maturity provides time for the new rules of competition to be established, this may not be necessary, provided the share leader has a commanding advantage as demonstrated by the U.S. long-distance industry. On the other hand, high relative share and the desire to enforce limited warfare may not be enough if the industry has high fixed and/or exit costs. In such cases, we conjecture that individual players may come to the conclusion that the gains from participating in cooperative equilibrium are outweighed by the (expected) losses due to high fixed costs, especially if they perceive that *their* share of industry sales will not cover the costs of their installed capacity.

17. Al Ries and Jack Trout, *Marketing Warfare* (New York: McGraw-Hill, 1986).

18. "Mega Trouble in the Air," *The Sunday Times,* November 22, 1987, London, England, p. 87.

19. George S. Day, *Analysis For Strategic Market Decisions* (St. Paul, MN: West Publishing Co., 1986) Chapter 3; Philip Kotler, *op. cit.;* Wasson, *op. cit.;* Anderson and Zeithaml, *op. cit.*

20. Anderson and Zeithaml, *op cit.*

21. Strictly speaking, there is a third alternative: Rejuvenate industry growth by changing technologies and/or markets.

22. The situation is different in the emerging stage of industry evolution. In this case, the technology or the market is changing so rapidly that industry leadership may pass back and forth. Furthermore, the age of the industry may be deceptive when evaluating the stage of evolution. For example, the U.S. microwave oven industry was founded by Amana in 1957, built slowly but steadily until the mid-1970s but did not really take off into its growth stage until the late 1970s. "Note on the Microwave Oven Industry" (Boston, MA: Harvard Business School, 1979).

23. More formally, we are assuming that price competition creates a secular downward pressure on overall industry price levels, which is difficult to reverse in the absence of externalities such as the oil-price shock of 1973.

Further, our statement regarding buyer power could be relaxed to include the case where price elasticity of demand is high, that is, react to price increases by reducing purchases almost immediately.

24. Buzzell and Gale, *op. cit.,* p. 187.

25. This caveat is important because, as we shall see, during the decline stage it is usually to the leader's advantage to play win/lose and drive lesser competitors out of the industry. Also see Michael Porter, "How to Attack the Industry Leader," *Fortune,* April 29, 1985, pp. 153–166.

26. Industry cost characteristics form necessary but sufficient conditions. Specifically, a stable equilibrium may be possible *only if* fixed or storage costs are low in relation to total cost.

27. Harry G. Summers, Jr., *On Strategy* (Novato, CA: Presidio Press, 1982). Also see Carl von Clausewitz, *On War,* Michael Howard and Peter Paret, (ed. and trans.) (Princeton, NJ: Princeton University Press, 1976) Book I, Chapter 2, pp. 92–93. The terminology used is the "ends" and the "means" of an offensive.

CHAPTER 8

1. R.E. Caves and M.E. Porter, "From Entry Barriers to Mobility Barriers: Conjectural Decisions and Contrived Deterrence to New Competition," *Quarterly Journal of Economics,* 1977, pp. 241–261.

2. In this context, we prefer the term "market areas" over "segments" or "niches" because it is more inclusive.

3. Ronald R. Gist, *Marketing and Society* (Hinsdale, IL: Dryden Press, 1971) pp. 6–7; Philip Kotler, *Principles of Marketing* (Englewood Cliffs, NJ: Prentice-Hall, 1980) pp. 16, 17, 231–232.

4. In this respect, our approach differs from Porter, *op cit.,* who focuses more on industry mapping.

5. Strictly speaking, perhaps we should include these markets in our analysis; however, it would complicate the problem considerably without providing additional insight. Furthermore, the situation we're describing corresponds very closely to actual conditions in the mid-1970s when Federal Express entered the market.

6. *Aviation Week and Space Technology,* March 22, 1971, p. 30; *Aviation Week and Space Technology,* November 30, 1984, p.36; *Purchasing,* April 29, 1982, p. 89.

7. *Federal Express (B),* Harvard Business School case, copyright President and Fellows of Harvard College, Boston, MA, 1978. Also additional references to Emery's relative profitability and cashflow comparisons, and so on.

8. "Anticipating the Evolution," *Forbes,* November 4, 1985, pp. 163–166; "Why ZapMail Finally Got Zapped," *BusinessWeek,* October 13, 1986, pp. 48–49.

9. *Forbes,* October 26, 1981, pp. 62–68.

10. "Why Federal Express Has Overnight Anxiety," *BusinessWeek,* November 9, 1987, pp. 62–66.

11. The military analogy is to the fighting in northern Europe in World War I, see for example, "Busch Fights to Have It All," *Fortune,* January 15, 1990, pp. 80–81; "Selected U.S. Farm Machinery Market Characteristics and Their Implications for the Future," *Agribusiness,* September 1989, pp. 437–447.

12. For example, in the ready-to-eat cereal industry such flanking activity is characterized by rapid proliferation of brands, created as much to counter competitive moves as to prevent entry. See Chapter 2.

13. "In Course and Climbing," *Barrons,* December 8, 1986, p. 53; "The Regional's Wider Reach," *BusinessWeek,* February 19, 1979, p. 77.

14. Milind M. Lele, *The Customer Is Key* (New York: John Wiley, 1987).

15. This is particularly important when group B contains low-volume customers and group A consists of the mass market. In this case, if products are substitutable, then learning curve and/or specialization effects must reduce group B's costs to the point that they are comparable to or below group A's costs at the higher volume. This nullifies the high-volume producer's cost advantages, which could otherwise be used to subsidize investments in product modification to meet any unique needs of group B customers.

16. Porter, *op. cit.,* Chapter 7.

17. "Mega Trouble in the Air," *The Sunday Times,* November 22, 1987, London, England, p. 87.

18. Porter, *op. cit.*

19. Theoretically, the cost to the larger carrier is the opportunity cost represented by lost revenues on routes from which capacity has been diverted. Given that in the short (and even medium) run an airline's costs are largely fixed, we could argue that the larger carrier can compete with marginal costs equal to the revenue difference between the *expected* number of passengers on the route(s) and the actual number carried in the smaller equipment. When overall demand is low, this difference is likely to be low or possibly even zero.

20. "Can't Get Off the Ground," *Barrons,* May 7, 1984, pp. 36–43; "Rooney, Pace Tries To Make It Big," *Financial World,* September 19/October 2, 1984, pp. 28–29; "The Wings of Mike Hollis," *Forbes,* December 3, 1984, pp. 111–112.

21. "*Up, Up and Away?*" *BusinessWeek,* November 25, 1985, p.80; "People Is Plunging But Burr Is Staying Cool," *BusinessWeek,* July 7, 1986, pp. 31–32.

22. "Dog Fight for Business Travelers," *Marketing and Media Decisions,* April 1984, pp. 70–71, 152.

CHAPTER 9

1. More formally, signaling has value primarily in situations where the payoff matrix of the N-person industry game is either zero-sum or declining-sum. In these situations, we use signals to prevent one-sided strategies and ensure cooperative equilibrium.

2. Michael Porter, *Competitive Strategy* (New York: The Free Press, 1980) Chapter 4, p. 79.

3. "Will Tenneco's Harvester Deal Turn Out to Be 'The Corporate Equivalent of Vietnam'?" *BusinessWeek,* February 4, 1985, pp. 80–81.

4. "AT&T: The Making of a Comeback," *BusinessWeek,* January 18, 1988, pp. 56–61.

5. "FCC to End Regulation of AT&T Profit," *Wall Street Journal,* March 17, 1987; "FCC Postpones Vote on AT&T Rate Regulation," *Wall Street Journal,* January 31, 1989, p. A4.

6. "Adolph Coors in the Brewing Industry," by the President and Fellows of Harvard College, Harvard Business School, Boston, MA, 1987.

7. Thomas C. Schelling, *The Strategy of Conflict* (Cambridge, MA: Harvard University Press, 1980).

8. An example of what Porter terms the "cross-parry."

9. Howard Raiffa, *The Art and Science of Negotiation* (Cambridge, MA: Harvard University Press, 1982) pp. 123–126.

10. Raiffa, *ibid.*

11. Strictly speaking, the number of participants with significant market shares.

12. Martin Shubik, "The Dollar Auction Game: A Paradox in Non-Cooperative Behavior and Escalation," *Journal of Conflict Resolution,* V. 15, March 15, 1971, pp. 109–111; Raiffa, *op. cit.,* p. 85.

CHAPTER 10

1. Here we are not distinguishing between *direct* entrants, that is, those creating/adding new capacity into the industry, and other types of entry such as related or acquisition entry (cf. George Yip, *Barriers to Entry* (Lexington, MA: Lexington Books, 1982) Chapter 2). It could be argued that entry should be restricted to describe direct entrants only, with other types of entrants being classified under the other three categories, depending on the types of firms acquired. The counter-argument is that either type of entrants has (at least temporarily) more freedom to change objectives and strategies than do existing players, and thus should be considered equally. We take the second approach.

2. Within the limits of existing antitrust policies.

3. Kathryn Rudie Harrigan, "Strategies for Declining Businesses" doctoral dissertation, Graduate School of Business, Harvard University, 1979.

4. More formally, when there is a stable, cooperative equilibrium to the N-person, constant-sum game.

5. An alternative is to change the game so that the total payoffs are increasing again. However, this requires an external agency such as technological change, sudden increases in population due to the creation of new demand segments, changes in usage patterns and so forth. If these externalities do not change, our rationale holds.

6. If entry barriers are low, the equilibrium is unlikely to be stable as participants leave and new players with different intentions or with no understanding of the (tacit) rules of the game enter the market.

7. Occasionally, they can enter a niche or fringe market, followed by a lateral entry into the core market (see George Yip, *op. cit.*). However, the issues remain the same: Should the firm accept the existing terms of competition or should it actively change them?

8. Note, for example, that ". . . (I)n six decades only 5 out of 25 brands lost their leadership position." Al Ries and Jack Trout, *Marketing Warfare* (New York: McGraw-Hill, 1986).

9. The concepts of the strategic and tactical offensives and defensives are described by Harry G. Summers, Jr., *On Strategy: A Critical Analysis of the Vietnam War* (Novato, CA: Presidio Press, 1982) pp. 109–110.

10. Examples being the farm equipment industry in the period 1983–87, the worldwide PBX industry, and the airframe industry rivalry between Boeing and Airbus.

11. We are using the terminology introduced by Porter when describing generic strategic choices. Michael E. Porter, *Competitive Strategy* (New York: Free Press, 1980) Chapter 2, p. 34 onwards.

12. "Across-the-board" is an important qualification; many firms consider themselves to be differentiated, but use narrow definitions of the served market.

13. The PIMS studies have clearly established that industry/segment leaders' profits are higher than those of other players. See, for example, Robert Buzzell and Bradley Gale, *The PIMS Principles: Linking Strategy to Performance,* (New York: Free Press, 1987).

14. Within the limits of prevailing antitrust policies, of course.

15. This is the classic "share versus margin" dilemma faced by leaders.

16. Proxy price cuts, for example, "cents-off" coupons and other, similar price-oriented promotional offers, are likely to trigger price wars because (1) overall demand is growing very slowly and (2) consumption is price-inelastic. Consequently any share gains by one brand will come at the expense of its competitors; as the latter are not likely to sit still, a price war is certain.

17. See, for example, Kathryn Rudie Harrigan, "Strategies for Declining Businesses" doctoral dissertation, Graduate School of Business, Harvard University, 1979, Chapter II, p. 51 onwards.

18. Marquise Cvar, "Competitive Strategy in Global Industries," doctoral dissertation, Graduate School of Business, Harvard University, 1984.

19. Pepsi's strategy for gaining share at the expense of Coke is a good example of "sawing the floor" around the leader. See the chapter on "The Cola War" in Al Ries and Jack Trout, *Marketing Warfare* (New York: McGraw-Hill, 1986).

20. Barbara Marsh, *A Corporate Tragedy* (Garden City, NY: Doubleday, 1985) p. 99 onwards.

21. Equally important, Deere had *strategic intent.* Their goal was clear and concise: Beat IH. Gary Hamal and C. K. Prahalad, "Strategic Intent," *Harvard Business Review,* May–June 1989, pp. 63–76.

22. See Porter, *op. cit.,* Chapter 1, p. 19.

23. For the purposes of this discussion we are not addressing the issue of whether the Japanese were guilty of dumping. Our objective is on the strategy they used after entering the market.

24. These being two major criticisms leveled at, respectively, the BCG share/growth matrix and the structure-conduct-performance paradigm.

25. A great many strategic blunders are traceable to flaws in the underlying managerial assumptions, i.e., to how many managers "framed" the various issues. See J. Edward Russo and Paul J.H. Schoemaker, *Decision Traps* (Garden City, NY: Doubleday, 1989).

CHAPTER 11

1. Milind M. Lele, "Technology Evolution and Product Development Objectives," Product Development and Management Association, Tenth Annual Conference, October 1986.

2. We are deliberately using the term "innovation evolution" as opposed to "technological" or "industry" evolution. First, we want to avoid the purely technical/scientific overtones of technological evolution; the pattern we are discussing, we believe, applies as well to nontechnology-based innovations, for example, new fashions or new services, such as credit card services, which are only partially based on technology. Secondly, we are not using "industry evolution" for the reason that industry evolution is synonymous with "innovation evolution" in the few cases where one major innovation is responsible for creating the industry. However, the pattern we are describing applies to smaller innovations within the industry, for example, process innovations in a mature industry. Note that there is considerable overlap in these terms, see for example, David Ford and Chris Ryan, "Taking Technology to Market" *Harvard Business Review,* March–April 1981, V. 59, No. 2, for a different (broader) definition of the technology life cycle.

3. The microwave oven is an example of all three issues. The basic design dates to 1957; however it was not until the late 1970s that microwave oven penetration in the United States took off. Early on, microwave ovens were large and expensive (technology). Secondly, prepared foods designed especially for the microwave had not appeared on supermarket shelves (infrastructure). Finally, convenience became a real issue only after women entered the workforce in large numbers (behavioral).

4. This term was introduced by William J. Abernathy and James M. Utterback, "A General Model," Chapter 4 in W.J. Abernathy, *The Productivity Dilemma* (Baltimore, MD: The Johns Hopkins Press, 1978) pp. 68–84.

5. Foster describes a number of such examples of rapid penetration. For example, ". . . in four years, 80 percent of the market for cash registers was lost to manufacturers of electronic products," and ". . . bias-ply tires lost 50 market share points in eighteen months." (Richard Foster, *Innovation: The Attacker's Advantage* (New York: Summit Books, 1986) pp. 141 and 161, respectively.)

6. Foster, *op. cit.,* p. 124.

7. The reasons for this are: Once a dominant design has emerged, there is a shift ". . . from radical to evolutionary product innovation and is accompanied by . . . increased emphasis on process innovation" (Abernathy and Utterback, *ibid.*). At this stage, therefore, designs that compete with the dominant design face a competitor (the producer of the dominant design) whose product technology has already evolved and who is now shifting his R&D resources to process improvements, that is, lowering manufacturing/operating costs. To succeed, competitive designs must simultaneously show that (1) their performance is superior, and (2) that their costs are comparable. This increases the technological and cost uncertainties. At the same time, producers of products compatible with the dominant design will see a reduction in their technological risks (they are now assured of a firm standard) and may be able to take advantage of "network externalities" such as interchangeability of complementary products, ease of communication and cost savings (see, for example, Joseph Farrell and Garth Saloner, "Installed Base and Compatibility: Innovation, Product Preannouncements and Predation," *The American Economic Review, 76,* No. 5, December 1986, pp. 940–955.

8. There has been considerable work done on the diffusion of innovations, particularly by Rogers and his co-workers, see Everett Rogers and F. Floyd Shoemaker, *Communication of Innovations* (New York: Free Press, 1971).

9. Philip Kotler and Gary Armstrong, *Principles of Marketing,* 4th ed. (Englewood Cliffs, NJ: Prentice-Hall, 1989) pp. 156–158; Rogers and Shoemaker, *ibid.*

10. While distinctions are difficult, they are important. We distinguish between the life cycle of the innovation, the product, and the brand. In this context, freeze-dried coffee is the innovation, decaffeinated freeze-dried, freeze-dried crystals, and so on are products and Sanka, Folgers et al. are brands that may offer any or all of these products.

11. Alternatively, until there is a sufficiently installed base of products based on the dominant design, the expected return from complements will be low. By the same token, until the dominant design has achieved a significant degree of market penetration, the market for specialty or niche products as well as variations of the basic product will be too small to be economical.

12. This is Foster's basic thesis. See Foster, *op. cit.,* especially Chapter 9.

13. "The PC revolution: IBM Sets the Industry Standard," *USA Today,* August 12, 1986. Figures are approximate due to preannouncements, industry secrecy, and difficulties in making precise distinctions due to confusion/lack of data.

14. *USA Today, ibid.*

15. Dataquest.

16. "The Pressure Builds at Big Blue," *New York Times,* August 10, 1986, Section 3 (Business), pp. 1, 23. Note that this was a third of a much larger market than in 1984.

17. Dataquest.

18. Milind M. Lele and Philip Maher, "Strategy: What Microcomputer Makers Are Missing," *Business Marketing,* November 1983.

19. "The Growth of PC Clones," *Computerworld,* November 12, 1986, pp. 35–36; "The PC Wars: IBM vs. the Clones," *BusinessWeek,* July 28, 1986, pp. 62–68.

20. Our reasoning is that while the dominant design (or innovation) is growing, its rate of technological improvement will be higher (or will be perceived to be higher) than that of competing innovations. Consequently, potential adopters will tend to choose the dominant design, *cet par.* This is an example of what Farrell and Saloner term "excess inertia." Farrell and Saloner, *op. cit.*

21. Al Ries and Jack Trout, *Marketing Warfare* (New York: McGraw-Hill, 1986) Chapter 14.

22. "AT&T Tries to Unsnarl Its Future," *New York Times,* February 15, 1987, Section 3 (Business) pp. 1, 26.

23. The list of failures is long: Chameleon, Syntrex, TeleVideo, Raytheon's Data Systems Division, Osborne Computer, Computer Devices, Gavilan Computer, Victor Technologies, Franklin Computer, Eagle Computer, Fortune Systems, Columbia Data Products, Monroe Business Systems, Vector Graphic, to name only a few. See Trout and Ries, *op. cit.*

24. "Why Compaq Must Try Harder to Stay No. 2," *BusinessWeek,* May 13, 1985, pp. 136–137; "Zenith: Tail Wags Dog," *Financial World,* November 3, 1987, pp. 22–24.

25. C. C. Swanger and Modesto Maidique, *Strategic Management of Technology and Innovation* (Homewood, IL: Richard D. Irwin, 1988) pp. 288–321.

26. Farrell and Saloner, *op cit.*

27. Which is not to say the other factors referred to were not important, but that the right timing was a necessary condition.

28. "Does This Lawsuit Compute for Apple?" *BusinessWeek,* April 4, 1988, pp. 32–33; "Imitation or Infringement?" *Time,* April 4, 1988, p. 60.

29. This may not be the case if imitation is riskless and feasible. In such situations, we could argue that emulators have lower relative product costs. On the other hand, in general the marketing costs of emulators will be higher and their prices lower.

30. This is, of necessity, a rather elementary treatment. It does not take into account discount rates or expected sales life cycles. In addition, we cannot proceed from the deterministic result to statements about expected sales without some consideration of probability distributions.

31. What Ries and Trout call ". . . the courage to attack oneself," Ries and Trout, *op. cit.,* p. 121.

32. Gillette is a rare example of a firm that has consistently (and successfully) replaced one innovation with its successor; such instances are few and far between.

33. Michael E. Porter, *Competitive Strategy* (New York: Free Press, 1980) p. 35.

34. In the personal computer industry both Apple and IBM have aggressively pursued alliances and acquisitions to round out their product lines, acquire technologies they needed, or ensure continued supply of, or control over, key components or complements.

35. Implicitly we are restricting ourselves to firms who specifically want to enter the particular market, not companies producing new innovations that displace the current design.

CHAPTER 12

1. This example is based on a combination of consulting experiences and research within the industry. Some figures have been changed to avoid inadvertent disclosure of confidential information. It is not intended to describe the specific actions taken by either company.

2. "The 'New' Old: Where the Economic Action Is," *Business Week,* November 25, 1985, pp. 138–140.

3. Most of these specialty manufacturers were absorbed in a major consolidation of the industry that occurred in the period 1986–1988. In addition, White Consolidated was acquired by Electrolux AB of Sweden, the leading European producer of large appliances. "Note on the Major Home Appliance Industry—1984," by the President and Fellows of Harvard College, HBS Case Services, Harvard Business School, Boston, MA, 1984.

4. This trend has continued with the consolidations referred to earlier.

5. "Those Big-Spending Middle-Aged Baby Boomers," *Business Week,* October 19, 1987, p. 20.

6. Note that the payoff matrix is symmetrical with respect to participants, so our analysis applies equally well to Whirlpool's choices.

7. Assuming that there is some uncertainty or lack of information about the likelihood of the aging market.

8. This payoff matrix is similar to that of the "Prisoner's Dilemma" discussed in Chapter 9. A cooperative (or collusive) solution would be for both GE and Whirlpool to refrain from introducing products for the aging until a smaller participant has proved the viability of the niche.

9. Capacity expansion in U.S. airlines in the regulated era was a similar game where ". . . it was better to guess wrong and conform with the other airlines than guess right and forfeit the benefits of superior efficiency (through the regulatory process)" from John MacDonald, *The Game of Business* (Garden City, NY: Anchor Press, 1977).

10. "Carmakers Are Driving the Risk Out of Buying," *Business Week,* October 24, 1988, p. 31.

11. Ester Gal-Or, "First Mover and Second Mover Advantages," *International Economic Review,* October 1985, pp. 649–653.

12. "A Market of the Future Gets Ahead of Itself," *Business Week,* August 12, 1985, p. 29.

13. Richard Foster, *Innovation: The Attacker's Advantage* (New York: Summit Books, 1986) pp. 129–130 and 151–152.

14. "Multi-Dimensional Product Differentiation and Price Competition," *Oxford Economic Papers,* November 1986, pp. 129–145. Oxford University, Oxford, England.

15. "What Do You Do for an Encore," *Fortune,* December 19, 1988, pp. 111–112.

16. Al Ries and Jack Trout, *Marketing Warfare* (New York: McGraw-Hill, 1986) pp. 121–122 and 149–151.

17. In terms of location models, this would imply one merchant trying to cover two areas of the market at once. If one assumes that his share at each location is proportional to the amount of time spent, then, given that the total potential market at one location (lower price) is much smaller than that at the main location, other things being equal, the merchant's total share will be lower than if he had concentrated all his attention on one location.

18. Michael Sedgwick, *The Motor Car 1946-56,* B.T. Batsford, London, England, 1979, pp. 144, 202, 253.

19. Milind M. Lele and Uday S. Karmarkar, "Good Product Support Is Smart Marketing," *Harvard Business Review,* November–December, 1983.

20. Gajanan Hegde, "Market for Product Supply," Ph.D. thesis, University of Rochester, 1985.

21. "The Test Pilot," *Business Marketing,* September 1988, pp. 8–12.

22. "VTR Wars," *Business Japan,* November 1985, pp. 55–59.

23. Adapted from Milind M. Lele, "How Service Needs Influence Product Strategy," *Sloan Management Review, 28,* No. 1, Fall 1986, pp. 63–70.

24. Lele and Karmarkar, *op. cit.*

25. Alvin von Auw, *Heritage and Destiny* (New York: Praeger, 1983) pp. 5–6.

CHAPTER 13

1. Jack Miller, "State of the Industry Report," Quill Corporation, Nov. 1990.

2. *New York Times,* April 17, 1986, and *Chicago Tribune,* July 21, 1985.

3. For example, the two case studies "General Electric—Component Motor Operation" and "Honeywell Information Systems" in E. Raymond Corey, Frank V. Cespedes and V. Kasturi Rangan, *Going to Market: Distribution Systems for Industrial Products* (Cambridge, MA: Harvard Business School Press, 1989) pp. 218–219.

4. Malcolm McNair, "Thinking Ahead," *Harvard Business Review,* July–August 1958, p. 25.

5. Note that we are not saying that these channels are less profitable, say, in the sense of return on their equity, merely that their gross (and in many cases their net) margins on sales are lower.

6. See Chapter 7 regarding the difficulty of clearly separating between these two. Especially in regard to channels, as very often products are marketed through different channels at different stages of their life cycle, all within the same industry.

7. Everett M. Rogers, *The Diffusion of Innovations* (New York: Free Press, 1982) p. 247.

8. A classic example of a "free-rider" problem.

9. The information in this example is drawn from two cases, "Note on the Microwave Oven Industry" and "Amana Microwave Ovens," copyright 1979 by the President and Fellows of Harvard College, Cambridge, MA, case numbers 9-579-185 and 9-579-182, respectively.

10. *The Wall Street Transcript,* June 13, 1978, p. 17; "Note on Microwave Oven Industry," *ibid.*

11. Under U.S. antitrust laws, territorial exclusives were difficult to justify (*Schwinn Bicycle Company vs. U.S.,* 1967), except when there were service-related reasons that would increase interbrand competition (*Continental TV, Inc. vs. GTE Sylvania, Inc.,* 1977).

12. "Amana Microwave Ovens," *op. cit.*

CHAPTER 14

1. Eliot B. Ross, "Making Money with Proactive Pricing," *Harvard Business Review,* November–December 1984, pp. 145–155.

2. Ross, *op. cit.*

3. "Extended Service Contracts, Still a Bad Idea," *Changing Times,* August 1988, p. 76.

4. Strictly speaking, the average repair cost plus the expected value of the catastrophic loss.

5. Essentially, it lowers their estimates of p_m, the probability of a major failure.

6. Using Williamson's terminology, this describes a condition of "information impactedness." Oliver E. Williamson, *Markets and Hierarchies* (New York: Free Press, 1975) pp. 31–32.

7. "IBM Moves to Demystify Service Options," *Computer World,* January 30, 1989, pp. 1, 6.

8. Even these volumes may be overstated, given that tools are bundled with fasteners and usually replaced more frequently than would be the case if they were purchased separately.

9. For simplicity, we have ignored the fact that some of the lost revenue could be regained over time by raising prices on the lower volume items, as it does not alter the substance of our argument.

10. We are restricting ourselves to *legal* price discrimination. In the United States, certain forms of price discrimination are considered anticompetitive and hence illegal; for the purposes of the present discussion we will assume that these conditions are not violated.

11. A good example would be GM reselling its telecommunications capabilities to dealers, distributors, and so forth.

12. *BusinessWeek,* September 2, 1985, p. 34.

13. See for example, E. Raymond Corey, Frank V. Cespedes and V. Kasturi Rangan, *Going to Market: Distribution Systems for Industrial Products* (Cambridge, MA: Harvard Business School Press, 1989) pp. 169–185.

14. Anthony Ramirez, "Blue vs. Gray: IBM Tries to Stop the Discounters," *Fortune,* May 27, 1985, p. 79.

15. "CAE Software: Still Bundled after All These Years," *Electronic Business,* June 1, 1988, pp. 94–98.

16. If manufacturer's prices are high enough, even the requirement of proprietary technology is not a barrier. For example, commonly used body parts such as fenders and side panels are available from third party suppliers, despite the high fixed costs of recreating tools and dies for such proprietary items; *Automotive News,* September 22, 1986, p. 20; *BusinessWeek,* October 14, 1985, p. 94.

Index